Employment and Inclusive Development

Issues relating to employment and labour have once again come to the fore of global policy debates in the wake of the widespread unemployment that has accompanied the recent financial crisis. In the developing world, there is a growing realization that productive employment promotion and social protection have to be at the core of inclusive growth and development.

This book supports the view that employment is a cross-cutting issue shaped by macroeconomic and microeconomic policy interventions, and provides a capacious framework to analyse the complexity of this global debate. It covers a wide range of issues that have received insufficient attention in the discourse of development and labour economics. These include the impact of macroeconomic policies on employment, labour rights, the development of human capabilities and employability, youth employment, the benefits and costs of labour market flexibility, and the importance of social protection for all.

This important book aims at filling this gap by revisiting old debates and reconnecting them to the contemporary context, combining analyses with relevant empirical evidence. It will appeal to a diverse readership of academic institutions and think-tanks, international organizations, bilateral donors working on development issues and policy makers in developing countries.

Rizwanul Islam is former Special Adviser, Employment Sector, ILO, Geneva, Switzerland.

Iyanatul Islam is currently Chief, Employment and Labour Market Policies Branch, ILO, Geneva, Switzerland.

Routledge studies in development economics

Employment and Inclusive Development

Rizwanul Islam and Iyanatul Islam

LONDON AND NEW YORK

First published 2015 by Routledge

2 Park Square, Milton Park, Abingdon, Oxfordshire OX14 4RN
52 Vanderbilt Avenue, New York, NY 10017

Routledge is an imprint of the Taylor & Francis Group, an informa business

First issued in paperback 2019

British Library Cataloguing in Publication Data
A catalogue record for this book is available from the British Library

Library of Congress Cataloging in Publication Data
Islam, Rizwanul
Employment and inclusive development / Rizwanul Islam, Iyanatul Islam.
   pages cm
   Includes bibliographical references and index.
   1. Labor market–Developing countries. 2. Economic development–
   Developing countries. 3. Employment (Economic theory) I. Islam,
   Iyanatul, II. Title.
   HD5852.I853 2015
   331.12–dc23   2014036826

ISBN: 978-0-415-82598-6 (hbk)
ISBN: 978-0-367-86781-2 (pbk)

Typeset in Times New Roman
by Wearset Ltd, Boldon, Tyne and Wear

To Gitasree and Shermeen
for their love and support

Contents

Figures

Tables

Preface

The idea of inclusive growth – also at times called 'inclusive development' – has, in recent years, become a major area of development discourse.[1] This is particularly the case in the context of the debate and discussion on the post-2015 development agenda. And yet, the literature on development suffers from a lack of clarity surrounding the concept, the process and its components. Moreover, it remains scattered in the form of unpublished or semi-published material that is often not easy to access. The gap in the development literature in this respect became apparent when the authors were looking for reference material for lectures they were delivering for various courses in academic institutions and for training courses organized by research institutes and international organizations. The motivation for writing the present book came from this need and received strong impetus from the interest expressed by our publisher.

Inclusive growth or development should embody the following essential elements: (1) rapid, stable and sustainable per capita GDP growth; (2) sustained decline in income poverty; (3) reduction in inequality; (4) growth of productive employment that matches or exceeds labour force growth; (5) sustained improvement in human development indicators, such as health, nutrition and education; and (6) basic social protection for all. Amongst these elements, productive employment is particularly important. It is a critical element not only for translating the benefits of economic growth into poverty reduction but also for reducing inequality in income distribution. Hence, this volume focuses particularly on employment and its linkages with growth, poverty, inequality and human capital. In doing so, it looks not only at labour market policies but also at the role of macroeconomic policies in promoting growth with productive employment. In addition, the book deals with policies to improve youth employment outcomes, right to work and rights at work, the debate on the benefits and costs of labour market flexibility, and the importance of social protection for all. Global and country-specific experiences are used to illustrate key propositions.

A good deal of the material for the present volume emerged from lectures delivered and papers presented by the authors at various academic and research institutions and international organizations. They include: the Institute of Social Studies, The Hague; New School University, New York; South Asian University,

New Delhi; Patna University, India; Dhaka University, Dhaka; North South University, Dhaka; Bangladesh Institute of Development Studies, Dhaka; Institute for Human Development, Delhi; REPOA, a development policy research institute in Dar Es Salaam; International Monetary Fund (IMF); International Labour Organization; International Training Centre, Turin. The authors are thankful to these institutions for the opportunities they provided to introduce the various ideas that were developed for the present volume. Thanks are due to the participants of the various seminars and lectures for very useful discussions on the ideas.

Both the authors have close links to the International Labour Organization (ILO) – one as a former official and the other as a current official. Not surprisingly, the core ideas expressed in this book have been shaped by the work of the ILO on employment and labour market issues. Nevertheless, the standard disclaimer applies: the views expressed here should be attributed to the authors and should not be interpreted to represent the official views of the ILO.

Several friends and professional colleagues read and commented on earlier drafts of the various chapters of the book. They include Muhammad Muqtada, Siddiq Osmani and David Kucera. Furthermore, the various chapters draw on work done jointly with David Kucera, Martina Hengge, Sarah Anwar and Anis Chowdhury. The authors would also like to thank Agustin Velasquez for his critical support in the processing of the various chapters and ensuring that they are aligned with the guidelines recommended by the publisher. He also provided considerable research assistance. While the authors are thankful to them, the usual applies: we take full responsibility for any remaining errors and omissions.

Finally, the authors would like to thank Routledge – and Lisa Thompson in particular – for supporting the publication of this book and for encouraging its continued progress even when it appeared at times to falter because of extraneous circumstances.

Note

1 The two terms 'inclusive growth' and 'inclusive development' will be used interchangeably throughout this book.

Acknowledgements

The authors would like to thank the following individuals and organisations for permission to reproduce text:

Islam, Iyanatul and David Kucera (eds): *Beyond Macroeconomic Stability: Structural Transformation and Inclusive Development*. Palgrave Macmillan and ILO, London and Geneva, 2013. (Pages from where material used: 9–12). Copyright International Labour Organization, 2013. Reproduced with permission.

International Labour Office: *Efficient Growth, Employment and Decent Work in Africa: Time for a New Vision*. ILO, Geneva, 2011. (Pages from which material used: 169–176). Copyright International Labour Organization, 2011. Reproduced with permission.

International Labour Office: *World of Work Report 2014: Developing with jobs*. ILO, Geneva 2014. (Material used: Table 7.1: Correlations between Social Protection Expenditure and Economic Growth, 1990–2012, p. 137). Copyright International Labour Organization, 2014. Reproduced with permission.

1   Introduction

It is tempting to analyse the role of labour in developing economies largely through the lens of standard theories of microeconomics. Such an approach usually deals with the demand for and supply of labour and determination of wages in a competitive setting enabling an analyst to spell out the negative employment consequences of interventions like minimum wage legislation and collective bargaining. This 'neoclassical' idea has influenced policy debates on the role of the labour market in developing countries and usually takes the form of a continuing debate between those who support 'labour market flexibility' and those who seek to sustain labour market regulations to protect wages and working conditions.

Labour market analyses in development economics have also been influenced by either a Lewisian (Lewis, 1954) or Harris–Todaro (Harris and Todaro, 1970) framework in which the policy debate turns to either urban-based industrialization to absorb rural surplus labour (as in Lewis) or to explore ways in which one can restrain excessive rural–urban migration.[1] There are a wide range of issues relating to employment and the world of work – such as the impact of macroeconomic policies on employment, the notion of labour rights, the development of human capabilities and employability, youth employment, guarding against a multitude of labour market risks – that receive insufficient attention in the discourse on development economics as well as labour economics. There is thus an important gap in the literature that needs to be filled.[2]

The gap mentioned above needs to be filled not just because it is intellectually challenging, but because issues relating to employment and labour have once again come to the fore of global policy debates. These debates are admittedly fuelled by the grim legacy of the Great Recession of 2008–09 that has led to a jobs crisis in rich countries. Even in the developing world that has weathered the most recent global recession far better than in the past, there is a growing realization that productive employment promotion and social protection have to be at the core of growth and development. At least this seems to be the message of the growing literature on 'inclusive growth'.

Apart from the short-term impact of economic crises on employment and labour market, experience with longer-term performance of economies with respect to economic growth and poverty reduction indicates that while economic growth is a necessary condition for poverty reduction, it is not sufficient. There are a number of studies (Islam, 2006a; Khan, 2007; and the country studies in Islam, 2006b, among others) showing that in addition to high rate of economic growth, the pattern and sources of growth and the manner in which its benefits are distributed are extremely important for poverty reduction. Productive employment plays an important role in that context. The studies mentioned above show that there is no invariant relationship between economic growth and poverty reduction,[3] and that development in employment and labour markets are critical variables influencing the poverty reducing outcome of economic growth. Hence, it is not surprising that although the Millennium Development Goal (MDG) of halving poverty has been attained at the global level (and also by a number of developing countries), many countries are witnessing a stubborn persistence of poverty despite good record in terms of economic growth.

Unfortunately, international development discourse during the last two decades of the twentieth century and in the early years of the new millennium by and large overlooked the importance of employment.[4] Of course, full and productive employment as a goal was included amongst the commitments of the World Summit on Social Development held in Copenhagen in 1995, but that was not followed up by specific targets and indicators. Other influential international instruments like the Poverty Reduction Strategy Papers or PRSPs (especially its first generation versions) almost entirely ignored the importance of employment. High rate of economic growth associated with expenditures on social sectors (e.g. education and health) was expected to be the major instrument of poverty reduction. The same was the case with the original list of MDGs; employment was not included in that list. And it took eight years for the international community to agree on incorporating the goal of full and productive employment in the list of MDGs.[5]

In the wake of the global economic crisis and the Great Recession of 2008–09, employment has become a subject of focus. This is apparent from the repeated mention of employment as an area of concern in the various fora of G20 countries that took place during and after the Great Recession. Between 2012 and 2014, four major global reports on the theme of jobs were released by various international organizations.[6] Also, the issue of employment is featuring prominently within the framework of the discussion on the post-2015 development agenda.[7] Given the urgency to accelerate the rate of poverty reduction by making economic growth more pro-poor and inclusive, and the potential role that can be played by productive employment in that regard, it is important to improve our understanding of why growth in some situations has not been accompanied by similar growth of productive employment and how growth can be made more employment friendly. This becomes particularly important in the context of the discussions on the post-2015 development agenda.

Recognition of the importance of employment has not, however, led to a resolution of the debate surrounding the issue of jobs, especially in relation to economic growth. At one extreme, there is still a tendency to deny the existence of the problem of slow growth of jobs in relation to economic growth. For example, the World Bank's World Development Report (WDR) on jobs (World Bank, 2012) attempts to dispel the notion of jobless growth by pointing out that economic growth is always accompanied by some growth in employment.[8] It has of course been pointed out (Islam, 2012) that there have been cases of zero growth of employment when economic growth has been positive. Moreover, as will be argued in Chapter 2 of the present volume, the term 'jobless growth' need not be interpreted in a literal sense of zero employment growth.

A more important point to note is the approach adopted to explain the slow growth of jobs. In this respect, the conventional wisdom is to argue that distortions in the labour market and its imperfect functioning act as constraints on employment creation. This view equates employment policy with labour market policies (read, policies for making labour markets flexible). Influential studies, like the report of the Commission on Growth (World Bank, 2008) and the IMF's report on job growth (IMF, 2013), are examples of this strand of work, although there are differences in details. For example, the report of the Growth Commission does recognize that governments may have to undertake measures to jump-start the process of job creation through encouraging the growth of new industries. Likewise, the IMF's 2013 report on job growth talks about 'selected policy interventions' that might lift barriers to private sector job creation and notes the importance of fiscal policies in that respect. However, when it comes to macroeconomic stability, all these reports remain unwavering in their focus and do not open up to the possibility of a debate on the relevance of macroeconomic policies (not to speak of inflation targeting) for employment. But it is not difficult to find practical illustrations to show that macroeconomic and other policies may result in distortions in factor prices which in turn act as constraints on employment creation.

The upshot of the above discussion is that employment as an element of inclusive development needs to be at the fore of development discourse with an open agenda where the approach will not be limited to labour market policies. The agenda is very broad, ranging from macroeconomic and sectoral policies to issues relating to structural transformation of an economy and its labour market.[9] Human capital development (including education and skill training) represents the supply side of the equation and is important not only from the point of view of its links to economic growth, but also for its role in addressing the issue of inequality. Furthermore, the role of human capital changes with the level of economic development of a country.

It would be unrealistic to keep the perspective of inclusive development narrowly confined to employment because, irrespective of the levels of productivity and returns, there may be situations, e.g. during old age and periods of unemployment (be it due to the normal process of job search or to economic downturns) and sickness, when people would need a degree of social protection. The agenda for inclusive development thus has to encompass a discussion on social protection. Measures of social protection can actually play an important role in the strategies of reducing poverty and inequality.

A readers' guide to the book

Chapter 2 *Employment and inclusive growth: a development perspective*

This chapter deals with the issue of low and declining employment intensity of growth in many developing countries that has given rise to the concern of 'jobless growth'. A number of related questions are addressed in the chapter. The first relates to the term 'jobless growth' itself. An important question in that regard is whether there could be growth of output without the growth of employment. The second question is whether the pursuit of employment intensive growth might result in a compromise with productivity and efficiency. The third question relates to the factors that make a difference in the relationship between growth and employment: how does one explain the phenomenon of low and declining employment intensity of growth and what are the real constraints on employment growth?

Chapter 2 of the book addresses the questions mentioned above. It starts with an attempt to place productive employment in the context of the debate on pro-poor and inclusive growth. In doing so, it aims at providing: (1) conceptual clarifications of the terms 'inclusive' and 'jobless growth'; (2) an empirical analysis of the possibility of trade-off between employment and productivity; (3) empirical evidence on the relationship between output growth and employment growth in a large cross-section of developing countries to examine whether growth has really been jobless; (4) diagnosis of factors that can explain the variation in the relationship between output and employment growth.

Chapter 3 *Macroeconomic policy, growth and employment*

The conventional view of macroeconomic policy is that governments should act as guardians of price stability, fiscal sustainability and a sustainable external balance. Such a role, when credibly conducted, can enhance investor confidence, promote growth and lead to employment creation both for adults and young people, given that basic labour market indicators are strongly positively correlated for both adults and youth. In practice, this view of macroeconomic policy has taken the form of attaining and sustaining prudential targets pertaining to debts, deficits, inflation and external balances. Thus, 'rule-of-thumb' targets – such as 40 to 60 per cent debt to GDP ratios supported by low fiscal deficits, low, single digit inflation, minimum foreign exchange reserve holdings – are often recommended by international financial institutions and some regional entities as hallmarks of good and growth-friendly macroeconomic management. It is also well known that many central banks in both developed and developing countries exercise inflation targeting and aim to attain low, single digit inflation over the medium term as one of the key goals of monetary policy.

Chapter 3 uses global and cross-country evidence to highlight the limits of the conventional macroeconomic policy framework. It shows that establishing a clear link between macroeconomic stability and growth is surprisingly difficult. This does not mean that macroeconomic stability is irrelevant, but more needs to be done beyond a mere emphasis on governments as guardians of stability. This serves as the background to highlight the various means through which macroeconomic policy managers can become active agents of development without forsaking their roles as guardians of stability. These include: sustainable resource mobilization through appropriate fiscal policies to support incentive-compatible policy interventions to promote employment and protect employment opportunities; pertinent changes to monetary and financial policies to enhance financial inclusion; maintaining stable and competitive real exchange rates combined with prudent capital account management to support economic diversification and new areas of employment opportunities.

Chapter 4 Structural transformation and productive employment creation: alternative pathways

In standard development discourse, the assumption is that the essence of a job creation strategy is to transfer low-productivity, 'surplus' labour from rural areas to urban-based manufacturing activities geared towards labour intensive exports. This transition of labour from rural to urban-based export-oriented activities is thus seen as a hallmark of both industrial development and structural transformation that promote durable employment. The success of East Asia in general and China in particular is regarded as a vindication of the effectiveness of this development strategy.

In many parts of the developing world, and most notably Sub-Saharan Africa, the evolution of national economies does not necessarily fit the predictions of standard development theory. The much-awaited transition and productive transformation from rural to an urban-based manufacturing export sector has not taken place.

In tandem with these structural realities, many developing economies have seen the persistence of a moderately sized manufacturing sector that has not managed to play the role of a leading sector in terms of productive employment generation. Instead, the service sector has played a major role in employment creation. Past policies have also entailed benign neglect of the agricultural sector. Rather than bemoaning the phenomenon of 'premature de-industrialization', one needs to find pathways to durable and productive job creation in the developing world that do not necessarily conform to standard models of industrial development and structural transformation.

Chapter 4 argues that it is fruitless to aim for a 'one size fits all' approach. Many developing countries will need to consider a multi-faceted strategy that emphasizes agricultural diversification and service sector driven growth. There is growing international evidence that the expansion of the productive segments of the service sector, rather than being seen as a retrograde step, can have a significant impact on aggregate GDP growth and thus spur both employment expansion and sustainable poverty reduction. In any case, the policy choice is not between either manufacturing or services, but a symbiotic relationship between the two. Modern services can provide intermediate inputs that can propel the expansion of the manufacturing sector.

The chapter also highlights the case of the non-renewable natural resources sector that has played a significant role in many countries in Sub-Saharan Africa and elsewhere. It notes that the natural resources sector cannot, given its characteristics, be a major source of employment creation. However, with the necessary political commitment and appropriate policies, the natural resource sector can support growth and employment-promoting structural transformation.

Chapter 5 Rights-based approach to employment

A rights-based approach to employment has its roots in economic and social rights. If one considers various declarations and agreements at the international level, a rights-based approach to development and employment can be seen to have a well established historical pedigree. But while adopting such an approach, one is confronted with a number of issues, not least of which is the basic question of whether the right to work can be treated as a human right. Related questions include that of specifying a duty bearer, especially in situations where employment results from the operation of market forces and from economic activities undertaken by many different individuals and enterprises. A point raised in this respect is whether it is absolutely essential to have a single duty bearer or whether one could argue for multiple duty bearers in the case of right to work. Another relevant question is whether the right to work should cover only wage paid employment, or self-employment as well.

Efforts to operationalize the rights-based approach to employment would involve identification of the roles and responsibilities of various agents in implementing the right, formulation of relevant policies, and monitoring the process of their implementation. An important question in that respect is whether legal frameworks are needed in order to formalize such procedures or whether it would be adequate to put in place governing procedures that clearly define and articulate the required steps. Employment related conventions and recommendations adopted by the ILO are relevant in this context.

Chapter 5 of the volume attempts to address the issues and questions raised above with respect to the rights-based approach to employment. It starts with a brief description of the historical background and how the right to work has been enshrined in various international protocols. The conceptual underpinnings of the rights-based approach to employment are discussed with a focus on whether it can be regarded as a human right, who the rights holders and duty bearers are, what their relative roles and responsibilities could be. In discussing the scope of the right to work, the difference between the right *to* work and rights *at* work is brought out. Issues relating to the operationalization of the rights-based approach to employment and the role of relevant instruments of the ILO are also discussed.

Chapter 6 Human capital and inclusive development

Human capital can make contributions in production that are different from those made by unskilled labour, and shortage of human capital may emerge as a constraint on the growth of economies in developing countries. However, from the point of view of inclusive development, it is important to look at the impact of human capital not only on the rate of economic growth but also on elements that make growth more inclusive. Following the characterization of inclusive growth presented in Chapter 1, the questions raised in Chapter 6 include the role of education and skill training in reducing poverty and inequality and in improving the employability of potential job-seekers.

Another issue that has not yet received detailed analysis in development literature is how the pattern of demand for education and skills changes with the level of economic development. For example, a country with a good base of elementary education may be able to achieve economic growth up to a certain level and yet face constraints arising from the shortage of skilled workers at a higher level of development. If that is the case, countries would need to keep upgrading the level of their human capital as they achieve higher levels of economic development.

Chapter 6 provides an overview of the role of human capital in attaining inclusive development combining economic growth with reduction of poverty and inequality and improvement in the employability of the labour force. In doing so, particular attention is given to differential education and skill requirement at different levels of development.

Chapter 7 Youth employment

There are several reasons why the issue of youth unemployment deserves special attention. It is well known that unemployment rates are much higher among the youth compared to overall and adult unemployment rates. And this is true of developing countries as well. Moreover, young people may face special difficulties in transiting from the world of learning to the world of work. This may not be a development issue as such in the sense that similar problems may be faced in countries irrespective of the level of development. However, in situations where levels of economic growth are either low or unstable and opportunities for productive employment remain inadequate even with high and stable growth, it is important to understand such specific difficulties that may put the youth in additional disadvantages.

While there are costs associated with unemployment itself, costs associated with youth unemployment may have implications for an economy in terms of missing the potential demographic dividend. This is an important issue in that development literature includes this as a factor that could contribute to economic growth in developing countries.

Moreover, the delay in entering the labour market and unemployment during the early phase of one's life and career is likely to have a 'scarring effect' on longer-term employment and earnings prospects of the youth. This would represent a cost not just for an individual but also for the economy and society as a whole in terms of lost productivity, earnings, tax revenue and other contributions to the economy.

Hence, a strategy for making economic growth more inclusive needs to include an understanding of why youth unemployment is so high and explore what special measures are needed to address the problem in addition to those that are required to promote the growth of productive employment as a whole. Chapter 7 purports to undertake this task. It starts by presenting some data to demonstrate that youth unemployment is much higher than overall and adult unemployment. The data presented also show that the situation worsened during and in the wake of the global economic crisis of 2008–09. The chapter analyses the costs associated with youth unemployment as well as its potential scarring effects, provides an overview of various factors that are responsible for youth unemployment, and reviews strategies, programmes and policies undertaken in response to the challenge of youth unemployment. The review is undertaken with a view to examining what has worked better.

Chapter 8 Labour market flexibility, informality and employment

This chapter reviews the contentious debate on labour market reforms in engendering desirable employment outcomes in developing countries. The orthodox variant of this debate regards all labour market regulations as a cost imposed on employers that induce them to reduce the demand for labour, especially for low-skilled workers. The result is either an increase in unemployment or a decrease in formal sector employment. Admittedly, there are a number of studies that empirically support this view, but one has to be much more circumspect in weighing the evidence. This is perhaps not surprising given that employment in developing countries – both in terms of quantity and quality – is the outcome of a complex interplay of various forces and factors, with labour market regulations being one such factor. Furthermore, labour market reforms need to strike the right balance between protecting workers from labour market risks and preserving broad-based employment opportunities. If reforms end up increasing inequality and imposing adverse short-run adjustment costs, then they militate against the goal of inclusive development.

Perhaps mindful of these concerns and the mixed nature of the evidence, the nature of the global discourse has become more nuanced, with the influential World Development Report of 2013 (World Bank, 2012) endorsing the notion of a 'plateau' effect of labour market regulations: too much regulation is paradoxically bad for workers, but so is too little regulation. Within these limits, there is 'plateau' in which the impact of labour market regulations on employment is benign while yielding redistributive benefits.

The chapter noted that this nuanced view is confronted by a G20-led initiative to make a renewed commitment to structural and labour market reforms as an effective way of promoting global growth and employment in the post-crisis era. The chapter has warned that the renewed emphasis on structural and labour market reforms as the way forward for the global community makes it difficult for a consensus to be reached that can serve as the basis for making progress on the agenda of employment and inclusive growth.

The chapter also notes that over 80 per cent of employers in more than 100,000 firms in over 100 low and middle income countries do not regard labour market regulations as a major impediment to their business operations. To such employers, the quality of governance, lack of a reliable transport network, lack of reliable supply of electricity, lack of access to finance and lack of a skilled workforce are much more pressing issues. Finally, the chapter argues in favour of a pluralist approach to labour market regulations. One should aim for an appropriate mix of policy instruments in attaining the broad goals of mitigating labour market risks and in dealing with chronic in-work poverty. Such an approach is well suited to the notion of striking the right balance between protecting workers against adverse circumstances and preserving broad-based employment opportunities. Only then can labour market reforms play their rightful role in promoting inclusive development.

Chapter 9 Labour market risks and social protection

In countries at all levels of development, the poor and the vulnerable face risks and shocks of various kinds that affect labour markets. While such shocks may make poverty more acute, they create the danger of even the non-poor lapsing into poverty. It is normally difficult to buy private insurance against labour market risks entailing spells of unemployment and underemployment as well as contingencies like old age. Hence, there is a strong case for countries at all levels of development to develop a comprehensive system of social protection that can provide individuals and households with necessary support during contingencies. A number of developments have taken place in this field in recent years.

One is a movement (at the international level) towards developing an agenda for social protection for all. This idea found its expression through the notion of 'social protection floor' which was endorsed by the UN system as a whole in 2009. It calls for initiatives towards ensuring that all citizens in both rich and poor countries at least have access to a minimum bundle of services that would enable people to cope with labour market risks and provide access to affordable healthcare, child benefits and incomes for those who are too old to work.

Another initiative worth noting in the context of a discussion on social protection is a programme under the rubric of 'conditional cash transfers' (CCTs) that started in the Latin American region and gradually gained circulation in other developing regions of the world. The basic premise is that income transfers directed towards poor and vulnerable households can be made incentive-compatible if such transfers are conditioned on ensuring that prospective beneficiaries use the resources received to invest in children's education and health.

Third, employment generation programmes (e.g. the national rural employment guarantee programme in India) are being used as a safety net measure through guaranteeing jobs and livelihoods for the poor.

The above represents a broad agenda for addressing labour market risks through social protection. Chapter 9 adopts this broader approach to analyse the contribution of social protection in making economic growth more inclusive. The chapter first provides an overview of definitional issues relating to various types of risks and modalities of social protection, including the notion of social protection floor. That is followed by a brief discussion on the challenge of social protection faced by developing countries in view of the particular characteristics of their labour markets. The chapter analyses the relationship between social protection and economic growth (from analytical as well as empirical angles) with particular attention to CCT programmes and their role in attaining inclusive development. The interrelationship between social protection and employment is examined, and the questions of cost, financing and affordability of social protection from the point of view of developing countries are addressed.

Notes

1 In the original Harris–Todaro model the use of wage subsidies to lower institutionally determined urban wages is seen as one mechanism for dealing with rural–urban migration. A complementary strategy is rural development to reduce the 'urban bias' in development policies. The model is revisited in Chapter 4.
2 Cazes and Verick (2013) offer a collection of essays that reflect wide ranging issues pertaining to the topic of labour economics from the perspective of developing countries. This book can be seen as a complement to that volume.
3 Islam and Kucera (2014) describe the case of Equatorial Guinea, a small country in Africa where per capita gross domestic product (GDP) grew five-fold between 1990 and 2000, and is classified by the World Bank as a high income non-OECD country. In ten years, the country's economy was transformed from an agrarian economy to an oil-dependent one. But that transformation has not led to real development, much less inclusive development. The incidence of poverty in the country was 77 per cent (based on US$2 per capita per day) in 2006, and life expectancy at birth was 51.4 years (in 2012) which is below the average for Sub-Saharan Africa. Moreover, mean years of schooling declined during 1980 to 2012. The country is also suffering from an acute youth unemployment problem. Quite clearly, high rate of economic growth has not been sufficient to reduce poverty or solve the problem of unemployment.
4 See Islam and Hengge (2015) for a good overview of the evolution of the full employment agenda in both developed and developing countries.
5 The goal of full and productive employment for all women and men and a few indicators relating to that goal were incorporated into the goal of poverty reduction as MDG 1B.
6 IFC (2013); ILO (2014); IMF (2013); World Bank (2012).
7 For example, the report of the High Level Panel of Eminent Persons on the post-2015 development agenda includes job creation as one of the five 'transformative shifts' that are considered to be essential. It asserts: 'There must be a commitment to ... sustained long-term inclusive growth that can overcome the challenge of unemployment' (UN, 2013, p. 8).
8 See World Bank (2012), pp. 98–99.
9 Islam and Hengge (2015) points out the need for a 'dual mandate' in formulating macroeconomic policies maintaining stability and facilitating structural transformation.

Bibliography

Cazes, Sandrine and Verick, Sher (2013) *Perspectives on Labour Economics for Development*, ILO, Geneva.

Harris, J.R. and Todaro, M.P. (1970) 'Migration, Unemployment and Development: A Two-Sector Analysis', *American Economic Review*, vol. 60, pp. 126–142.

IFC (International Finance Corporation) (2013) *Private Sector Contributions to Job Creation*, Washington, D.C.

ILO (International Labour Organization) (2014) *World of Work Report: Developing with Jobs*, Geneva.

IMF (International Monetary Fund) (2013) *Jobs and Growth: Analytical and Operational Conditions for the Fund*, Washington, D.C., available at: www.imf.org/external/np/pp/eng/2013/031413.pdf (accessed 14 July 2014).

Islam, I. and Hengge, M. (2015) 'Renewing the Full Employment Compact: Issues, Evidence and Policy Implications', in Janine Berg (ed.) *Labour Market Institutions and Just Societies*, ILO, Geneva.

Islam, I. and Kucera, D. (2014) *Beyond Macroeconomic Stability: Structural Transformation and Inclusive Development*, Geneva, and Palgrave Macmillan, Basingstoke.

Islam, R. (2006a) 'The Nexus of Economic Growth, Employment and Poverty Reduction: An Empirical Analysis', in Islam, R. (ed.) *Fighting Poverty: The Development-Employment Link*, Lynne Rienner, Boulder and London.

Islam, R. (ed.) (2006b) *Fighting Poverty: The Development-Employment Link*, Lynne Rienner, Boulder and London.

Islam, R. (2012) 'Addressing the Jobs Challenge', blog at ODI's site on 'Development Progress', available at: www.developmentprogress.org/blog/2012/11/08/addressing-jobs-challenge (accessed 10 December 2013).

Khan, A.R. (2007) 'Asian Experience on Growth, Employment and Poverty: An Overview with Special Reference to the Findings of some Recent Case Studies', ILO, Geneva and UNDP, Colombo.

Lewis, A. (1954) 'Economic Development with Unlimited Supplies of Labour', *Manchester School*, vol. 22, pp. 139–191.

UN (United Nations) (2013) *A New Global Partnership: Eradicate Poverty and Transform Economies through Sustainable Development*, Report of the High Level Panel of Eminent Persons on the Post-2015 Development Agenda, New York.

World Bank (2008) *The Growth Report: Strategies for Sustainable Growth and Inclusive Development*, Commission on Growth and Development, Washington, D.C.

World Bank (2012) *World Development Report 2013 Jobs*, Washington, D.C.

2 Employment and inclusive growth

A development perspective

Introduction

As economic growth is usually expected to result in employment growth and poverty reduction, the major concern in both academic literature on economic development and in development debate in policy circles has been with analysis of rates and determinants of economic growth and with policies for boosting economic growth. This has been the case, for example, in influential studies like the one on the East Asian miracle (World Bank, 1993) and the report of the Commission on Economic Growth (World Bank, 2008). However, by now, there is sufficient empirical evidence to cast doubt on the conventional view about the automaticity in the relationships between economic growth, employment and poverty (Islam, 2006a, 2006b; Khan, 2007). Neither the relationship between economic growth and employment nor the one between growth and poverty is invariant.

The notions of pro-poor growth, and later, of inclusive growth, came into circulation in the wake of the realization that economic growth does not necessarily result in reduction of poverty and growth of employment at rates commensurate with economic growth. However, the notion of inclusive growth still lacks rigour and clarity both in terms of definition and empirical application. For example, even though the relationship between economic growth and poverty is not invariant and there is evidence that employment-intensity of output growth plays an important role in explaining the variation (Islam, 2006a), the role of employment is not clear in the debates on pro-poor and inclusive growth.

Recent research[1] has also shown that the employment intensity of economic growth in many developing countries has been rather low and declining despite the existence of surplus labour. That has given rise to the concern that many countries are experiencing 'jobless growth'. While the work mentioned above has drawn the attention of the research community to the issue of employment intensity of economic growth, a number of related questions also arise. The first relates to the term 'jobless growth' itself. Can there be growth of output without the growth of employment? Second, would the pursuit of employment intensive growth not result in a compromise with productivity and efficiency? Third, what are the factors that make a difference in the relationship between growth and employment? How does one explain the phenomenon of low and declining employment intensity of growth and what are the real constraints on employment growth? The present chapter addresses these questions.

The basic purpose of the present chapter would be to place productive employment in the context of the debate on pro-poor and inclusive growth. It aims at providing (1) conceptual clarifications of the terms 'inclusive' and 'jobless growth', (2) empirical evidence on the relationship between output growth and employment growth in a large cross-section of developing countries to examine whether growth has really been jobless, and (3) diagnosis of factors that can explain the variation in the relationship between output and employment growth.

The chapter is organized as follows. First, some analytical and conceptual issues, specifically the terms 'inclusive growth' and 'jobless growth' and the possibility of trade-off between employment and productivity are discussed. Cross-country data on economic growth and employment growth are then examined in order to see whether growth was indeed jobless. The issue of possible trade-off between productivity and employment growth is taken up next, which is followed by a discussion on constraints on the growth of employment. The chapter ends with some concluding observations.

Conceptual and analytical issues

Interpreting the notion of jobless growth

Before the global economy went into recession in 2008, healthy growth was achieved for several years. And yet, the employment situation did not improve in many countries, especially in the developing ones.[2] Indeed, in some of them, employment growth lagged far behind overall economic growth rates.[3] The phenomenon was particularly noticeable in the formal sectors of the economies. The term 'jobless growth' came back into currency in that context.[4] But several questions arise in this regard. First, what is meant by the term 'jobless growth'? In other words, can there at all be output growth without any growth of jobs? Or, for that matter, does jobless growth imply, in a literal sense, output growth without any employment growth? Second, from the point of view of moving towards the goal of full employment, is employment growth irrespective of output growth a desirable outcome? In other words, when one talks about the desirability of job-rich (or employment intensive) growth what is really meant? Some clarifications on these questions may be useful before embarking on a discussion in this important field.

While looking for a definition of the term 'jobless growth', it is found that although the term has been widely used, especially at the level of international agencies, there is not much by way of a carefully articulated definition. One of the early uses of the term and some indication of a definition is found in the 1993 *Human Development Report* of the United Nations Development Programme (UNDP) which states: 'Many parts of the world are witnessing a new phenomenon: *jobless growth*. Even when output increases, increase in employment lags way behind' (UNDP, 1993, p. 36). From this description, it appears that to the UNDP, jobless growth means employment growth lagging substantially behind output growth. Another UNDP report (UNDP, 1996) uses low employment growth relative to output growth as an illustration of jobless growth. This kind of definition has the problem that it does not specify any quantitative indicator of how far employment has to lag behind output growth in order for growth to be called jobless.

ILO's World Employment Report 2004–05 (ILO, 2005) talks about jobless growth specifically in the context of economic recovery in the USA from the recession in 2001, and points out not only the lag with which employment growth followed economic growth but also the sluggishness of employment growth till 2004. This seems to imply that the term 'jobless growth' was used in the same sense as the UNDP, to imply a situation where employment growth was much lower than output growth.

Of course, the term 'jobless growth' can be interpreted in other ways, for example by comparing employment growth with that of labour force growth, and by looking at the overall employment/unemployment situation of a country in relation to its economic growth rate. Using this approach, Bhorat and Oosthuizen (2006) suggested three different 'tests' of jobless growth: (1) positive economic growth associated with zero or negative employment growth; (2) positive economic growth associated with employment growth lagging behind labour force growth and hence rising unemployment; (3) positive output growth associated with employment growth below a 'satisfactory level'. A comparison of employment growth with that of labour force is extremely important from the point of view of policies and measures for moving towards full employment; but it may be easy to pass the test of non-zero and non-negative employment growth while employment growth is very slow compared to economic growth. As for the second test, employment growth could be less than the growth of labour force even with positive economic growth if growth is very low; and in that kind of situation, it is not simply low employment growth but also low economic growth itself that is the main problem. The same observation would apply about the third test if economic growth is low; even with a 'satisfactory' level of employment growth, the overall rate of employment may be insufficient to achieve a significant improvement in the employment situation or prevent its deterioration. The upshot of this discussion is that from the point of achieving full employment, it would be important to simultaneously achieve high rates of economic as well as employment growth. The point may be clarified by using a simple diagram as in Figure 2.1 where a stylized picture of various possible combinations of output and employment growth is presented.

The four quadrants of Figure 2.1 show different combinations of output and employment growth in a typical developing economy. While quadrants III and IV represent high rates of output growth, I and II represent low levels of output growth. The growth experience that has been referred to above, namely one of high output growth accompanied by low growth of employment growth, is

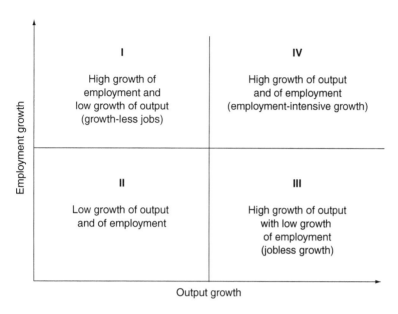

Figure 2.1 Combinations of output and employment growth (source: author's elaboration).

represented by quadrant III. It may be noted that observations in this quadrant need not be literally on the *x*-axis denoting zero employment growth with positive and high output growth. Observations inside the quadrant also represent situations that are not helpful from the point of view of achieving full employment, and are perhaps being referred to as indicating 'jobless growth'.

On the other hand, it is conceivable to find countries where, despite low output growth, employment growth may be high if employment is driven by a supply push and people find jobs in low productivity activities of a residual nature. Such a situation would reflect distress and employment of last resort where the alternative is unemployment and starvation (in the absence of any social protection measures). Quadrant I of Figure 2.1 could depict other types of situations, e.g. public sector enterprises creating jobs without regard to output growth or even private enterprises 'hoarding labour' during a period of economic downturn in the hope of a quick recovery. In an empirical exercise involving estimation of the elasticity of employment growth with respect to output growth, observations in quadrant I will demonstrate high values. In such a situation, if employment elasticity alone is used as an indicator of whether growth in an economy has been employment intensive and hence good from the point of view of achieving full employment and accelerating poverty reduction, it will provide misleading signals.

Quadrant IV represents situations where high growth of employment goes together with high growth of output. This naturally would be the desirable outcome of economic growth in situations where growth is expected to be the means for achieving the goals of full employment and rapid rate of poverty reduction using the employment route. Hence, from a policy point of view, the goal would have to be to move a country towards quadrant IV, wherever it is currently placed. And when one talks about employment intensive (or job-rich) growth, it should be interpreted as referring to a growth scenario depicted in quadrant IV (*not* in quadrant I).

The concept and indicators of inclusive growth

Critical overview of various definitions and interpretations of the term 'inclusive growth'

The term 'inclusive growth' has been brought into use by agencies providing support to developing countries – working at both international and bilateral levels. The international agencies instrumental in this regard are the World Bank, the regional development banks (e.g. the Asian Development Bank (ADB)) and the UNDP. Amongst the bilateral development support institutions, the UK's Department for International Development (DFID) has been active in putting this term in circulation. What has led them to do so? In answering this question, it may be useful to briefly recall the evolution of the development paradigm during the past five decades or so.

It may be noted that in the wake of limitations of development strategies applied during the 1960s and 1970s, a major shift in paradigm took place in the early 1980s. Steered primarily by the World Bank and the IMF (and supported by major developed countries of the world), the paradigm at that time was characterized by the centrality of market and of economic growth which is expected to result from unhindered operation of market forces. The package of policies put together around this basic theme that included privatization and liberalization, and later dubbed the 'Washington Consensus', became the cornerstone of so-called stabilization and structural adjustment policies prescribed by the international development financial institutions and imposed on a large number of developing countries throughout the 1980s and 1990s. However, the limitations of that prescription – even in achieving higher rate of economic growth, not to speak of achieving the goals of economic development and poverty reduction – became apparent and the need to look at alternatives was being widely recognized even within the organizations that promoted the paradigm. The result was the introduction, in the late 1990s and the early 2000s, of Poverty Reduction Strategy Papers (PRSPs) and the notion of pro-poor growth.

In the debate on pro-poor growth that ensued, two broad approaches and definitions emerged – absolute and relative. Under the absolute definition, growth is considered to be pro-poor as long as the poor benefit in absolute terms, as reflected in some agreed measure of poverty (Ravallion and Chen, 2003). In contrast, in the relative definition, growth is pro-poor if and only if the incomes of the poor people increase faster than those of the population as a whole, i.e. if inequality declines[5] (Kakwani and Pernia, 2000; Kakwani, 2002). Thus, the basic difference between the two approaches to pro-poor growth turned out to be in the emphasis on inequality. And that is what gave rise to a degree of uneasiness around the notion itself. Even though the absolute definition – which recognized any growth that resulted in some poverty reduction as pro-poor irrespective of the outcome on inequality – was favoured by the World Bank, there was an apprehension that strategies for pro-poor growth may focus only on relatively poorer people and may thus ignore the impact on the others who may be critical from the point of view of investment and economic growth in an economy. This apprehension eventually resulted in the replacement of pro-poor growth by 'inclusive growth' as the favoured paradigm.

How is inclusive growth [IG] defined? The answer is not straightforward because there is no universally accepted definition of the term. In fact, there are differences in approaches adopted by different organizations, e.g. the World Bank, the ADB and the UNDP.[6] Take the World Bank, for example:

> Rapid and sustained poverty reduction requires inclusive growth that allows people to contribute to and benefit from economic growth. Rapid pace of growth is unquestionably necessary for substantial poverty reduction, but for this growth to be sustainable in the long run, it should be broad-based across sectors, and inclusive of large part of the country's labour force. This definition of inclusive growth implies a direct link between the macro and micro determinants of growth. [...] Inclusive growth refers to both to the pace and pattern of growth which are considered interlinked, and therefore in need to be addressed together.
>
> (World Bank, 2009, pp. 1 and 2)

The tension about the treatment of inequality is apparent from the following statements:

> The inclusive growth definition is in line with the absolute definition of pro-poor growth, but not the relative definition.... By focusing on inequality, the relative definition could lead to sub-optimal outcomes for both poor and non-poor households. [...] IG focuses on productive employment rather than income distribution.
>
> (World Bank, 2009, pp. 3 and 4)

A few aspects of the notion of inclusive growth that stand out clearly from the World Bank's definition may be noted:[7]

- There is a renewed emphasis of the centrality of economic growth, enlarging the size of an economy and the importance of investment. While growth is a necessary condition for poverty reduction, and measures to raise growth are important, what is notable is the almost single-minded pursuit of this goal suggested for many developing countries. Note the following statement: 'When it comes to poor countries growing at very low rates, the main focus of inclusive growth approach should be on getting the fundamentals for growth right' (World Bank, 2010, p. 2).

However, not much is said about what kind of strategy should be adopted except for pointing out the usefulness of the growth diagnostic analysis developed by Hausmann *et al.* (2005).

- There is some internal contradiction in the definition or elaboration of the notion of inclusive growth by the World Bank. For example, mention is made of the importance of both the rate and pattern of growth; yet, when it comes to matters of details, it is mentioned that there is no need to have policies for promoting labour intensive industries. What then is implied when the pattern of growth is mentioned?

- The importance of productive employment is mentioned explicitly, and yet there is no indication of how growth of productive employment can be enhanced. In contrast, as mentioned above, the possibility of favouring a pattern of growth focused on labour intensive sectors is ruled out (World Bank, 2009, p. 11, footnote 20). The experience of countries that succeeded in combining high rate of economic growth with growth of productive employment shows that the pattern of growth is extremely important, and labour intensive sectors have played an important role during the early stages of their development (Islam, 2010a, 2010b). For economic growth to result in poverty reduction at high and sustained rate, two more conditions need to be fulfilled. For the wage employed, real wages need to rise in line with increases in labour productivity. For the self-employed, productivity and real earnings have to increase. In both respects, the main focus in the World Bank definition seems to be on business environment and employability rather than on how demand for labour can increase and how workers and the poor self-employed could benefit from the process.

- The shift away from income distribution is very clear from the definition of inclusive growth suggested by World Bank. Indeed, a view that is implicit in the World Bank's definition is that strategies to improve income distribution may be inimical to raising the rate of economic growth. Note, for example, the statement: 'Inclusive growth focuses on ex-ante analysis of sources of, and constraints to sustained, high growth, and not only on one group – the poor' (World Bank, 2009, p. 3).

Asian Development Bank (ADB) is another organization where considerable amount of discussion has taken place on inclusive growth. Yet it appears that a single, agreed-upon definition has not emerged from there. Reports coming out of the ADB itself recognize this. Klasen (2010, p. 1), for example, mentions that various ADB documents reveal conflicting definitions – some are vague and do not lend themselves to quantification, while others are specific but do not capture the essence of the concept. Another ADB document (Rauniyar and Kanbur, 2009) summarizes the situation thus:[8]

> According to ADB literature ... there is no agreed-upon and common definition of inclusive development. The concept, however, is understood to refer to 'growth coupled with equal opportunities'. It focuses on creating

opportunities and making them accessible to all, not just to the poor. There is inclusive growth when all members of a society participate in and contribute to the growth process equally, regardless of their individual circumstances. In the same way, inclusive growth is one that emphasizes that economic opportunities created by growth are available to all, particularly to the poor, to the maximum extent possible.

(Rauniyar and Kanbur, 2009, p. 3)

The same paper goes on to state that efforts to achieve inclusive growth and inclusive development should involve a combination of mutually reinforcing measures including (1) promoting efficient and sustainable economic growth, (2) ensuring a level playing field, (3) strengthening capacities, and (4) providing social safety nets.

The definition mentioned above was earlier suggested in another ADB study (Ali and Son, 2007, pp. 1–2). However, Ali and Son's listing of the key elements of inclusive growth is different from the above-mentioned list. Their list includes: (i) productive employment, (ii) developing human capabilities through adequate investment in basic social services like education and health, and (iii) social safety nets.

Based on the characterization of inclusive growth within ADB (and recognizing that it does not have a unique definition of the term) a few observations may be made:

- First, whatever may be the official definition of inclusive growth within ADB, the renewed focus on economic growth is quite clear. This is clear from the list of elements emerging from Rauniyar and Kanbur (2009) as mentioned above where growth and level playing field appear as the first two items.
- Relegation of the distributional issue is also clear from the emphasis on opportunities for all and not just for the poor (see Klasen's definition mentioned above).

Thus, with regard to the emphasis on growth and moving away from inequality, there is similarity between the definitions adopted by the World Bank and the ADB. However, there are also differences:

- ADB seems to be at odds with the World Bank in its focus on social safety nets. Although ADB's focus on this element does not go beyond safety nets for the poor, this represents at least a thinking of how the poor can be provided with support in the event of their inability to benefit adequately from the process of economic growth. Of course, ADB's treatment of safety nets falls short of the idea of a basic social protection floor which has been adopted by the UN system as part of the strategy to provide social protection for all.
- Individual studies emerging from the ADB also appear to define IG differently from the organization's 'official' definition. Rauniyar and Kanbur

(2010), for example, characterize IG as growth with declining inequality.[9] And in that sense, their definition appears to be similar to the relative definition of pro-poor growth. Another study coming out from ADB (Ali and Son, 2007) defines IG very differently from the official definition. This study focuses on the distribution in the access to employment and social opportunities like education and health services. It defines IG as 'growth that not only creates new opportunities, but also one that ensures equal access to the opportunities created for all segments of society' (Ali and Son, 2007, p. 1). The methodology developed by the study for measuring inclusive growth explicitly introduces the notion of equity in order to examine how the opportunities are distributed.

UNDP does not appear to have come up with an official definition of inclusive growth. However, the website of UNDP's International Policy Centre for Inclusive Growth (IPC-IG) introduces inclusive growth as follows:

Inclusive growth is both an outcome and a process. On the one hand, it ensures that everyone can participate in the growth process, both in terms of decision making for organizing the growth progression as well as in participating in the growth itself. On the other hand, it makes sure that everyone shares equitably the benefits of growth. Inclusive growth implies participation and benefit sharing.

It is quite clear from the above that for UNDP, IG implies not only participation in the process of growth but also equity in the sharing of the outcome of growth. This way of defining IG is not only at odds with that of the World Bank, but it goes some way in making the term IG meaningful. If one simply talks about participation in the process of growth, it should not be difficult to argue that in almost all situations, everybody in a society participates in the process of growth in some way or the other. Hence, in order to make the concept of inclusiveness meaningful, it is essential to bring in the aspect of equity with regard to the distribution of the outcome of growth. And it appears that the approach of the UNDP (as well as that suggested by some of the studies emerging from the ADB as mentioned above) addresses this important aspect.

Inclusive growth: a suggested characterization

It is quite clear that in order to define the concept of inclusive growth in a meaningful manner, it would be necessary to go beyond an approach focused only on process and on a concept like participation which is not amenable to quantification and can be interpreted in a variety of ways. Indeed, in a broad sense, every member of the work force participates in the growth process in the sense that (s)he does something that contributes to the economy. Hence, in order to bring a real meaning in the definition, it would be important to focus on both the process and outcome. While the process of inclusion can be captured through measures relating to employment, the outcomes can be assessed in terms of income relative to some benchmark of poverty, inequality or other dimension of human development (e.g. education and health). Another important element of inclusiveness is the degree of social protection provided by a society. The following elements would be important from the point of view of making growth inclusive:[10]

• Stable economic growth that is sustainable;
• Reduction of poverty and inequality in the distribution of income;
• Improvement in the access to education and health services;
• Opportunities for productive employment; and
• Basic social protection floor for all citizens.

A few words may be in order about the elements suggested above. First, in order for *economic growth* to play its role in reducing poverty, it has to be stable over time and sustainable in the context of a country's macroeconomic situation. The latter, in turn, may be looked at in terms of macroeconomic stability with respect to inflation, budgetary situation and the situation with regard to other macroeconomic variables like debt, exchange rate, etc.

While economic growth is a necessary condition for poverty reduction, there are studies showing that it is not sufficient. Indeed, there is no invariant relationship between growth and poverty reduction (Islam, 2006a, 2006b). Hence, the degree to which economic growth results in a *reduction of poverty* needs to be looked at in specific terms. Now the question would be: what rate of poverty reduction (or poverty reduction in relation to economic growth) could be regarded as consistent with the notion of inclusive growth? While no specific figure can be prescribed in this respect, a useful benchmark is provided by the MDGs with respect to reduction of poverty and hunger.

As for *inequality*, although there is a degree of uneasiness about its inclusion in the concept of inclusive growth, it needs to be understood that an exclusive focus on process without any attention to the outcome would make the concept ineffective. Once one focuses on outcome, one would note that even in order to achieve reduction in absolute poverty it would be necessary to be mindful of what happens to inequality because the poverty reducing effect of growth can be neutralized (or at least countered) by the adverse effect of increase in inequality. Hence, a reduction in inequality in the distribution of income (or at least preventing a rise in inequality) has to be an important element in the effort to achieve inclusive growth.

Education and health are among the basic ingredients that are critical for creating and improving capabilities of the people that are vital from the point of view of benefiting from the benefits of growth. As for indicators of progress in these respects, there are clearly articulated MDGs that could be utilized as benchmarks to measure progress made by a country.

Productive employment is critical from the point of view of translating the benefits of economic growth into poverty reduction. Indeed, there are studies (for example, Islam, 2006a, 2006b) demonstrating that employment intensity of growth is an important variable influencing the poverty reducing outcome of economic growth. Hence the degree of employment intensity of economic growth should be an important indicator of inclusive growth. In addition to a quantitative measure of the degree of employment intensity of growth (which does not capture the level of productivity), it would be useful to look at the changes in the structure of employment in order to examine whether a shift is taking place towards more productive and remunerative sectors of employment. In addition, there are targets within the framework of MDGs (target 1B) that provide some indicators of progress in the field of employment: (1) growth rate of labour productivity (GDP per person employed); (2) employment-to-population ratio; (3) the incidence of working poor (measured by the proportion of employed people living below poverty line); (4) the incidence of vulnerable employment (measured as the ratio of own-account and contributing family works to total employment).

Basic social protection is a human right. It may be recalled that Article 22 of the Universal Declaration of Human Rights (UN, 1948) states: 'Everyone, as a member of society, has the right to social security'. The idea of a 'social protection floor' has been developed in the wake of the global economic crisis of 2008–09 as a means of providing protection against risks and uncertainties of various types (ILO and WHO, 2009; see also the documents at ILO's 'Social Protection Floor Initiative', available at: www.socialsecurityextension.org). If people, especially the poor, are not to be left to the vagaries of market forces, the idea of inclusive growth has to incorporate a minimum package of social protection measures. While this package could vary from country to country depending on the level of development and capabilities, a basic minimum suggested by the ILO is: (1) access to basic/essential healthcare benefits; (2) income security for children at least at the poverty level through various family/child benefits or transfers; (3) targeted income support to the poor and the unemployed; (4) income security for the old and the disabled – at least at the poverty level – through pensions for old age and disability benefits for survivors (ILO, 2008).

Employment intensive growth and labour productivity[11]

Mention has already been made above of the inverse relationship between employment elasticity and labour productivity which implies the possibility of a trade-off between employment growth and labour productivity. In reality, however, this trade-off does not have to be very serious. One can see this easily if one remembers that in an accounting framework, both the quantity of labour input and labour productivity contribute to output growth. Depending on the policies pursued, a country may be able to achieve a balanced contribution of both these elements towards output growth. This proposition is explained further below.

For an economy as a whole, output is equal to the product of the labour force employed and labour productivity. This can be expressed through the following identity:

$$Y = L \times Y / L, \tag{1}$$

where Y and L stand respectively for output and employment.
For small changes, one can write the above as

$$\Delta Y = \Delta L + \Delta(Y/L), \tag{2}$$

where Δ indicates growth rate.

Expression (2) implies that growth in output is the sum of the growth of employed labour force and growth of labour productivity. Thus, both employment in quantitative terms and labour productivity can potentially contribute to output growth. Indeed, if output growth is sufficiently high, there could be scope for substantial increases in both employment and productivity growth.[12] And that has been the experience of East and South East Asian economies like those of the Republic of Korea, Taiwan, China, Malaysia and, to a lesser extent, Indonesia and Thailand (especially before they were hit by the East Asian economic crisis in 1997–98).

Jobless growth in the developing world: some empirical evidence

Employment and output growth in manufacturing industries in developing countries

It needs to be noted that employment growth in developing countries cannot often be taken as a reflection of labour demand because, for a variety of reasons, employment growth may reflect both demand and supply of labour force. However, for the organized sectors, e.g. manufacturing, employment would perhaps reflect the demand side more closely than overall employment, and hence it may be more meaningful to look at the relationship between employment and output growth for such sectors. Figures 2.2a and 2.2b present such data for selected developing countries for two periods – 1980s and 1990s. The countries and the periods covered by these figures are dictated by the availability of data. However, these two figures bring out interesting points concerning the relationship between employment and output growth.

First, in terms of the conceptualization of the terms 'jobless growth' and 'employment intensive growth', it appears from the figures that not many can be said to belong to the category of employment intensive growth. This would be the case if combinations of 10 per cent or more output growth and fiver per cent or more employment growth are regarded as employment investive growth. While this is, admittedly, arbitrary, the experience of countries that have succeeded in achieving high growth of both output and employment in manufacturing in the past (e.g. those in some countries of East and South East Asia) indicates that such growth is quite possible. More disconcerting from the point of view of achieving high growth of productive employment is that the number

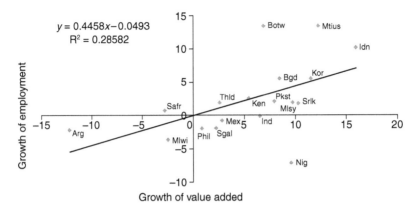

Figure 2.2a Annual growth of employment and value added in manufacturing, 1980–89 (source: prepared by the authors using data from UNIDO (2005)).

Notes
Arg: Argentina; Bgd: Bangladesh; Botw: Botswana; Ind: India; Idn: Indonesia; Ken: Kenya; Kor: Korea; Mlwi: Malawi; Mlsy: Malaysia; Mtius: Mauritius; Mex: Mexico; Nig: Nigeria; Pkst: Pakistan; Phil: Philippines; Sgal: Senegal; Safr: South Africa; Srlk: Sri Lanka; Thld: Thailand.

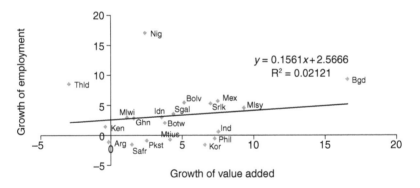

Figure 2.2b Annual growth of employment and value added in manufacturing, 1990–2002 (source: prepared by the authors using data from UNIDO (2005)).

Notes
Arg: Argentina; Bgd: Bangladesh; Botw: Botswana; Ind: India; Idn: Indonesia; Ken: Kenya; Kor: Korea; Mlwi: Malawi; Mlsy: Malaysia; Mtius: Mauritius; Mex: Mexico; Nig: Nigeria; Pkst: Pakistan; Phil: Philippines; Sgal: Senegal; Safr: South Africa; Srlk: Sri Lanka; Thld: Thailand.

of countries achieving employment intensive growth is lower in the second period.

Second, a comparison of the slopes of the two lines showing the employment output relationship indicates clearly that the strength of the relationship between the two variables has weakened in the second period. This is also confirmed statistically by the lower value of the regression coefficient of value added for the second period. This simply implies that output growth in the second period has been less employment intensive as a whole for the sample countries.

Third, there are quite a few cases of negative employment growth when output growth was positive. In fact, the number of such cases is larger during the second period. This provides further support for the conclusion that output growth in the second period has been less employment intensive than in the first period. It is also clear that positive output growth is not necessarily associated with positive employment growth. Output growth in several cases has not only been 'jobless' in a literal sense, there has been a decline in employment when output has grown.

Elasticity of employment with respect to output

Asia

Table 2.1 presents some estimates of the elasticity of employment with respect to output – for manufacturing as well as for the economy as a whole – for selected countries of Asia.

A few important conclusions emerge from the data presented in Table 2.1. First, there appears to have been a general decline in the employment intensity

Table 2.1 Output elasticity of employment (OEE) in selected Asian countries

Country	OEE (economy-wide)		OEE (manufacturing)	
	1980s	*1990s*	*1980s*	*1990s*
Bangladesh[a]	0.55[b]	0.50[b]	0.76[c]	0.72[c]
Cambodia	n.a.	0.48	n.a.	0.56
China	0.33[b]	0.13[b]	0.5	0.25[d]
India	0.4	0.15	0.37	0.29
Indonesia	0.44[b]	0.38[b]	0.79[e]	0.61[f]
Malaysia	0.55	0.48	0.67[g]	0.71[g]
Sri Lanka	0.51	0.46	0.55[h]	0.45[h]
Thailand	0.56	0.1	0.64	0.47
			0.55	0.53

Notes and sources
Unless specified otherwise, the figures have been taken from recent ILO-UNDP country case studies, a synthesis of which can be found in Khan (2007).
a Islam, (2006a).
b Asian Development Bank (2005)
c These figures are based on data at three-digit level. Figures based on four-digit level data show a sharper decline – from 0.74 to 0.60. See Chapter 5 in Islam (2006b).
d Figure for 2002.
e Figure for 1980–84.
f Figure for 1990–94.
g Khan (2007).
h Elasticity with respect to value added.

of growth in the manufacturing sector of the developing countries of Asia during the 1990s compared to the 1980s. While the declines in countries like Malaysia and Thailand could be taken as reflecting the tightening of their labour markets, the same cannot be said about other countries which are still characterized by surplus labour. Second, during the 1980s, the level of employment intensity in manufacturing in some countries (e.g. Cambodia, China and India) was rather low in relation to their factor endowment. Indeed, those levels appear quite conspicuous if compared with the levels in Korea and Malaysia during their early stages of industrialization when their economies still had surplus labour. Third, the degree of employment intensity seems to have declined further from such low levels. Fourth, although for reasons mentioned earlier, we prefer to look at employment elasticity figures for the economy as a whole with more caution, the figures presented in Table 2.1 tend to go along the same line as those on manufacturing. They generally point to a trend towards falling employment intensity of economic growth as a whole.

Data on economy-wide employment elasticity for broad regions presented in Table 2.2 generally confirms the tendency towards a decline over time for developing regions including Asia.

A look at country level data on growth of output and employment for different sub-periods brings out further interesting aspects of the phenomena of jobless and employment intensive growth. Such data for selected countries of Asia are presented in Figure 2.3 and Table 2.3. An example of how the situation can change within the same country is provided by the experience of Indonesia during 1975–96 and 2001–03. During the earlier period, manufacturing industries in that country attained high growth of both output and employment. Indeed, that provides a good example of employment intensive growth that is close to the stylized version of quadrant IV of Figure 2.1. The situation changed

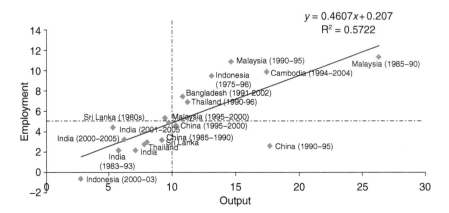

Figure 2.3 Growth of manufacturing output and employment in selected countries of Asia (source: the data are from the in-depth country-level studies referred to in Khan (2007), except for the figures for Bangladesh which are from Ahmed *et al.* (2009)).

Table 2.2 Elasticity of employment with respect to output in different regions of the world, 1984–2008

Regions	Output growth		Employment growth		Elasticity of employment	
	1984–98	*1999–2008*	*1984–98*	*1999–2008*	*1984–98*	*1999–2008*
All countries	3.0	4.2	1.3	1.6	0.43	0.38
Developed countries	2.9	2.7	1.1	1.6	0.38	0.59
C and SE Europe, CIS	−0.3	5.8	−0.7	0.8	n.c.	0.14
Developing countries	4.3	4.4	2.3	2.1	0.53	0.48
Asia	5.5	5.7	2.1	1.8	0.38	0.32
LAC	3.2	3.5	2.6	2.4	0.81	0.69
MENA	n.a.	4.5	n.a.	2.2	n.a.	0.49
SSA	n.a.	4.1	n.a.	1.2	n.a.	0.29

Source: Authors' estimates based on data from Kucera and Roncolato (2012).

Notes
C and SE = Central South East; CIS = Commonwealth of Independent States; LAC = Latin America and Caribbean; MENA = Middle East and North Africa; SSA = Sub-Saharan Africa; n.a. = not available; n.c. = not calculated.

Table 2.3 Growth of manufacturing employment and output in selected countries of Asia

Country (period)	Annual growth of employment (%)	Annual growth of output (%)
Bangladesh (1991–2002)	7.5	10.9
Cambodia (1994–2004)	9.8	17.4
China (1985–90)	3.1	9.2
China (1990–95)	2.6	17.7
China (1995–99)	4.6	10.3
India (1983–93)	2.1	5.8
India (1993–99)	2.1	7.1
India (2000–05)	3.2	6.2
Indonesia (1975–96)	9.4	13.0
Indonesia (2000–03)	−0.7	2.8
Malaysia (1985–90)	11.2	26.3
Malaysia (1990–95)	10.8	14.7
Malaysia (1995–2000)	4.9	9.8
Sri Lanka (1980s)	4.3	5.3
Sri Lanka (1990s)	2.9	8.0
Thailand (1980–89)	5.3	9.4
Thailand (1990–96)	6.8	11.2
Thailand (2001–04)	2.7	7.8

Source: the data are from the in-depth country-level studies referred to in Khan (2007), except for the figures for Bangladesh which are from Ahmed *et al.* (2009).

completely after the economic crisis of 1997–98. It not only took several years for the country to return to a path of sustained growth, the labour market responded with an even longer lag (Islam, 2003, 2010a). During 2000–03, employment growth in the manufacturing sector was negative although output growth was positive. Thus, from a case of employment intensive growth, Indonesia turned into a case of jobless growth.

In fact, employment elasticity in Indonesia's manufacturing had already started to decline since the mid-1980s (0.66 during 1986–92 compared to 0.76 during 1981–85). For some industries like textiles, garments, furniture and food manufacturing, employment elasticity during 1993–97 was lower compared to 1985–88 (Islam, R., 2002). It appears that the trend not only continued during the post-crisis period, but may have accelerated. From a policy point of view, it would be important to understand the factors behind such a phenomenon – an issue to which we shall return in the subsequent sections.

A change similar to that of Indonesia (although not so sharp) is noticeable in the case of Thailand where both output and employment growth in manufacturing was higher during 1990–96 compared to 1980–89. However, both output and employment growth declined sharply during 2001–04. If only the elasticity of employment declined, it could probably have been ascribed to a change in the labour market situation. But the simultaneous decline of output and employment growth and a sharper decline in the latter point to possibilities that are deeper than simple changes in the labour supply situation.

The change in China presents a contrast to the changes observed in Indonesia and Thailand. Elasticity of employment in manufacturing declined in China during 1990–95 (when output growth increased sharply) compared to 1985–90, but increased during 1995–99. Again, it would be useful to find out if any policy changes contributed to the above-mentioned improvement.

Sub-Saharan Africa

Detailed country level studies of the kind from which data on the Asian countries presented in Table 2.1 have been obtained are not available for Sub-Saharan Africa (or for that matter for countries in other developing regions). However, an attempt has been made to estimate elasticity of employment with respect to value added in the manufacturing sector for selected countries (for which necessary data are available from the United Nations Industrial Development Organization (UNIDO) source mentioned in the appendix to this chapter). The results are presented in Table 2.4. However, the figures presented in Table 2.4 have to be interpreted with caution for a variety of reasons. First, in some cases, the sign of the coefficient is negative because of negative growth rate in either value added or employment. Second, in some cases, the regression equation did not provide statistically significant coefficient or a good fit in terms of R-squared. The results may be looked at with these caveats.

In several cases, there has been a decline in employment elasticity during the 1990–2002 period compared to 1980–89; they include Botswana, Malawi and Mauritius. Indeed, in Mauritius, employment growth during the second period was negative. In Kenya, the problem appears to be a decline in value added rather than a decline in employment intensity of growth. The countries which demonstrate improvement in terms of employment intensity of growth are Nigeria and Senegal. The former moved from a situation of negative growth of employment during the 1980s to one with positive and reasonable employment elasticity. Senegal also moved in the same direction and the employment elasticity registered for the 1990s is very high (in fact, higher than one – implying a decline in labour productivity). In the case of South Africa, a comparison becomes difficult because in the 1980s, the country's manufacturing sector registered negative value added growth while during 1990–2002, employment growth was negative despite positive value added growth.

Figures presented in an earlier study (Khan, 2006) on some countries of Sub-Saharan Africa also showed mixed results. Ethiopia and Uganda showed rather low employment intensity of growth in manufacturing, although both demonstrated a slight increase during the 1990s compared to the earlier decade. Increases were also seen in the cases of Ghana, Côte d'Ivoire, Kenya and Nigeria. But there were declines in Burkina Faso, South Africa, Zambia and Zimbabwe. On the whole, the conclusion was that most countries of Sub-Saharan Africa were not able to get on to a path of industrialization that would enable them to move labour away from low productivity sectors and raise their incomes on a sustained basis.

Table 2.4 Elasticity of employment with respect to output for selected developing countries, 1980–2002

Countries	Employment and output			Employment and value added		
	1980–90	1990–2002	1980–2002[a]	1980–90	1990–2002	1980–2002[a]
Argentina	0.03	0.02	−0.38	0.19	0.18	0.49
Bangladesh	0.70	0.71	0.86	0.62	0.64	0.86
Bolivia	0.18	0.20	0.15	0.15	0.16	0.10
Botswana	−0.08	−0.04	0.40	0.85	0.86	0.92
Brazil	n.a.	n.a.	n.a.	n.a.	n.a.	n.a
Ghana	0.08	0.09	0.01	0.07	0.08	−0.004
India	0.08	0.08	0.16	0.08	0.08	0.15
Indonesia	0.62	0.63	0.71	0.64	0.64	0.66
Kenya	0.13	0.14	0.25	0.09	0.10	0.38
Korea, Republic of	0.22	0.21	0.13	0.24	0.24	0.12
Malawi	−0.35	−0.34	−0.25	0.01	0.01	0.04
Malaysia	0.41	0.42	0.58	0.40	0.41	0.58
Mauritius	1.52	1.51	1.17	1.01	1.00	0.77
Mexico	0.67	0.66	0.54	0.79	0.78	0.62
Nigeria	0.49	0.47	0.13	0.15	0.14	−0.02
Pakistan	0.22	0.23	0.29	0.24	0.24	0.32
Philippines	0.81	0.80	0.68	0.39	0.38	0.36
Senegal	0.34	0.34	0.35	−0.09	−0.09	−0.08
South Africa	−0.02	−0.01	−0.01	−0.13	−0.13	−0.15
Sri Lanka	0.88	0.87	0.81	0.59	0.59	0.61
Thailand	0.39	0.40	0.58	0.16	0.18	0.46

Source: authors' estimates based on data from Unido (2005).

Note
a Through a simple regression: lnE = a + lnVAt, t = 1980,..., 2002.

For Sub-Saharan Africa as a whole, the employment elasticity for the period 1999–2008 is found to be rather low (Table 2.2) – and much lower than for other developing regions.

Middle East and North Africa

Data on countries in the Middle East and North Africa region are limited and do not permit inter-temporal comparison. However, data available for nine countries of the region for the period 1991–2003 are presented in Table 2.5, from which several points emerge.

First, the degree of employment intensity of growth in the industrial sector of these countries varies considerably – from a low of 0.14 in Egypt to 1.27 in Jordan. A few countries, namely Morocco, Tunisia, Syria and Yemen, demonstrated healthy employment elasticity of between 0.5 and 0.8.

Second, in some cases, low growth of output is a more fundamental problem. In five of the nine countries (Algeria, Egypt, Iran, Morocco and Tunisia), growth of value added in industry was less than 5 per cent per annum during the period mentioned above. Annual GDP growth was over 5 per cent in only three of the countries (Jordan, Sudan and Yemen). Thus the challenge before the countries of the region is to simultaneously achieve higher growth of output and of employment. In terms of Figure 2.1, most countries of the region are in either quadrant II or I; from the point of view of healthy employment intensive growth, they will need to move to a growth regime that characterizes quadrant IV.

The issue of growth and its stability comes out more sharply when one goes beyond annual averages to the actual trends. For example, the economy of Syria suffered from a recession in 1999 and GDP growth remained rather low for several years after that (Islam, I., 2005). In Egypt, after growth rates of 5 to 6 per cent per annum during the second half of the 1990s, the economy went into recession during 2000–03. After 2003–04, growth resumed to 5 per cent per annum (El Laithy and El Ehwany, 2006). Thus, it is not only low growth but also its stability that appears to be a major problem in the countries of the region.

The elasticity of employment with respect to overall GDP for the countries of MENA region was 1.0 during 2000–05 (Radwan, 2006). This high overall employment elasticity is, however, misleading because both output and employment growth appear to have been higher for the informal segments of the economies compared to the formal sectors. Such growth, either in output or in employment, cannot be very helpful from the point of view of raising incomes of the poor and reducing poverty.

Latin America

For Latin America, the availability of data limits us to estimate employment elasticity for manufacturing only for Argentina and Mexico. For both countries, the estimates indicate very little change in the employment intensity of growth. It may be mentioned here that an earlier study (Khan, 2006) using data up to

Table 2.5 Real GDP growth, sectoral output growth and employment elasticity in selected countries of Middle East and North Africa, 1991–2003

| Country | Sectoral value added growth and employment elasticity (1991–2003) | | | | | | Total GDP growth |
| | Agriculture | | Industry | | Services | | |
	Growth	Elasticity	Growth	Elasticity	Growth	Elasticity	
Algeria	3.70	1.22	2.30	0.75	3.20	0.51	2.60
Egypt	3.10	0.27	3.80	0.14	4.60	0.81	4.40
Iran	4.70	1.50	0.30	0.30	7.30	0.20	4.10
Morocco	0.30	0.63	3.20	0.52	2.90	1.06	2.50
Sudan	9.30	0.53	5.70	0.37	3.30	0.10	5.60
Tunisia	2.20	2.05	4.60	0.77	5.30	0.57	4.60
Jordan	0.60	1.61	6.00	1.27	4.60	1.28	5.10
Syria	4.20	1.89	7.30	0.63	3.40	1.50	4.40
Yemen	6.30	1.14	5.30	0.72	5.60	0.77	5.60

Source: Adapted from Messkoub (2009).

1998 found that the elasticity of employment in manufacturing in both Brazil and Mexico during 1991–98 was lower than during 1981–90. It thus appears that there has been a reversal from the trend observed earlier.

For the region as a whole, elasticity of employment appears to have declined substantially over time, as is indicated by figures presented in Table 2.2 – decline from 0.81 during 1984–98 to 0.69 during 1999–2008.

Summing up

A few observations may be made by way of summing up the findings and discussions of the present chapter. First, there is a clear trend towards declining employment outcome of output growth, although there are exceptions (in terms of countries as well as periods within countries). Second, there are countries whose growth experience changed from employment intensive to jobless type. Third, there is at least one case (China) of a change in the opposite direction. Fourth, there are countries that are characterized by high elasticity of employment with respect to output, but growth is dominated by the informal sector. So, mere high elasticity of employment should not be the goal of policies for achieving full employment; the type and quality of employment are important considerations. High elasticity of employment can be achieved with a regime of low and unstable output growth. In such cases, the goal should be to move towards a regime of high growth of output associated with high employment growth.

Contribution of labour productivity and employment to output growth

From the point of view of the impact of the pattern of growth on employment and the possibility of a trade-off between productivity and employment, it is important to identify the relative contribution of labour productivity and the quantity of labour input to output growth. Here, we shall do that for selected countries of Asia, with a particular focus on possible difference between East and South East Asian (ESEA) countries on the one hand and the countries of South Asia on the other. The reason for taking this comparative perspective is that the former group of countries is by now regarded as having been more successful in achieving more employment intensive growth compared to the countries of South Asia.

The pattern of economic growth that unfolded in the countries of ESEA has been widely debated. But that debate focused mainly on the relative contribution of capital accumulation and total factor productivity (the latter being used as an indicator of disembodied technological progress) in explaining the impressive growth performance of those countries. While the well-known World Bank study of 1993 (World Bank, 1993) argued that East Asia's superior economic performance was mainly caused by rapid technological progress, there are many (especially Kim and Lawrence, 1994; Krugman, 1994; Young, 1995) who challenged this view and argued (on the basis of alternative empirical analysis) that the contribution of total factor productivity (TFP) growth to East Asia's labour productivity growth has been relatively small.[13]

Storm and Naastepad (2005) undertook a decomposition exercise of output growth into productivity and employment growth for some countries of the ESEA region and came to the conclusion that 'labour productivity growth has been the major source of East Asian per capita income growth' (Storm and Naastepad, 2005, p. 1062). However, in an empirical analysis (using cross-country data on 24 developing countries) of the relationship between labour productivity growth and employment growth, they find East Asian countries to be 'outliers'. And on the basis of that, they conclude that 'East Asia managed to escape the trade-off between labour productivity growth and employment growth'. The apparent contradiction between these two sets of findings could probably be explained by the employment creating effect of labour productivity growth exceeding the employment displacing effect. Be that as it may, it appears from Storm and Naastepad (2005) that the pattern of growth in East Asia enabled them to combine high growth of employment and productivity. How do the countries of South Asia compare with those of ESEA in this respect?

In order to address the above question, decomposition of output growth (both total GDP and manufacturing output) into contributions by employment and productivity growth has been carried out by using the methodology outlined in the earlier section, and the results are presented in Tables 2.6a, 2.6b and 2.7. A number of interesting conclusions can be drawn, at least tentatively, from these results.

The first observation (and an important one from the point of view of trade-off between employment and labour productivity growth) that can be made on the basis of Tables 2.6a and 2.6b is that during the 1980s and 1990s, the contribution of labour productivity growth to GDP growth in Korea, Malaysia, Taiwan and Thailand left sufficient scope for employment to increase. That, combined with the high rates of GDP growth achieved by them, meant that they were able to combine fairly high rates of employment growth with substantial growth in labour productivity. In other words, it was not only employment growth but growth of productive employment that was achieved by those countries.

Second, when one compares the countries of South and South East Asia, one does not find a systematic difference (although one would expect the contribution of labour productivity growth to be lower in the former). The figures for India, for example, especially for 1990–96 and 2000–06, are not much different from those of Korea – although given the levels of development and the labour market situation in the two countries, one would expect the figures for Korea to be substantially higher. Likewise, during the 1980s, the contribution of productivity growth in Pakistan and Sri Lanka was higher than in countries like Malaysia and Thailand. Quite naturally, growth in the latter countries was more employment intensive than in the former.

Third, when one looks at the trend over time, some figures do not appear to be consistent with what one would expect. For example, the contribution of labour productivity growth to GDP growth increased over time in Bangladesh, China, India, Indonesia and Malaysia, but not in Korea. The increase in the

Table 2.6a Decomposition of GDP growth into productivity and employment growth (South Asia)

Countries	Growth rate of GDP			GDP growth due to employment growth			GDP growth due to productivity growth			Contribution of productivity growth to GDP growth (%)		
	1980–90	1990–2000	2000–06	1980–90	1990–2000	2000–06	1980–90	1990–2000	2000–06	1980–90	1990–2000	2000–06
Bangladesh	3.84	4.80	5.65	2.69	2.09	2.27	1.15	2.71	3.37	29.97	56.40	59.77
India	5.59	5.46	7.35	2.60	1.87	2.52	3.00	3.59	4.83	53.60	65.82	65.75
Pakistan	6.29	4.43	5.45	2.25	2.01	4.10	4.04	2.42	1.35	64.19	54.64	24.82
Sri Lanka	4.33	5.24	4.50	1.53	2.29	2.02	2.80	2.96	2.48	64.60	56.39	55.15

Source: author's calculations by using data available from www.conference-board.org/economics/downloads/flat_file_08l.xls.

Table 2.6b Decomposition of GDP growth into productivity and employment growth (East and South East Asia)

Countries	Growth rate of GDP			GDP growth due to employment growth			GDP growth due to productivity growth			Contribution of Productivity Growth to GDP Growth		
	1980–90	1990–96	2000–06	1980–90	1990–96	2000–06	1980–90	1990–96	2000–06	1980–90	1990–96	2000–06
China	7.39	8.79	11.56	2.85	1.11	1	4.54	7.68	10.56	61.48	87.37	91.35
Indonesia	5.04	7.83	4.86	3.97	2.09	0.97	1.07	5.74	3.88	21.2	73.34	79.94
Malaysia	5.96	9.56	4.91	3.34	3.96	1.75	2.62	5.6	3.16	43.95	58.55	64.34
Philippines	1.69	2.77	4.63	2.99	3.4	3.13	–1.3	–0.63	1.51	–77.19	–22.67	32.53
South Korea	9.05	7.68	4.63	2.88	2.44	1.53	6.17	5.23	3.1	68.16	68.19	66.99
Taiwan	6.71	7.08	3.49	2.42	1.54	1.07	4.29	5.54	2.42	63.97	78.27	69.42
Thailand	7.85	8.16	5.09	2.94	0.56	2.24	4.9	7.6	2.85	62.48	93.11	55.96

Source: author's calculations by using data available from www.conference-board.org/economics/downloads/flat_file_08l.xls. Access to that website is through www.ggdc.net.

Table 2.7 Decomposition of manufacturing value added growth into productivity and employment growth

Countries	Value added growth		Value added growth due to employment growth		Value added growth due to productivity growth		Contribution of productivity growth to value added growth (%)	
	1980–89	1990–2002	1980–89	1990–2002	1980–89	1990–2002	1980–89	1990–2002
Bangladesh	8.21	14.57	5.51	9.38	2.70	5.19	32.88	35.59
India	7.10	6.36	-0.09	0.57	7.19	5.79	101.32	91.00
Indonesia	16.57	4.17	10.18	2.95	6.39	1.21	38.55	29.13
Korea, Republic of	10.20	7.12	5.52	-1.62	4.68	8.74	45.91	122.81
Malaysia	9.23	10.00	1.96	4.58	7.27	5.43	78.79	54.24
Pakistan	8.54	2.20	2.14	-1.10	6.41	3.30	74.99	149.81
Philippines	-1.20	4.64	-1.95	-0.61	0.74	5.26	-61.90	113.23
Sri Lanka	5.45	6.05	1.80	5.27	3.65	0.78	67.01	12.95
Thailand	5.30	-0.13	1.92	8.54	3.38	-8.67	63.72	64.95

Source: Calculated from UNIDO (2005).

contribution of labour productivity growth in Bangladesh, China and India is rather unexpected, given that those countries are still far away from experiencing a tight labour market. That, in turn, indicates that the pattern of industrial growth in these countries has not been conducive to generation of productive employment for the large amount of surplus labour that is available in those countries.

Constraints on employment growth and the pattern of growth

Factors that may influence growth of employment

The notion of employment growth is often treated as synonymous with employment *creation*, especially by the government, through special programmes. As a result, it gets associated with the perception of welfare. It needs to be recognized, however, that employment growth can play an important role in shaping up the pattern of income distribution and effective demand, which, in turn, can be important from the point of view of sustaining economic growth.[14] Hence, the present study does not regard employment growth simply as a welfare proposition, and as synonymous with employment creation, although employment programmes by governments should not be ruled out as a means of enhancing employment growth.[15] It is concerned with growth of employment that is associated with growth of output.

From the point of view of using employment as a route to poverty reduction and a mechanism for improving (or at least, preventing a worsening of) the distribution of income, the goal would be to achieve high rates of both output and employment growth. However, the recent experience with economic growth in many developing countries shows (as recounted in the section on 'Jobless growth in the developing world' of the present chapter) that high rate of output growth may be associated with different rates of employment growth. From the point of view of employment policy, it would, therefore, be important to identify the factors that constrain employment growth when output is growing at high (or reasonably high) rate.

The framework of employment growth that is linked to output growth would involve recognizing the key elements that determine/influence the employment outcome associated with output growth. The broad elements are: (1) growth of output; (2) labour market policies and institutions; (3) the sector and sub-sector composition of output; (4) the technology used. In any particular situation, there could be a variety of factors hindering employment growth; and policy interventions may not be able to focus simultaneously on all of them. From that point of view, it may be useful to narrow them down to a small number (say, two or three) that may be the 'binding constraints',[16] and gear policies towards addressing them effectively rather than diluting efforts in various directions.

Growth of output

That employment growth would be influenced by the growth of output is to state the obvious. A good deal of work has been undertaken to identify the constraints on output growth. One line of work – referred to as the 'growth diagnostics' analysis, à la Hausmann *et al.* (2005) – tries to identify what are called 'binding constraints' on growth. The other line which tries to link employment to output (e.g. Heintz, 2006) categorizes the constraints broadly as 'demand constraint' and 'capital constraint'. The basic idea behind the diagnostic approach outlined by Hausmann *et al.* (namely, identifying the distortion whose removal would give the highest marginal welfare benefit) may be useful in the context of identifying constraints on employment growth. But in examining the role of the growth factor in employment growth, it would be important to relax the assumption of constant labour productivity. Output growth is the sum of the growth of labour productivity and of employment. Hence, from the point of view of raising employment growth, the division of output growth between productivity and employment growth would be critical (refer to the discussion in the earlier section). It would also be necessary to understand the factors that can help achieve an optimum combination of productivity and employment growth. It may be noted here that the assumption of constant labour productivity is not realistic for economies with unemployment and under-employment. The experience of the East and South East Asian countries demonstrates that high rates of economic growth may be associated with a good mix of labour productivity and employment growth[17] (although there is controversy as to how much of the growth can be ascribed to total factor productivity and how much to mere increases in inputs).

Labour market policies and institutions

According to the standard neoclassical theory, output growth is supposed to lead to employment growth, and interventions in the labour market, e.g. through labour laws, trade unions, or minimum wages, distort the labour market and prevent it from producing the optimal outcome in terms of employment. It is argued on the basis of that theory that employment growth, especially in developing countries, is constrained by restrictive labour laws and trade union interventions that create rigidities in the labour market. However, the debate on this issue is far from settled; and available evidence does not lend support to this hypothesis. For example, it remains to be established whether greater flexibility in the labour markets does indeed result in higher employment growth.

There are studies pointing out that labour market institutions do not necessarily hinder the growth of employment (for example, Auer and Islam, 2006; Bean, 1994; Forteza and Rama, 2002; Kapsos, 2005; Nickel, 1997). On Europe, a widely cited article by Bean (1994) argues that the available evidence does not show that the existence of generous unemployment benefits was the cause of persistent unemployment. Nickel (1997) also shows that all types of labour market rigidities do not have an adverse effect on unemployment rates. He concludes:

Labour market rigidities that do not appear to have serious implications for average levels of unemployment include the following: (1) strict employment protection legislation and general legislation on labour market standards; (2) generous levels of unemployment benefits, so long as these are accompanied by pressures on the unemployed to take jobs by, for example, fixing the duration of benefit and providing resources to raise the ability/willingness of the unemployed to take jobs; and (3) high levels of unionization and union coverage, so long as they are offset by high levels of coordination in wage bargaining, particularly among employers.

(Nickel, 1997, p. 72)

A study by Forteza and Rama (2002) covering 119 countries (both developed and developing) shows that minimum wages and mandated benefits do not hinder economic growth. They argue that curtailing social security benefits might not contribute much to economic performance. An econometric exercise undertaken by Kapsos (2005) demonstrates that rigidities in the labour market do not have a negative effect on employment elasticity. In his cross-section analysis with data from 100 countries, he uses the World Bank's 'employment rigidity index' (which is the average of three indices, namely, difficulty of hiring, difficulty of firing and rigidity of hours) and finds that there is no statistically significant relation between employment elasticity and the employment rigidity index. Moreover, the sign of the coefficient is not in the expected direction.

What, then, constrains employment growth?

Technology

In response to the above question, one may be tempted to cite the choice of technology to be the major factor. Indeed, once the product composition of a country is determined, the employment outcome would depend, to a large extent, on the technology that is used in producing the given products. Premature capital deepening and the adoption of technology that is not in line with the factor endowment of a particular country could be a cause of slow employment growth. But the choice of technology may be limited due to a variety of reasons. First, the shelf of available technologies may indeed be limited. Second, even when there is a choice, there may be a tendency towards the use of the most modern (which often is the most capital intensive) technology. This may, of course, be justified from the point of competitiveness and efficiency which are important considerations in the current environment of growing globalization and liberalization. In such an environment, producers may try to use the best available technology, irrespective of whether the product is intended for the domestic or the external market. However, even within such an environment, some choice of alternatives may be available. And whether the choice would be exercised would depend on a variety of factors, such as relative factor prices, access to the entire shelf of available technologies, level of skills, management. It would, therefore, be important to examine the availability of alternative technologies as well as factors that influence decisions concerning the type of technology that is used.

The pattern of growth

In the circumstances mentioned above, the search for factors responsible for slow employment growth may lead one back to output growth. It has been demonstrated earlier that similar output growth can be obtained through different combinations of employment and labour productivity growth. The particular combination that would prevail in a particular country would depend on a variety of factors which in turn are influenced by the overall development strategy pursued by the country. If a country with surplus labour consciously pursues a development strategy that focuses on optimal utilization of its abundant factor (i.e. labour), that may be reflected in the relative contribution of employment and labour productivity growth to overall growth of output. This has already been examined in the present chapter, and it was found that the pattern of growth is indeed important from the point of view of the employment outcome of growth. One particular element in the pattern of growth is the sector and sub-sector composition of output.

Sector and sub-sector composition of output

Studies that have attempted to identify the binding constraints on employment growth (e.g. Heintz, 2006) remain limited to linking aggregate employment to total output, and do not take into account the possibility of a variation in the employment outcome that may result from a variation in product-mix. Total demand may be an important constraint on the growth of output. But the *pattern* of demand is important in shaping up the *pattern* of growth, which, in turn, can influence the employment outcome of growth. In fact, the product-mix (or sector-composition) of an economy is also linked to demand, but the pattern of demand and income elasticity of demand for various products are important here. And that brings one to the consideration of the composition of output.

As indicated above, the amount of employment associated with a given amount of output would be influenced by what is being produced. Recent research (e.g. Auer and Islam, 2006; Islam, 2006a, 2010a) argues that the overall employment intensity of output growth would depend on the sector composition of output. At the level of broad sectors of an economy, manufacturing, construction and services usually demonstrate higher employment elasticity compared to sectors like agriculture, mining, utilities, etc. In the Kaldorian framework, manufacturing should serve as the engine of growth, and it is high growth in that sector (in relation to sectors like agriculture) that helps an economy move on to an increasingly higher growth path and creates conditions for a gradual transfer of labour away from low productivity activities. It needs to be noted, however, that growth of manufacturing would not automatically enable an economy to absorb surplus labour from the traditional sectors; the sub-sector composition of manufacturing would also be important in that regard. At the initial stages of development, higher growth of labour intensive industries is essential from the point of view of transferring labour to higher productivity activities. In that context, it may be useful to look at the experience of Asian developing countries. Data presented in Tables 2.8 and 2.9 are intended to throw some light on the issue of sector and sub-sector composition of growth. In order to examine the Kaldorian issue of the role of the manufacturing sector in overall economic growth, data on growth of GDP and of manufacturing output for selected countries of Asia are presented in Table 2.8.

What comes out clearly from Table 2.8 is the higher growth of manufacturing output in relation to GDP growth achieved by the countries of ESEA compared to those of South Asia. In the Republic of Korea, for example, the elasticity of growth of manufacturing output with respect to GDP growth was over 2 in the 1960s and dropped to just below 2 in the 1970s. The figure dropped below 1.5 only during the 1980s. In Malaysia, the figure was between 1.5 and 2 for almost three decades (1970–96). Indonesia and Thailand had a similar experience. In contrast, this figure has been in the range of 1.3 to 1.4 in India, and lower in Pakistan. In Bangladesh and Sri Lanka, there has been a considerable degree of fluctuation in the elasticity of manufacturing growth with respect to GDP growth. On the whole, not only has overall economic growth been higher in the countries of ESEA (except Philippines) than in South Asia, the manufacturing sector has been the major driver of growth in the former. It thus appears that only those countries were able to achieve a sectoral pattern of growth outlined by Kaldor and others like Clark, Fisher and Kuznets.[18] Not surprisingly, they are also the countries that were able to achieve more employment intensive growth and Lewis type transformation of their labour markets – albeit at varying speed.

As mentioned earlier, growth in countries of ESEA was more employment intensive compared to those of South Asia. As a result of high rates of growth of manufacturing industries and labour intensive nature of such industries in the former group of countries, surplus labour from agriculture was quickly transferred to the modern manufacturing sector. The Republic of Korea was able to achieve the so-called Lewis turning point by mid-1970s, and Malaysia followed during the 1980s. Indeed, apart from Korea and Taiwan, Malaysia and Thailand are the only other countries of developing Asia that appear to have used up their surplus labour in agriculture. Indonesia was on its way towards that stage, but her journey was disrupted by the Asian economic crisis of 1997–98. The countries of South Asia (e.g. Bangladesh, India, Nepal, Pakistan and Sri Lanka) are still quite distant from that point.[19]

In order to get further insight into the sectoral pattern of economic growth, it would be useful to look at the composition of the manufacturing sector. Using UNIDO (2005) data,[20] an attempt has been made to rank sub-sectors of manufacturing industries (at the three digit level) of various countries according to their capital–labour ratios. Based on such rankings, five most labour intensive and five most capital intensive industries for each country were identified for 1980, 1990 and 2002. The shares of the five most labour intensive and five most capital

Table 2.8 Growth rate of overall GDP and manufacturing output (annual compound rate of growth in percentage)

Country	1960–70			1970–80			1980–90			1990–96			2000–05		
	GDP	Man	Em	GDP	Man	Em	GDP	Man	Em	GDP	Man	Em	GDP	Man	Em
Bangladesh	n.a.	n.a.	n.a.	2.3	5.1	2.2	4.3	3.0	0.7	4.3	7.3	1.7	5.4	6.7	1.2
Cambodia	n.a.	n.a.	n.a.	n.a.	n.a.	n.a.	n.a.	n.a.	n.a.	6.5	7.8	1.2	8.9	14.1	1.6
China	n.a.	n.a.	n.a.	5.5	10.8	1.96	10.2	11.1	1.1	12.3	17.2	1.4	9.6	11.1	1.2
India	3.6	4.8	1.3	3.4	4.6	1.4	5.8	7.4	1.3	5.8	7.5	1.3	7.0	6.9	0.99
Indonesia	3.5	3.3	0.9	7.2	14.0	1.9	6.1	12.8	2.1	7.7	11.1	1.4	4.7	5.2	1.1
Korea, Republic of	8.5	17.2	2.02	10.1	17.7	1.8	8.9	12.1	1.4	7.3	7.9	1.1	4.6	7.0	1.5
Malaysia	6.9	n.a	n.a	7.9	11.7	1.5	5.3	9.3	1.8	8.7	13.2	1.5	4.8	5.2	1.1
Nepal	n.a	n.a	n.a	2	n.a	n.a	4.6	9.3	2.0	5.1	12.0	2.4	2.8	-0.6	n.a
Pakistan	6.7	9.4	1.4	4.9	5.4	1.1	6.3	7.7	1.2	4.6	5.5	1.2	4.8	9.1	1.9
Philippines	5.1	6.7	1.3	6.0	6.1	1.0	1.0	0.2	0.2	2.9	2.6	0.9	4.7	4.3	0.9
Sri Lanka	4.6	6.3	1.4	4.1	1.9	0.5	4.0	6.3	1.6	4.8	8.8	1.8	4.2	2.9	0.7
Thailand	8.2	11.0	1.3	7.1	10.5	1.5	7.6	9.5	1.3	8.3	10.7	1.3	5.4	7.2	1.3
Vietnam	n.a	n.a	n.a	n.a	n.a	n.a	4.6	n.a	n.a	8.5	n.a	n.a	7.5	11.5	1.5

Sources: World Bank, *World Development Indicators* (1998, 2004, 2007), available at: http://data.worldbank.org/products/wdi; World Bank *World Development Reports* (1978 and 1999).

Notes
Man = Manufacturing output.
Em = Elasticity of manufacturing growth with respect to GDP growth.

Table 2.9 Share of the five most labour intensive and five most capital intensive industries in total manufacturing value added in Asia

Countries	Share of the labour-intensive			Share of the capital-intensive		
	1980	*1990*	*2002*	*1980*	*1990*	*2002*
Bangladesh	1.78	12.36	22.54[b]	3.09	8.74	32.35[b]
India	9.47	4.01	5.21[d]	21.76	25.01	26.48[d]
Indonesia	30.90	18.34	3.91	14.61	18.02	17.21
Korea, Republic of	8.26	9.53	4.21[d]	22.64	10.10	28.18[d]
Malaysia	4.09	12.21	5.27[d]	9.37	18.25	20.93[d]
Pakistan	15.79	4.14[a]	3.62[e]	21.69	11.61[a]	24.51[e]
Philippines	7.20	8.80	7.89[b]	23.58	21.50	23.01[b]
Sri Lanka	22.99	4.42	23.25[c]	5.28	10.96	12.57[c]
Thailand	n.a	4.77	14.34[f]	n.a	17.06	20.07[f]

Source: Calculated from UNIDO (2005).

Notes
a 1991.
b 1997.
c 2000.
d 2001.
e 1996.
f 1994.

intensive industries in total manufacturing value added were then calculated.
These shares are presented in Table 2.9.[21] The idea behind this exercise is to see
whether there has been a systematic change in the sector composition of the
manufacturing sector in either direction.

Data presented in Table 2.9 point out a few interesting aspects of the sectoral
pattern of industrialization in the selected countries of Asia. First, both the
Republic of Korea and Malaysia show an increase in the share of labour intensive industries up to 1990 and a decline thereafter. Korea also experienced a fall
in the share of capital intensive industries till 1990 and a rise thereafter. In
Malaysia, on the other hand, the share of such industries in 1990 was already
higher than in 1980, although there was a slight decline after that. The above
figures indicate that, while Korea provides a classic example of labour intensive
industrialization in its early phase of development, Malaysia comes close to that.
Thailand also witnessed a rise in the share of labour intensive industries between
1990 and 2002. In contrast, India witnessed a gradual decline in the share of
labour intensive industries and a rise in the share of capital intensive industries.
Pakistan and Sri Lanka also show similar trends, although not so clearly.

The figures for Bangladesh presented in Table 2.9 need to be interpreted with
caution. They indicate a substantial rise in the shares of both top five labour
intensive and top five capital intensive industries. These figures themselves are
not implausible, and might indicate growth taking place at two ends of the spectrum. Indeed, there has been very rapid growth of one labour intensive industry,
i.e. ready-made garments, which may be reflected in the sharp increase in the

share of the top five labour intensive industries. It should, however, be noted that apart from this single industry, there has not been a similar growth in any other labour intensive industry. In fact, the performance of another major labour intensive industry of the country, i.e. leather and leather products, has been rather disappointing, resulting in a decline in its share in total manufacturing value added (Ahmed *et al.*, 2009).

In the case of India, data from national sources (Annual Survey of Industries (ASI)) corroborate the findings based on UNIDO data. One study (Palit, 2008) based on the ASI data shows that the overall share of the labour intensive industries in total manufacturing output declined significantly between 1990–91 and 2003–04. In 1990–91, the top five labour intensive industries (food and other food products; beverages and tobacco; wood products and furniture; other textiles; leather and fur products) accounted for nearly 41 per cent of manufacturing output. In 2003–04, the share of the top five (which in that year were: other textiles; leather and fur; beverages and tobacco; food products; other manufacturing) dropped to 28.32 per cent (Palit, 2008).

The figures for Sri Lanka in Table 2.9 raise a couple of questions. First, the share of the top five labour intensive industries declined sharply during the 1980s and then increased to the level of 1980 by 2002. Second, the share of capital intensive industries increased gradually over the two decades. While a full explanation of the observed phenomenon is not possible without going into a detailed analysis of the situation and policies pursued at the country level, some tentative remarks may be made. As for the growth of manufacturing as a whole, there was a major acceleration during the 1990s (compared to the 1980s); and there were specific initiatives by the government to promote the growth of labour intensive industries such as garment manufacturing.[22] As a result, such industries achieved higher growth. For example, the annual growth rates achieved by textiles, and leather and footwear during 1993–2001 were 9.8 and 5.9 per cent respectively. At the other end of the spectrum, capital intensive industries like chemicals, petroleum, rubber and plastic (together as a group) and metal products also achieved moderate growth of 4.1 per cent and 4.3 per cent per annum during the same period.[23] That may explain the steady rise in the share of capital intensive industries.

Employment implications of alternative sector composition of output: methodologies and illustrations

Once the relevance of the pattern of economic growth is recognized, it would be necessary to monitor the sector and sub-sector composition on a periodic basis at the country level. At the broad sector level, it would be useful to first examine which sectors are characterized by higher employment intensity of growth. In a developing economy, manufacturing, trade, transport and construction and some service sectors are expected to be more employment intensive than agriculture, mining, utilities, etc. If that is found to be the case, an employment-focused strategy would involve strategies to achieve higher growth in such sectors and a transfer of labour from traditional sectors like agriculture to these sectors.

Within the manufacturing sector, an attempt should be made to identify sub-sectors that are more employment intensive. In order for such an exercise to be useful from an operational point of view, it should be done at a disaggregated level (at least at three digit level). Once employment intensive sub-sectors are identified, their growth performance should be monitored on a regular basis. In addition, the policy environment having a bearing on their growth should be analysed, and strategies and policies should be based on such analysis. The analysis of the policy environment faced by the employment intensive sub-sectors should be carried out from the point of view of identifying factors that may be constraining their growth.

An example of the kind of exercise mentioned above is provided by a recent study on Bangladesh (Ahmed *et al.*, 2009) which starts from empirically examining the growth performance of employment intensive manufacturing industries and goes on to analyse the policy environment faced by selected industries from that category. The study not only provides useful insight into the question of the composition of the manufacturing sector of Bangladesh (i.e. whether it has been conducive to an employment intensive pattern of growth), but also attempts to identify constraints that the selected sub-sectors face. Based on the analysis, the study provides useful policy guidelines for promoting higher growth of those sub-sectors.

For India, a study on manufacturing industries (Palit, 2008) shows that during 1990–91 to 2003–04, the structure of manufacturing industries has not shown any change towards labour intensive industries, although economic and trade liberalization undertaken in the country since 1991 was expected to engender a process of labour intensive industrialization. In fact, that study shows that the overall share of the labour intensive industries in total manufacturing output declined significantly between 1990–91 and 2003–04. In 1990–91, the top five labour intensive industries (food and other food products; beverages and tobacco; wood products and furniture; other textiles; leather and fur products) accounted for nearly 41 per cent of manufacturing output. In 2003–04, the share of the top five (which in that year were: other textiles; leather and fur; beverages and tobacco; food products; other manufacturing) dropped to 28.32 per cent (Palit, 2008).

As mentioned earlier, Islam (2010a) shows that the composition of growth in terms of contribution of various sectors plays a key role in rendering growth more or less employment intensive. However, for drawing operational implications of this proposition, it is necessary to assess the relative employment content of sectors and sub-sectors of economic activity at such a disaggregated level that is relevant for policy and programme application. In other words, it is necessary to broadly quantify the amount of employment that would be generated in producing a given quantum of output in different lines of activities so as to identify sectors whose fast growth would make a good contribution to employment. However, such quantification at broad aggregated level may not be adequate because the policy actions that may be utilized to facilitate higher growth of some lines of production than others could only be applied at the level of sub-sectors and individual commodities. Thus, prioritizing agriculture for employment generation may, in fact, imply emphasizing sub-sectors like horticulture, animal husbandry and fisheries. In the case of industry, it may imply specially promoting growth of labour intensive industries generally, and textiles, light engineering, agro-based products and so on, specifically. Assessment of the employment impact at the appropriate level of disaggregation of economic sectors is, therefore, required for determining the output structure of growth and evolving suitable policy intervention to ensure its realization, in order to bring employment into focus in growth strategy.

Employment impact analysis (EIA)[24] involves not only an assessment of changes in the employment numbers resulting from a given expansion of output in a particular sector/industry, but also the indirect and induced employment effects[25] such expansion produces in each of the other sectors and industries through backward and forward linkages. It involves an analytical framework to assess the direction and magnitude of impact on employment and also identify the transmission channels due to a change in policy at macro and/or sectoral level. To undertake EIA, various tools are used such as Time Series and Cross-Sectional Analysis, Location Quotient, Shift-Share Analysis and Economic Modelling.

Economic Modelling encompasses a variety of analytic approaches, such as input-output analysis and economic simulation. Input–output analysis is among the most direct and relatively simple tool to undertake EIA. Besides the direct effects, it enables measurement of the effects from suppliers of inputs (raw materials, etc.) and thus gives a measure of the total effect of the activity in question. For example, direct employment in manufacturing activities of X product is seen as the first link in a chain of employment effects. Secondary links are employment associated with the production of components and raw materials used in the production of X. The ratio of the total employment generated in all linked sectors together as a result of a unit of investment/increase in output in the reference sector is also referred to as its employment multiplier. What one actually requires to estimate the total employment impact (or employment multiplier) of a sector is (1) the amount of output of each of the other sectors required as input for a unit of output in this sector and (2) the employment coefficient of each sector defined as the number of persons employed in that sector for a unit of value added/output. Aggregate employment coefficient of a sector is derived as the ratio of employment generated directly in it and in other linked sectors as a result of a unit expansion of output in the reference sector and the amount of output in other sectors required as input in the reference sector. It may be noted that employment coefficients or employment multipliers estimated using input-output analysis account for direct and indirect employment effects and not the 'induced' effects. Also for a sector, these estimates include employment effects of output and its backward linkages only (output of other sectors used as input), and not the forward linkages (output of the other sectors resulting from use of this sector's output as input).

The application of the methodology described above can be illustrated by an exercise undertaken for India which is based on the input–output table for

2003–04 providing data for 130 sectors. To estimate the employment coefficient, the employment data have been taken from the sixty-first National Sample Survey (NSS) round (2004–05) on employment and unemployment. Since the input-output table and the employment data are based on different industrial classifications, adjustments have been made to have one-to-one correspondence at a two digit level of classification, and 130 sectors have been aggregated into 19 broad sectors.[26]

Table 2.10 presents the results of this exercise, which includes the direct employment coefficient (number of persons per million rupees of gross value added in the sector) and indirect employment coefficient which is the sum of employment coefficient in all other sectors. For instance, one million rupees of gross value added in manufacturing sector directly creates around 15 employment opportunities, and another eight employment opportunities due to changes in the production/demand of other sectors linked to manufacturing. Thus 1 million rupees of gross value added in manufacturing will create a total of 23 employment opportunities in the economy. Within manufacturing, the agro-based

Table 2.10 India: direct and indirect employment coefficient (employment per million rupees of gross value added)

Sl. No	Sector description	Direct	Indirect	Total
1	2	3	4	5
1	Agriculture, livestock and others	50.15	0.96	51.10
2	Forestry and logging	6.27	0.49	6.76
3	Fishing	5.58	0.70	6.27
	Agriculture and allied (1 to 3)	46.25	5.18	51.43
4	Mining and quarrying	4.13	0.91	5.04
5	Food, food processing, beverages and others	24.71	95.84	120.55
6	Textiles (cotton, wool, jute etc.) and products	39.51	20.93	60.44
7	Wood, furniture, paper and leather and their products	50.36	10.05	60.41
8	Rubber, plastic and their products	8.50	17.94	26.43
9	Chemical, petroleum and non-metallic mineral products	5.87	8.27	14.14
10	Basic metal	6.62	6.62	13.24
11	Machine tools and non-electrical machinery	6.47	7.03	13.51
12	Electrical machinery and other transport equipments	2.73	6.80	9.54
	Manufacturing (5 to 12)	14.75	7.77	22.52
13	Construction	16.59	6.00	22.59
14	Utilities	2.49	4.87	7.36
15	Transport, storage and communications	8.85	4.22	13.07
16	Trade, hotels, and restaurants	12.40	3.34	15.74
17	Banking and insurance	1.91	0.89	2.80
18	Real estate etc.	0.79	0.30	1.09
19	Education, health and other services	9.75	0.67	10.43
	Services (15 to 19)	8.55	5.11	13.66

Sources: ILO (2009) and Papola (2008).

industries such as food and food processing and textiles have both higher direct and indirect employment impact as compared to the non-agro-based industries. Unlike many sub-sectors of manufacturing, the indirect employment effects in service sector are very low. Among the 19 sectors, food products, textiles and wood and paper products top the list with over 60 jobs created directly and indirectly for each million of rupees of value added, while real estate, banking and insurance and mining and quarrying figure at the bottom with only five or less jobs for similar value added. Based on future growth scenarios, these employment coefficients can be used to forecast corresponding employment growth for the whole economy as well as for various sectors.

Social Accounting Matrices (SAMs) may also be used to analyse the total impact on employment (i.e. taking into account both direct and indirect effects) of a particular measure, and thus could be applied to identify sectors or sub-sectors that could yield the maximum impact on employment.

Indeed, SAM is a powerful tool to investigate the distributional and employment implications of given structures of production in an economy and the way they are affected by policy interventions.[27] An illustration of how SAMs can be applied to work out the employment implications of the growth of various sectors of an economy (taking into account the direct employment in a sector as well as employment created through linkage effects on other sectors of the economy) is provided by a recent exercise on South Africa by Capaldo (2007). That exercise divides the economy into 26 sectors that include agriculture, mining, sub-sectors within manufacturing and a number of service sectors. The results obtained from the exercise indicate that within the manufacturing sector, food, textiles and paper have the highest impact on employment while commercial equipment, transport equipment and machinery have low employment impact. Among the other sectors, agriculture, construction and most of the services are found to be highly employment intensive.

Identifying constraints on the growth of employment intensive sectors/sub-sectors

Constraints on the growth of labour intensive sectors/sub-sectors may arise from both demand and supply sides. On the demand side, both domestic and external demand will have to be considered, while on the supply side, a range of issues starting from the policy environment to factors operating at the sector and enterprise level would be important.

Domestic demand

Domestic demand depends on the level as well as the distribution of income. With an unequal distribution of income and rising inequality, the pattern of demand may shift towards more capital intensive and imported goods, which, in turn, may have an adverse employment implication. An analysis of the income elasticity of demand for various products would, therefore, be an important element in the identification of constraints on employment growth. However, a literature search indicates that such studies on an up-to-date basis are not readily available. However, early studies on the topic (e.g. ILO, 1970 on Colombia; Islam, 1976 on Bangladesh; Sinha *et al.*, 1979 on India) do provide some useful insight.[28] The study on India, for example, shows that expenditure elasticity of demand for products of labour intensive sectors like cotton textiles and footwear are much higher for lower and middle income groups than for higher income groups.

More recent studies on India indicate significant changes in the consumption pattern that have taken place in country. However, the differences in the pattern of consumption between the rich and the poor continue to remain. For example, the difference in average expenditure on consumer durables is much more marked than that in the case of food and other basic items (Shukla and Kakar, 2007). And as income inequality widens, the consumption pattern (and hence the pattern of domestic demand) is getting tilted more towards consumer durables which are more capital intensive by nature.[29]

Some illustrative estimates (presented in Table 2.11) of income elasticity of demand for selected consumer goods in Bangladesh indicate a pattern similar to that observed in India. For example, some items like *gur* (traditional sweetening agent produced from sugarcane or date juice) and firewood clearly emerge as inferior goods at high levels of income (top 10 per cent of households), implying that an increase in income at that level leads to a decline in the amount spent on these items. And it is quite well known that these items are more labour intensive compared to similar products (for example, *gur* compared to sugar, firewood compared to gas and electricity). Second, for some items which use labour intensive techniques in their production (for example, *lungi* (traditional item of dress), furniture, shirt and pants, leather shoes), the income elasticity of demand at high income level (i.e. the top 10 per cent of households) is lower than for households as a whole. This implies that an increase in income at the topmost level would increase the demand for such items by smaller amounts than if income increases at lower income levels. Third, for items like refrigerators, pressure cookers, etc. (which not only involve the use of capital intensive technology in their production but in Bangladesh are mostly imported), the income elasticity of demand is much higher for the top 10 per cent of the households compared to the overall sample. So, an increase in the demand for such products is unlikely to create much employment within the country (except perhaps in the sales of such items).

The pattern of consumer demand (which in turn has its roots in the pattern of income distribution) mentioned above has implications for the growth of sectors that are more employment intensive. An early study on India (Gupta, 1977), for example, demonstrates that a redistribution of private consumption expenditure in favour of the poorer classes of population would change the output mix in India in such a way that the average annual growth rate of employment would register an increase of 11 per cent (year of reference was early 1970s). A study on Bangladesh (Islam, 1976) also found positive employment impact of a redistribution of

Table 2.11 Income elasticity of demand for selected consumer goods in Bangladesh (2005–06)

Items of expenditure	Income elasticity of demand	
	Top 10% of the households	All households
Milk	0.327	0.498
Milk powder	0.300	0.363
Tea	0.316	0.456
Bottled drinks	0.191	0.325
Sugar	0.171	0.408
Gur	−0.001	0.164
Firewood	−0.031	0.179
Electricity	0.313	0.398
Lungi	0.100	0.231
Shirt and pants	0.353	0.616
Mill made cloth	0.149	0.306
Handloom cloth	1.453	0.338
Leather shoes	0.328	0.516
Plastic shoes	0.216	0.184
Kitchen items	0.502	0.438
Refrigerator, pressure cooker, cutlery	1.169	0.566
Furniture	0.623	0.743
Consumer durables	−1.180	1.080

Source: authors' estimates based on primary data from the Household Income and Expenditure Survey 2005 conducted by the Bangladesh Bureau of Statistics, and available at the Bangladesh Institute of Development Studies.

Notes

a Coefficients estimated by running double logarithmic regressions;

b Except for *gur*, firewood, and mill made cloth for top 10 per cent of the households, all coefficients are statistically significant either at 1 per cent or 5 per cent level.

income from upper to lower income groups, although the magnitude was much less notable. One could thus conclude, at least tentatively, that an unequal income distribution and increase in inequality poses a constraint on the growth of sectors that are employment intensive in nature.

The impact of income distribution on the pattern of consumer demand gets exacerbated when demand gets boosted through credit and subsidy. Indeed, when developing countries move to higher levels of development, it is not uncommon to find consumer demand boosted through such incentives. But it is usually the demand for consumer durables that is supported by such measures; and the employment outcome of the growth of such demand is not necessarily very positive. Credit-driven growth of domestic demand in China and India provides examples of such pattern of growth. In China, the Government's stimulus programme adopted in response to the global economic crisis of 2008–09 included a 13 per cent subsidy in rural areas on the purchase of appliances like televisions, refrigerators, washing machines, air conditioners and computers ('Market Watch' in *Beijing Review*, 25 June 2009). Likewise, in India, credit for the purchase of such items has boosted their demand during the period of high growth (Chandrasekhar and Ghosh, 2008).

External demand

External demand plays a major role, especially in open economies. Conventional trade theory suggests that labour-abundant countries have a comparative advantage in the production and export of labour intensive goods. Hence, an outward-looking and export-oriented development strategy should result in a high growth of such sectors and a high growth of employment. The critical question here is whether such a growth strategy automatically results in a change in the structure of production towards more labour intensive sectors and in high employment growth.

In order to understand whether exports can help developing countries in promoting the growth of their more labour intensive lines of production, it would be necessary to have estimates of the elasticity of export demand for various categories of products. Unfortunately, a search for such studies yielded few results, hence it was necessary to look for alternative (and somewhat indirect) evidence concerning the type of external demand.

According to the standard theory of comparative advantage, developing countries endowed with an abundance of labour are expected to specialize in and export goods that require more labour compared to other scarce factors of production. But data presented above (Table 2.8) has already pointed to exceptions to this standard prediction. While trade openness has been associated with specialization in and export of labour intensive manufactures in some countries, there are exceptions, e.g. India. In the latter case, exports are found at both the labour intensive and the capital intensive ends of the spectrum of manufacturing industries. How does one explain this?

It needs to be noted in the context of the question raised above that developing countries may export goods to both developed and developing countries. While the standard prediction based on the theory of comparative advantage may apply to the former, it does not necessarily apply to the latter. Indeed, there is evidence to show that the latter category of exports may include goods, e.g. metal products, machinery, chemicals, transport equipment (Murakami, 1968), which may not fit into the conventional description of labour intensive items. The importance of such goods in total exports may, of course, vary depending on the level of development achieved and the strategy of industrialization pursued by a developing country. But in reality, it is possible that the weight of such goods in total exports and production may be quite substantial, and their share may not change much (or may increase) even when an open trade regime is introduced. And as a result, the emerging pattern of industrialization may not be very employment intensive. While the case of India has already been mentioned above, a look at Pakistan's export structure also indicates a similar pattern.

In India, the shares of labour intensive manufactures like garments and leather in total exports have not registered a significant increase after the economic reforms and liberalization were introduced in 1991. For example, the share of ready-made garments was 12.3 per cent in 1990–91 and actually declined to 11.1 per cent in 1997–98, and thereafter increased to 12.5 per cent in 2000–01, which implies a return to the level of 1990–91 (Reserve Bank of India, 2008). The share of leather and leather products declined substantially from 7.9 to 4.7 per cent during the same period. On the other hand, the shares of chemical and allied products and engineering products increased respectively from 7.2 to 9 per cent and from 12.4 to 15.2 per cent (Sharma, 2000). A more recent study (Burange and Chaddha, 2008) found that India enjoys comparative advantage in the exports of labour intensive items like textiles as well as in scale intensive items such as chemicals, and iron and steel (the latter belonging to the capital intensive category).

In Pakistan, a study (Ansari, 2007) undertaken for the Export Promotion Bureau shows that the growth rates of exports of labour intensive items like garments and leather witnessed notable escalation during 1999–2005 compared to 1993–98 (from 2.66 and –1.74 per cent respectively during 1993–98 to 11.19 and 10.45 per cent during 1999–2005). But in terms of the structure of exports, the shares of chemicals and pharmaceuticals, petroleum products and engineering goods registered significant increases (from 0.56, 0.82 and 0.41 respectively to 1.33, 1.83 and 1.65 per cent respectively between the two periods mentioned above) – thus demonstrating the growth in the exports of both labour intensive and capital intensive goods. In fact, average growth rates registered by the latter mentioned industries were several times higher than those of the labour intensive goods mentioned above.

The upshot of the findings reported above may be summarized as follows. Greater trade openness may help labour-abundant countries to achieve accelerated growth of labour intensive industries. But a divergence from this standard prediction may occur, and countries may indeed export goods that are at the capital intensive end of the production spectrum. Such a divergence can act as a constraint on employment growth.

Supply side constraints

Supply side constraints can arise from a variety of sources, e.g. the supply of needed raw materials, and the availability of specific skills that may be required. The price structure of inputs in relation to that of outputs may affect the profitability of industries, and thus act as a constraint on its growth. A study on Bangladesh (Ahmed *et al.*, 2009) brings out these constraints in the context of specific labour intensive industries like food products, furniture and leather products. For example, in the case of food manufacturing, a weak technological base resulting in an inability of enterprises to meet the health and sanitary conditions of export markets is found to be an important constraint. For leather and leather products, low level of technology, lack of appropriate skills, shortage of raw materials, low level of entrepreneurial skill, etc. are found to be important constraints on the growth of the sector. Likewise, in the case of furniture, scarcity of raw material, high customs duty on imported inputs and shortage of skills are found to be the major constraints. Frequent changes in policy that result in an uncertain business environment are also regarded as a problem. This kind of sector-focused study that revealed the constraints mentioned above are important in identifying the constraints that specific industries face.

Policy environment

The policy environment prevailing in an economy may affect the growth of a sector from both the demand and supply sides. For example, the pattern of domestic demand may be the outcome of the way in which income is distributed, which in turn may be due to the overall development strategy and policies pursued. Likewise, macroeconomic and sector level policies are critical in determining the relative prices of factors and other inputs that are important in the production of various goods and services in an economy. An important question to address in this context is whether relative factor prices of the key factors of production (i.e. capital and labour) reflect their true scarcities. Another key question is whether there is anything in the policy environment (e.g. relating to taxes and tariffs on inputs and competing imports) that go against the profitability and competitiveness of the employment intensive sectors/sub-sectors.

For example, there are studies on India (e.g. Chandrasekhar, 2008; Palit, 2008) demonstrating the existence of a number of elements in the country's policy framework that have led to a cheapening of capital which is the relatively scarce factor of production. On the other hand, there is nothing in the policy environment to encourage the use of labour. As a result, the relative factor prices do not reflect their true scarcities, and the growth of employment has been lower than what it should have been in a country with surplus labour. This appears to be consistent with the findings mentioned earlier (Palit, 2008) of a sectoral pattern of growth characterized by an increase in the share of capital intensive sectors and a decline in the share of labour intensive ones. This, clearly, is an area for further investigation and possible policy intervention.

Concluding observations

The present chapter starts by providing clarifications regarding the concept and terminology of jobless growth, and points out that the term need not be interpreted in a literal sense. The term is used to capture situations of low growth of employment in relation to output growth in countries that are still characterized by surplus labour. It is pointed out that the term employment intensive growth does not imply employment creation without output growth. Indeed, this term is used to describe a situation where high output growth is associated with high employment growth. It is pointed out that in a growing economy, there should be room for growth of both employment and labour productivity, and that it should be possible to avoid a trade-off between the two.

The discussion on the concept of jobless growth is followed by a critical review of the various interpretations of the term inclusive growth. After pointing out the ambivalence regarding the precise characteristics of inclusive growth, a characterization is suggested which would include reduction in income inequality, growth of productive employment and a social protection floor for all citizens.

By using cross-country data on manufacturing industries in developing countries, it is shown that the relationship between employment and output growth has weakened during the 1990s compared to the 1980s. In addition, there are countries where positive output growth has been found to be associated with zero or negative employment growth, thus pointing to situations of jobless growth in a literal sense. For a number of Asian countries for which estimates of elasticity of employment with respect to output growth in manufacturing could be found for the 1990s and the 1980s, the figures for the 1990s were found to be lower, thus indicating a decline in the employment intensity of growth in the sector. In cases where data are available, the fall in the employment intensity of growth is found to continue during the 2000s. Interestingly, this happened in countries where surplus labour continues to exist, so that a decline in the employment intensity of growth cannot be explained by the labour market situation.

The present chapter points out that it is important to go beyond estimates of employment elasticity and look at actual figures on output and employment growth. By doing so, it is found that there are countries (e.g. in the Middle East and North Africa region) where the problem is not only one of low employment growth but also one of low growth of output. In such situations, the policy concern would be how to raise both output and employment growth. But there are countries (e.g. China, India and other South Asian countries) where employment growth has been low despite high or moderate output growth. The policy concern in such situations would be to raise employment growth.

A decomposition of output growth into employment and productivity growth presented in this chapter showed that the trade-off between the two is not inevitable. There are countries (e.g. Republic of Korea, Malaysia, Indonesia and Thailand) which have been able to combine employment growth with productivity growth. On the other hand, there are countries (e.g. Bangladesh, China and India) where the contribution of labour productivity to total output growth has not only been high (especially considering the fact these economies are still characterized by the existence of surplus labour), but has also been increasing. These findings point towards a pattern of growth in those countries that has not been conducive to the growth of employment.

The present chapter argues that the pattern of economic growth in terms of the sector and sub-sector composition of output is important in determining the employment outcome of growth. In that context, a high rate of growth of manufacturing in relation to overall GDP growth would be important because such a pattern of growth is potentially conducive to a high rate of employment growth. High rate of growth of manufacturing at the initial stage of development is necessary for creating conditions for transfer of surplus labour from sectors characterized by low labour productivity to those with higher productivity. However, for that process to succeed, it is also important for more labour intensive subsectors of manufacturing to grow at high rates – at least at the initial stages of development.

It is by now well-known that a few countries of East and South East Asia (especially the Republic of Korea and Malaysia, and Indonesia and Thailand, to some extent) were able to achieve the kind of growth pattern mentioned above. In general, the countries of ESEA not only had higher growth manufacturing in relation to overall GDP growth, the sector composition of the manufacturing sector was also more labour intensive (at least during the initial stages of their growth) than in countries of South Asia. As a result, the employment intensity of growth during the initial stages of their development was also higher than in the latter.

This chapter outlines alternative methodologies (e.g. those based on input-output analysis and SAMs) for assessing the direct as well as the total impact on employment of alternative sectoral patterns of growth. The application of such methodologies is illustrated with examples from India and South Africa.

Constraints on the growth of employment intensive sectors can arise from demand and supply sides. The pattern of income distribution can have significant influence on domestic demand for various products and, hence, on the sectoral pattern of output growth. An important point that has come out is that greater trade openness does not necessarily lead labour-abundant countries to specialize and export *only* labour intensive goods. Depending on the level of development and the strategy of industrialization pursued, a developing country may have, in its export basket, both labour intensive and capital intensive goods. The pattern of external demand thus could be an important factor in explaining the low employment intensity of output growth.

The findings and analysis of the present study have important implications for countries that need to make economic growth more employment intensive. If it is found that the sectoral pattern of growth is such that there is room for higher growth of labour intensive industries and growth of additional labour intensive lines of production than at present, the next step from a policy point of view would be to examine the factors responsible for the observed pattern. In fact, one study mentioned above (Palit, 2008) already points out that the sector composition of India's manufacturing sector has changed towards more capital intensive industries from labour intensive ones. As mentioned above, the sector composition could be a reflection of the pattern of demand in an economy which in turn is influenced by the level and distribution of income. On the other hand, it could also be due to distortions in the incentive structure created by the policy environment prevailing in the economy. In the latter case, it should be possible to identify appropriate reforms in policies that would modify the policy environment and make it more conducive for higher growth of labour intensive sectors.

Distortions in the incentive structure could also be created in the process of implementing the so-called stimulus programmes that were implemented by various countries in response to the economic crisis. In Indonesia, for example, the stimulus package included subsidies for the purchase of machinery under the Machinery Revitalization Programme (Hailu, 2009). In China, the industries that benefited from government support include steel, automobiles, machinery, ship-building, textiles, electronics and petrochemicals (Riskin, 2010). It is quite clear that apart from textiles and electronics, the others in this list are at the capital intensive end of the spectrum.

While capital is being made cheaper than it would otherwise have been, in none of the countries whose examples are cited above (China, India and Indonesia) is there any measure to encourage the use of labour in industries. Thus, relative factor prices may not often reflect the true scarcities of the factors of production and may not be conducive to employment intensive growth.

The analysis of the present chapter also brings out a number of gaps in the literature relating to the sector composition of output and point to what needs to be done if an employment diagnostic exercise were to be carried out in a particular country. The starting point of such an exercise has to be an assessment of the direct as well as the total employment impact of alternative sectoral growth scenarios. That kind of exercise would require an input-output table or SAM on an up-to-date basis at a disaggregated level. While there has been a good deal of improvement in this respect in many developing countries, the availability of up-to-date data at an appropriate level of disaggregation is often a problem. Once the employment impact has been assessed, the next step would be an analysis of the pattern of demand – both domestic and external – for the products of various sectors. This is where the real data gap lies. And this also is an important issue because demand is one of the major factors that influence the sectoral pattern of output growth. Once the demand pattern is known, the next step would be to examine the policy environment that prevails in the country at the macro, sector as well as sub-sector levels and identify reforms that are needed in that sphere from the point of view of promoting the growth of sectors/sub-sectors, the products of which are characterized by high income/price elasticity of demand, and growth is constrained more by factors in the policy environment than by demand.

Appendix: Brief description of the data used

1 UNIDO data

UNIDO publishes industrial statistics on a periodic basis; 'Indstat 3 rev 2' brought out in 2005 is the latest available in that series. Data pertaining to manufacturing industries classified at the three digit level of the International Standard Industrial Classification (ISIC) are presented by country, industry and year. The following items are covered by this data set: number of establishments, employment, wages and salaries, output, value added, gross fixed capital formation, number of female employees and index number of industrial production.

The data cover 28 industries. The period covered ends in 2003, but the latest year for most of the data is 2002. Moreover, the coverage differs across countries and variables; and there are important gaps for a number of countries.

While data from the member countries of the Organisation for Economic Co-operation and Development (OECD) are first collected by OECD and then provided to the UNIDO, data for non-OECD countries are collected by the UNIDO directly from the national statistical offices of the respective countries.

The data are originally stored national currency values at current prices. The system allows conversion of values from national currency into US dollars using the average period exchange rates as given in the International Financial Statistics. For purposes of the present chapter, all values (both value added and values of fixed assets) have been converted into constant prices by using a deflator for the manufacturing sector calculated from data available in the World Bank's *World Development Indicators*.

2 Data used for decomposition of GDP

Data used in Tables 2.6a and 2.6b for decomposing GDP growth into productivity and employment growth has been obtained from the database provided by the Groningen Growth and Development Centre and the Conference Board. That database, which covers 125 countries of the world, is available online at www.ggdc.net. The data included in it are compiled from a variety of well-known international sources, e.g. the World Bank, the regional development banks (like the Asian Development Bank), and the International Labour Organization.

Notes

1 See, for example, Khan (2007) and the country studies referred to in that report, as well as ADB (2005).
2 ILO's Global Employment Trends Brief 2006 noted that there was an increase in unemployment in 2005 compared to 2001, although the global economy achieved a growth of 4.3 per cent. Likewise, in 2006 also, robust economic growth failed to translate into significant reductions in unemployment, and global unemployment in 2006 was higher than in 2005. See ILO (2006, 2008).
3 Data in this regard will be presented in the third section.
4 It is difficult to say how and when this term came into use in the literature on growth and development. However, it seems that the term 'jobless recovery' was being used in the USA in the early 1990s to describe the situation where the economy was emerging from recovery and yet the labour market was not responding by creating sufficient number of new jobs. Rifkin (1996) pointed to the situation where human labour is being systematically eliminated from the economic process.
5 It may be noted that Kakwani's deifinition does not ensure an avoidance of increased inequality. All it does is ensure that the distribution between two broad groups – the poor and the non-poor – improves. It is possible for inequality to increase even if the income share of the poor increases.
6 The term is also being used at the country level by governments, e.g. in India. The strategy for the Eleventh Five-Year Plan of that country was 'Towards Faster and More Inclusive Growth' although the Government of India has not provided any official definition of the term. See Suryanarayana (2008) for the development of a measure of inclusive growth and its application to India. His measure focuses basically on consumer expenditure distribution, and he measures 'inclusion coefficient' for various social groups and rural and urban areas.

7 See, also, Saad-Filho (2010) for a description of the evolution of the concept of inclusive growth and a critique of the World Bank's definition of the term.

8 It may be noted that this paper reviews, among other documents, a number of ADB studies, speeches delivered by the organization's high level officials at various meetings, discussions at a regional Forum on Inclusive Growth and Poverty Reduction organized by ADB in 2007, and the report (in 2007) of the Eminent Persons Group established by the organization.

9 This study uses the terms 'inclusive growth' and 'inclusive development' almost interchangeably.

10 It may be noted in this context that a country may do well in one or more of the indicators listed here but not in others. In such a situation, the issue of how to characterize growth in that country would arise. In order to fully address such a question, it would be useful to have a composite measure of inclusive growth. But then the issue would be one of devising such a measure and quantifying it. At the present state of knowledge on the subject, it is not possible to do so.

11 The term 'labour productivity' has been distinguished by A.R. Khan (2002) from 'output per worker'. In the present chapter, the term is used in the sense of 'output per worker'.

12 Equation (2) which can be used for a decomposition exercise basically provides an accounting framework, and does not imply anything about the existence or absence of an interlinkage between the two terms on the right hand side, i.e. employment and labour productivity. These two are obviously related; growth in labour productivity may have an employment displacing as well as an employment creating effect, and the net effect will depend on the relative magnitudes of the two effects.

13 Khan (2002) appears to take the view that TFP was an important source of growth for the countries of East Asia. Helpman (2004) makes the point that there is a problem of interpreting causality in the TFP estimates because high investment rates are at least partly in response to high productivity growth. And that would further weaken the position taken by Krugman and others.

14 Indeed, employment itself is an important macroeconomic variable, especially in the Keynesian framework.

15 Such programmes can play an important role in sustaining effective demand in low income economies.

16 The term 'binding constraints' has been used by Hausmann *et al.* (2005) in the context of identifying constraints on output growth. More on this will be said shortly.

17 The present chapter has already presented a comparative decomposition exercise showing the contribution of productivity and employment growth in overall and manufacturing output growth for selected countries of East and South East Asia on the one hand and South Asia on the other.

18 For a discussion on this, see Islam (2010a).

19 See Islam (2008) for an analysis of that aspect.

20 A brief description of this data is presented in the appendix to this chapter.

21 The names of the industries are not mentioned in Table 2.9 in order to keep it simple. However, the names have been examined carefully to see if there are cases of factor intensity reversal (i.e. the same industry appearing as labour intensive in one country and as capital intensive in another, or changing factor intensity over time in the same country). The only such case that could be noted is tobacco which appeared amongst the top five capital intensive industries in Korea in 1980, changed to become the third most labour intensive industry in 1990, only to change position again in 2001. Apart from this case, industries like wearing apparel, footwear, leather products, wood products and furniture rank as labour intensive in all the selected countries. On the other hand, petroleum products, chemicals, iron and steel, metal products, and paper and paper products generally appear as capital intensive.

22 One example is the so-called '200 Garment Factory Programme' initiated by the

Government in the early 1990s which led to an increase in the export of non-quota garments and the capacity of garment industry.

23 Data and information presented in this paragraph are from Tilakaratna *et al.* (2006).

24 The methodology and the illustration described here are based on Papola (2008) and ILO (2009).

25 *Direct effect* represents the first round changes in output, employment and value added (e.g. change in output which directly affects employment and value added) for a given industry as a consequence in change in final demand. *Indirect effects* are the output, employment and value added changes in inter-industry purchases as they respond to the new demands of the directly affected industries. *Induced effects* represent the response by all local industries caused by the expenditures of new household income generated by direct and indirect effects due to the changes in final demand for a given industry.

26 For further details, see ILO (2009) and Papola (2008).

27 SAM models were first introduced more than three decades ago by Stone (1978) and Pyatt and Round (1979).

28 In fact, studies carried out during the 1970s under the auspices of the ILO pointed out the importance of income distribution in influencing the mix of products that is produced in a country as the income elasticity of demand for various consumer goods varies between income/expenditure classes.

29 Chandrasekhar and Ghosh (2008) note such a shift in the pattern of consumer demand.

Bibliography

Ahmed, N., Yunus, M. and Bhuyan, H.R. (2009) *Promoting Employment-Intensive Growth in Bangladesh: Policy Analysis of the Manufacturing and Service Sectors*, Employment Sector Working Paper, ILO, Geneva.

Ali, I. and Son, H.H. (2007) *Defining and Measuring Inclusive Growth: Application to the Philippines*, ERD Working Paper No. 98, ADB, Manila.

Ansari, J. (2007) 'Structural Change in Pakistani Exports 1992–2005', *Market Forces*, vol. 3, no. 2, July 2007.

ADB (Asian Development Bank) (2005) *Labour Markets in Asia: Promoting Full, Productive and Decent Employment*, Manila.

Auer, P. and Islam, R. (2006) 'Economic Growth, Employment, Competitiveness and Labour Market Institutions', in World Economic Forum, *The Global Competitiveness Report 2006–07*, Geneva.

Bean, C. (1994) 'European Unemployment: A Survey', *Journal of Economic Literature*, vol. 32, June, pp. 573–619.

Bhorat, H. and Oosthuizen, M. (2006) 'Evolution of the Labour Market 1995–2002', in Bhorat, H. and Ravi Kanboor, S.M. (eds) *Poverty and Policy in Post-Apartheid South Africa*, Human Science Research Council, Cape Town.

Burange, L.G. and Chaddha, S.J. (2008) 'India's Revealed Comparative Advantage in Merchandise Trade', *Artha Vijnana*, vol. L, no. 4, December 2008, pp. 332–363.

Capaldo, J. (2007) *Employment Impact Assessment with Social Accounting Matrices*, Levy Economics Institute, New York.

Chandrasekhar, C.P. (2008) 'Re-visiting the Policy Environment for Engendering Employment Intensive Economic Growth', draft paper, ILO, Geneva.

Chandrasekhar, C.P. and Ghosh, J. (2008) 'Employment and the Pattern of Growth', in Kapila, R. and Kapila, U. (eds) *Economic Developments in India*, Academic Foundation, Delhi.

El Laithy, H. and El Ehwany, N. (2006) 'Employment-Poverty Linkages towards a Pro-Poor Employment Policy Framework in Egypt', unpublished paper, ILO, Geneva.

Forteza, A. and Rama, M. (2002) *Labor Market 'Rigidity' and the Success of Economic Reforms Across More than One Hundred Countries*, World Bank, Washington, D.C.

Gupta, A.P. (1977) *Fiscal Policy for Employment Generation in India*, Tata-McGraw Hill Publishing, New Delhi.

Hailu, D. (2009) 'The Indonesian Response to the Financial and Economic Crisis: Is the Developmental State Back?', *One Pager*, no. 86, International Policy Centre for Inclusive Growth, Brazil.

Hausmann, R., Rodrik, D. and Velasco, A. (2005) *Growth Diagnostics*, John F. Kennedy School of Government, Harvard University, Cambridge, MA.

Heintz, J. (2006) *Growth, Employment and Poverty Reduction*, paper presented at a workshop on 'Growth, Employment and Poverty Reduction', organized by Department for International Development, UK.

Helpman, E. (2004) *The Mystery of Economic Growth*, Belknap, Cambridge, MA.

ILO (International Labour Organization) (1970) *Towards Full Employment: A Programme for Colombia*, Geneva.

ILO (International Labour Organization) (2005) *World Employment Report*, Geneva.

ILO (International Labour Organization) (2006) *Key Indicators of Labour Markets (KILM)*, 4th edition, Geneva.

ILO (International Labour Organization) (2008) *Can low-income countries afford basic social security?* Social Security Department, Social Security Policy Briefings, Paper 3, Geneva.

ILO (International Labour Organization) (2009) *Towards an Employment Strategy for India*, unpublished report, Delhi and Geneva.

ILO (International Labour Organization) and WHO (World Health Organization) (2009) *Manual and Strategic Framework for Joint UN Country Operations*, Geneva.

Islam, I. (2005) *Managing without Growth: Challenges Confronting the Syria Labour Market*, unpublished paper, UNDP, Beirut.

Islam, R. (1976) *Factor Intensity and Labour Absorption in Manufacturing Industries: The Case of Bangladesh*, unpublished PhD dissertation, London School of Economics and Political Science, London.

Islam, R. (2002) 'Poverty Alleviation, Employment, and the Labour Markets: Lessons from Asian Experiences and Policies', in Edmonds, C. and Medina, S. (eds) *Defining an Agenda for Poverty Reduction: Proceedings of the First Asia and Pacific Forum on Poverty*, ADB, Manila.

Islam, R. (2003) *Labour Market Policies, Economic Growth and Poverty Reduction: Lessons and Non-lessons from the Comparative Experience of East, South-East and South Asia*, Issues in Employment and Poverty Discussion Paper 8, Recovery and Reconstruction Department, ILO, Geneva.

Islam, R. (2006a) 'The Nexus of Economic Growth, Employment and Poverty Reduction: An Empirical Analysis', in Islam, R. (ed.) (2006) *Fighting Poverty: The Development-Employment Link*, Lynn Rienner, Boulder and London.

Islam, R. (ed.) (2006b) *Fighting Poverty: The Development-Employment Link*, Lynn Rienner, Boulder and London.

Islam, R. (2008) 'Has Development and Employment through Labour-Intensive Industrialization Become History?', in Basu, K. and Kanbur, R. (eds) *Arguments for a Better World: Essays in Honour of Amartya Sen. Vol. II: Society, Institutions, and Development*, Oxford University Press, Oxford.

Islam, R. (2009) 'What Kind of Economic Growth is Bangladesh Attaining?', in Sha-habuddin, Q. and Islam Rahman, R. (eds) (2009) *Development Experience and Emerging Challenges: Bangladesh*, Bangladesh Institute of Development Studies and University Press Limited, Dhaka.

Islam, R. (2010a) 'Pattern of Economic Growth and its Implication for Employment', in Banerjee, L., Dasgupta, A. and Islam, R. (eds) *Development, Equity and Poverty: Essays in Honour of Azizur Rahman Khan*, Macmillan India and UNDP, Delhi and New York.

Islam, R. (2010b) *Addressing the Challenge of Jobless Growth in Developing Countries: An Analysis with Cross-Country Data*, Occasional Paper Series No. 1, Bangladesh Institute of Development Studies, Dhaka.

Kakwani, N. (2002) *Pro-Poor Growth and Policies*, Asia-Pacific Regional Programme on Macroeconomics of Poverty Reduction, UNDP, Colombo.

Kakwani, N. and Pernia, E.M. (2000) 'What is Pro-Poor Growth?', *Asian Development Review*, vol. 18, pp. 1–16.

Kapsos, S. (2005) *The Employment Intensity of Growth: Trends and Macroeconomic Determinants*, Employment Strategy Papers, 2005/12, ILO, Geneva.

Khan, A.R. (2002) *Employment, Productivity and Poverty Reduction in Developing Countries: A Background Document for the World Employment Report 2003*, draft paper, ILO, Geneva.

Khan, A.R. (2006) 'Employment Policies for Poverty Reduction', in Islam, R. (ed.) (2006) *Fighting Poverty: The Development-Employment Link*, Lynn Rienner, Boulder and London.

Khan, A.R. (2007) *Asian Experience of Growth, Employment and Poverty: An Overview with Special Reference to the Findings of some Recent Case Studies*, ILO, Geneva and UNDP, Colombo.

Kim, J. and Lawrence J.L. (1994) 'The Sources of Economic Growth in the East Asian Newly Industrializing Countries', *Journal of Japanese and International Economics*, vol. 8, no. 3, pp. 235–271.

Klasen, S. (2010) *Measuring and Monitoring Inclusive Growth: Multiple Definitions, Open Questions, and Some Constructive Proposals*, Sustainable Development Working Paper Series No. 12, ADB, Manila.

Krugman, P. (1994) 'The Myth of Asia's Miracle', *Foreign Affairs*, November/December 1994, pp. 62–78.

Kucera, D. and Roncolato, L. (2012) *Structure Matters: Sectoral Drivers of Growth and the Labour Productivity-Employment Relationship*, unpublished paper, ILO, Geneva.

Messkoub, M. (2009) *Economic Growth, Employment and Poverty in the Middle East and North Africa*, Employment Sector Working Paper No. 19, ILO, Geneva.

Murakami, A. (1968) 'Two Aspects of the Export of Manufacturing Goods from Developing Countries', *The Developing Economies*, vol. 6, no. 3, pp. 261–283.

Nickel, S. (1997) 'Unemployment and Labour Market Rigidities: Europe versus North America', *Journal of Economic Perspectives*, vol. 11, no. 3, pp. 55–74.

Palit, A. (2008) *Policies Responsible for Excessive Use of Capital Relative to Labour in India's Manufacturing Industries*, draft paper, ILO, Geneva.

Papola, T.S. (2008) *Mainstreaming Employment in Economic Policy Making*, unpublished draft, ILO, Geneva.

Pyatt, G. and Round, J.I. (1979) 'Accounting and Fixed Price Multipliers in a Social Accounting Matrix Framework', *Economic Journal*, vol. 89, December, pp. 850–873.

Radwan, S. (2006) *Economic Growth, Employment and Poverty Reduction: Linkages, Challenges and Policies in the MENA Region*, presentation at the ILO-UNDP Seminar on 'Economic Growth, Employment and Poverty in Middle East and North Africa', Cairo, 20–21 November.

Rauniyar, G. and Kanbur, R. (2009) *Inclusive Growth and Inclusive Development: A Review and Synthesis of Asian Development Bank Literature*, Occasional Paper No. 8, Independent Evaluation Department, ADB, Manila.

Rauniyar, G. and Kanbur, R. (2010) *Inclusive Development: Two Papers on Conceptualization, Application, and the ADB Perspective*, ADB, Manila.

Ravallion, M. and Chen, S. (2003) 'Measuring Pro-Poor Growth', *Economic Letters*, vol. 78, pp. 93–99.

Reserve Bank of India (2008) *Handbook of Statistics on Indian Economy, 2008*, available at: http://rbidocs.rbi.org.in/rdocs/Publications/Docs/87513.xls.

Rifkin, J. (1996) *The End of Work: The Decline of the Global Labour Force and the Dawn of the Post-Market Era*, Penguin, New York.

Riskin, C. (2010) 'Inequality and Economic Crisis in China', in Banerjee, L., Dasgupta, A. and Islam, R. (eds) *Development, Equity and Poverty: Essays in Honour of Azizur Rahman Khan*, Macmillan, India and UNDP, Delhi and New York.

Saad-Filho, A. (2010) *Growth, Poverty and Inequality: From Washington Consensus to Inclusive Growth*, UNDESA Working Paper No. 100, UN, New York.

Sharma, K. (2000) *Export Growth in India: Has FDI Played a Role?*, Economic Growth Center Yale University Discussion Paper No. 816, Connecticut.

Shukla, R. and Kakar, P. (2007) 'Consumption Level Up as India Shines', *The Economic Times*, 9 February.

Sinha, R., Pearson, P., Kadekodi, G. and Gregory, M. (1979) *Income Distribution, Growth and Basic Needs in India*, Croom Helm, London.

Stone, J.R.N. (1978) *The Disaggregation of the Household Sector in the National Accounts*, paper presented at the World Bank Conference on 'Social Accounting Methods in Development Planning', Cambridge, UK, 16–21 April 1978.

Storm, S. and Naastepad, C.W.M. (2005) 'Strategic Factors in Economic Development: East Asian Industrialization 1950–2003', *Development and Change*, vol. 36, no. 6, pp. 1059–1094.

Suryanarayana, M.H. (2008) 'What is Exclusive about "Inclusive Growth"?', *Economic and Political Weekly*, 25 October.

Tilakaratna, G., Jayawardena, P. and Kumara, T. (2006) *Economic Growth, Employment and Poverty Reduction in Sri Lanka*, unpublished paper, ILO, Geneva.

UN (United Nations) (1948) *The Universal Declaration on Human Rights*, available at: www.un.org.en/documents/udhr (accessed 7 August 2014).

UNDP (United Nations Development Programme) (1993) *Human Development Report 1993*, New York.

UNDP (United Nations Development Programme) (1996) *Human Development Report 1996: Economic Growth and Human Development*, New York.

UNIDO (United Nations Industrial Development Organization) (2005) *Industrial Statistics Data (Indstat 3)*, electronic version, Vienna.

World Bank (1978) *World Development Report 1978*, Oxford University Press, New York.

World Bank (1993) *The East Asian Miracle: Economic Growth and Public Policy*, Oxford University Press, New York.

World Bank (1999) *World Development Report 1999/2000: Entering the 21st Century*, Oxford University Press, New York.

World Bank (2008) *The Growth Report: Strategies for Sustained Growth and Inclusive Development*, Commission on Growth and Development, Washington, D.C.

World Bank (2009) 'What is Inclusive Growth?'. Online, available at: http://siteresources. worldbank.org/INTDEBTDEPT/resources/468980–1218567884549/WhatIsInclusive-Growth20081230.pdf (accessed 27 September 2011).

World Bank (2010) 'Inclusive Growth: Key to Identifying Development Priorities'. Online, available at: http://web.worldbank.org/WBSITE/EXTERNAL/EXTABOUTUS/ORGANIZATION/EXT (accessed 27 September 2011).

World Bank (various years) *World Development Indicators*, available at: http://data. worldbank.org/products/wdi.

Young, A. (1995) 'The Tyranny of Numbers: Confronting the Statistical Realities of the East Asian Growth Experience', *Quarterly Journal of Economics*, vol. 110, no. 3, pp. 641–680.

3 Macroeconomic policy, growth and employment

Introduction

The conventional view of macroeconomic policy is that governments should act as guardians of price stability, safeguard fiscal sustainability and ensure that the external account is viably financed. Such a role, when credibly conducted, can enhance investor confidence, support growth and lead to employment creation. In practice, this view of macroeconomic policy has taken the form of attaining and sustaining prudential targets pertaining to debts, deficits, inflation and external balances. Thus, 'rule-of-thumb' targets – such as a 40 to 60 per cent debt to GDP ratio supported by low fiscal deficits, low, single digit inflation, minimum foreign exchange reserve holdings – are often recommended by international financial and regional institutions as hallmarks of good and growth-friendly macroeconomic management. It is also well known that many central banks in both developed and developing countries exercise inflation targeting and aim to attain low, single digit inflation over the medium term as one of the key goals of monetary policy.

The notion that macroeconomic stability is crucial to growth and job creation seems to have become an article of faith among key international organizations. Thus, the World Bank, in its World Development Report of 2013 (World Bank 2012c) proclaims that macroeconomic stability is 'fundamental' to growth and job creation. The IMF, in its 2013 *Jobs and Growth* report (IMF, 2013a) expresses a rather similar sentiment as does an OECD report (2014) which proclaims: 'Monetary and budgetary policy settings aimed at low and stable inflation and sound public finances are conducive to long-term growth'.

Despite this prevailing orthodoxy, the present chapter argues that the mere pursuit of prudent macroeconomic policies, while necessary, is not sufficient to promote rapid growth and broad-based employment creation. The chapter, using a combination of global and country-specific evidence, highlights the various means through which macroeconomic policy managers can become active agents of development without forsaking their roles as guardians of stability. These include: counter-cyclical policies to cope with economic volatility; pertinent changes to monetary and financial policies to enhance financial inclusion; maintaining stable and competitive real exchange rates (RERs) combined with prudent capital account management to support economic diversification and new areas of employment opportunities; sustainable resource mobilization through appropriate fiscal policies to support incentive-compatible policy interventions to promote productive employment.

The conventional approach to macroeconomic policy and its relevance to developing countries: genesis, characteristics, scope and scale

The conventional approach to macroeconomic policy and its relevance to developing countries bears the hallmarks of a conservative strain of thinking that was nurtured in the institutional environment of advanced countries. Thus, in the sphere of monetary policy, the emphasis is on a so-called 'single instrument–single objective' framework in which the overriding goal is to attain and maintain low, single digit inflation using one instrument, the so-called 'policy rate'. This approach is widely known as 'inflation targeting' and was first formally adopted in New Zealand in 1990. This subsequently spread – after about a lag of a decade – to developing countries and emerging economies.

The lack of any reference to an employment objective in the monetary policy framework can be justified on the ground that policy rules that have been used to guide inflation targeting – often called the Taylor rule – also uses information on the so-called 'output gap', that is the deviation of actual output from potential output that measures full capacity utilization, including full utilization of the workforce.[1] One could then argue that if there is no output gap, the inflation rate will be stable. Thus, maintaining low and stable inflation also means that the output gap is minimal. This is a restatement of the view that the long-run Phillips curve is vertical, that is, there is no long-run trade-off between inflation and unemployment. Hence, one can target an inflation rate without affecting the unemployment rate which is determined by supply side factors. Such supply side factors work best in a context of full wage and price flexibility, ensuring that an economy settles at full employment equilibrium and is associated with a 'non-accelerating rate of inflation', or NAIRU. At this 'bliss point', the rate of inflation is stable because private sector expectations pertaining to the future course of inflation is anchored to the prevailing inflation rate. It is, in principle, possible for NAIRU to be compatible with different rates of inflation, but the pertinent literature displays a distinct preference for low, single digit inflation.

The inflation targeting approach to monetary policy has turned out to be rather influential as it has implications for other areas that typically form the domain of macroeconomic policy: the exchange rate regime, capital account management and fiscal policy. Thus, the effective practice of inflation targeting should be combined with both market-determined and flexible exchange rate regimes and capital account liberalization.

A monetary policy regime that is influenced by inflation targeting also means that fiscal policy needs to be aligned with the imperatives of such a regime. Thus, one leading advocate of this view expresses the monetary policy–fiscal policy interaction in the following way: '(r)estraining the fiscal authorities from engaging in excessive deficit financing … aligns fiscal policy with monetary policy and makes it easier for the monetary authorities to keep inflation under control'.[2] This is probably the basis for advocating 'fiscal rules' in which countries impose numerical limits on debts, deficits, expenditures and revenues, as well as advocating for balanced budgets. The Eurozone's Maastricht Treaty fiscal rules that are combined with inflation targeting are, of course, well known, but this idea has spread to the developing world on a significant scale.[3]

What is important to emphasize is that the Maastricht Treaty combines inflation targeting and fiscal rules within a currency union, thus providing another institutional variant to the view that inflation targeting is predicated on the premise that a country runs a market-determined, flexible exchange rate regime and combines this with full capital mobility. This institutional variant means that developing countries face a binary choice with respect to exchange rate regimes: either a fully flexible exchange rate regime or a fully fixed exchange rate regime both of which are combined with an open capital account. Fixed exchange rate regimes can be adopted in a number of ways, such as membership of a currency union, a currency board or de jure dollarization.

In sum, a developing country can, in principle, fully embrace the conventional approach to macroeconomic policy by incorporating the following institutional arrangements:

- Inflation targeting;
- Fully flexible or fully fixed exchange rate regime;
- Open capital account;
- Fiscal rules.

Such institutional arrangements will foster macroeconomic stability and thus anchor private sector expectations. This in turn will boost business confidence, promote savings and investment and thus support growth. Beyond these virtues, one has to rely on structural and labour market reforms to induce greater product and labour market flexibility. This view is based on the premise that product and labour market rigidities represent binding constraints on private sector-led growth. Hence, the attenuation or removal of such binding constraints promotes growth and enhances employment opportunities.[4]

While, in principle, developing countries in particular and all countries at large, can and do adopt the aforementioned elements of the conventional framework, how widespread is this in practice? Here, one can refer to the IMF's annual report on 'exchange arrangements and exchange restrictions'. Despite its title, the report also describes a country's monetary policy framework and documents restrictions on the capital account. The report has the advantage of describing policy regimes based on de facto rather than de jure arrangements.

Table 3.1 draws on the 2013 IMF *Annual Report* (IMF, 2013b) on the above subjects. It shows that, despite its seemingly dominant intellectual influence for more than two decades, only 34 countries in the world – out of 188 member states that report to the IMF on these matters – actually claim that in practice

Table 3.1 Number of IMF member states by typology of monetary policy frameworks, 2013

Exchange rate anchor	Monetary aggregate target	Inflation targeting	Other
92	26	34	39

Source: adapted from IMF (2013b: 5–6).

Table 3.2 Percentage of IMF member states by typology of exchange rate arrangements, 2013

Hard pegs	Soft pegs	Floating with some intervention	Free floating	Other managed arrangement
13.1	42.9	34.0	15.7	9.9

Source: adapted from IMF (2013b: 7).

they implement inflation targeting regimes. The majority of the countries are split between using the exchange rate as a nominal anchor, targeting of monetary aggregates and using a 'multiple indicators' approach.

What about exchange rate regimes? Is there a bi-modal distribution with countries split between fully flexible and fully fixed exchange rates? The available evidence does not support that proposition. As Table 3.2 shows, fully flexible exchange rate regimes are a rare occurrence and are limited to a handful of high income countries. At the other extreme, fully fixed exchange rate regimes are also not widespread. The dominant types of exchange rate regimes are 'managed' and take the form of what the IMF describes as 'soft pegs', floating regimes with some interventions and other regimes in which there is also some degree of intervention in foreign exchange markets. Similarly, full capital account liberalization is not common. The aforementioned 2013 IMF report found 57 instances of tightening of capital controls in 2011 and 2012 ranging across its member states. This has happened in response to the 'increased volatility of capital flows and the changing global environment'.[5]

Consider now the case of fiscal rules. Are they widespread? In 1990, they were indeed rather uncommon, with five known cases. By mid-2012, there were 76 countries incorporating fiscal rules in their policy frameworks, with emerging economies being responsible for the major share of recent adoptions of fiscal rules.[6] Hence, in terms of popularity, fiscal rules seem to outperform the implementation of inflation targeting regimes and either fully flexible or fully fixed exchange rate regimes.

The conventional approach to macroeconomic policy and its relevance to developing countries: a critical appraisal

Ultimately, the popularity and persistence of particular institutional arrangements pertaining to the conduct of macroeconomic policy should be evaluated in terms of their impact on growth and employment. Hence, the discussion turns briefly to the consequences and implications of adopting inflation targeting regimes, specific exchange rate arrangements, open capital accounts and fiscal rules.

As far as inflation targeting regimes are concerned, the evidence is mixed. They seem to foster somewhat better inflation outcomes, but this does not extend to either a consistently superior growth performance or better labour market outcomes in terms of productivity and vulnerable employment – see Figures 3.1a, 3.1b and 3.1c. Hence, if the aim is to use inflation targeting regimes as a means of promoting growth and employment, developing countries aspiring to reap such benefits will be disappointed.

The key challenge facing many developing countries, especially those belonging to the low income category, is to deal with the implications of the robust

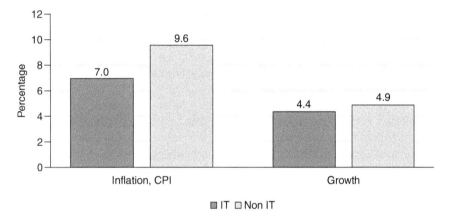

Figure 3.1a Inflation and growth differentials, inflation targeting (IT) vs non-inflation targeting (non IT) countries (source: IMF, *World Economic Outlook Data 2014*, Washington, D.C., authors' calculations). The period covered is 2000–2013 based on a sample of 24 countries.

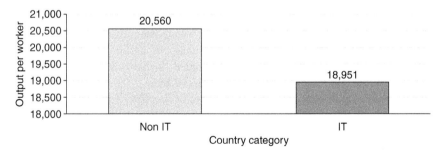

Figure 3.1b Labour productivity differentials, inflation targeting (IT) vs non-inflation targeting (non IT) countries (source: ILO (2014b) authors' calculations). The period covered is 2000–2012 based on a sample of 24 countries.

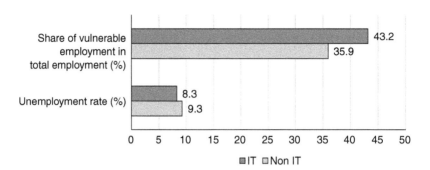

Figure 3.1c Unemployment and vulnerable unemployment, inflation targeting (IT) vs non-inflation targeting (non IT) countries (source: ILO (2014b) authors' calculations). The period covered is 2000-2012 based on a sample of 24 countries.

finding that the monetary transmission mechanism is weak and unreliable in these economies.[7] Such a finding casts doubts on the capacity of monetary authorities either to conform to the norms of inflation targeting or even to conduct counter-cyclical policies.

Even if one does not adopt a fully fledged inflation targeting regime, many developing countries could still opt for either an implicit or explicit inflation target. This is a reasonable aspiration as such countries set policy targets in other areas, most notably pertaining to growth. Furthermore, developing countries also subscribe to the Millennium Development Goals (MDGs) and often incorporate poverty reduction targets as part of this global framework.

What strikes one about the setting of inflation targets is their apparent arbitrariness. For example, the median targeted inflation rate for inflation targeting countries in the developing world is less than 5 per cent.[8] Such a number appears to have been chosen without much regard to the long-run behaviour (that is, over several decades) of inflation rates in developing countries or a reasonable approximation of a 'threshold' rate, that is the threshold beyond which inflation has a deleterious impact on growth. Take, for example, the case of India. The latest proposal is to aim for a medium-term inflation target of 4 per cent based on the CPI (consumer price index). Yet India's long-run inflation rate, calculated over 40 years, hovers around 7 per cent.[9] Hence, the current proposal entails a rather ambitious inflation target that, if adopted, is likely to put considerable pressure on the credibility of the Reserve Bank of India.[10]

The proclivity to aim for an inflation target of less than 5 per cent is also not consistent with the prevailing evidence on threshold rates based on the estimated growth–inflation trade-off. The implication of such evidence is that developing countries should avoid double digit inflation which is a much more eclectic formulation than the current preference for low, single digit inflation.[11]

The issue of setting appropriate inflation targets and the broader issue of the appropriateness of expanding the reach of inflation targeting regimes in the developing world acquires particular salience because of contemporary debates on the design and conduct of monetary policies in the advanced countries. In the wake of the global economic and financial crisis of 2007–09, several scholars and practitioners wonder whether the efficacy of inflation targeting regimes, so dominant over two decades, has run its course. Some have even proclaimed the 'death of inflation targeting', at least in its narrow sense.[12] The harsh reality is that long periods of low, single digit inflation can co-exist with a severe outbreak of financial instability. Alternative proposals to improve the efficacy of monetary policy include doubling the inflation target from its current tendency to use a 2 per cent norm, aiming for other targets (such as nominal GDP targeting) and broadening the scope of monetary policy to include macro-prudential instruments to cope with the risk and recurrence of financial instability.[13]

There is also considerable debate on the nature and shape of the Phillips curve, with some arguing that in the 2000s, characterized by a high degree of globalization and low inflation, the Phillips curve has become much flatter. This increases the costs of a disinflation strategy.[14] In light of such debates that are happening in advanced countries, it would be unconscionable for practitioners and policy makers not to reflect on the implications of such debates for developing countries.

On exchange rate regimes, the verdict is quite clear. Hard pegs are associated with growth collapses,[15] while the contemporary experience of the Eurozone shows that currency unions even in advanced economies lack the flexibility to empower individual members of such a union to cope expeditiously with recessions. It is unlikely that the typical developing economy will have the capacity or proclivity to rely on fully flexible exchange rate regimes. The continuing policy challenge for developing countries is to manage the trade-off between the exchange rate as a nominal anchor that enables it to play a major role as an anti-inflation strategy and the exchange rate as a tool for fostering international competitiveness and bring about structural change. As the subsequent discussion will suggest, active management of the exchange rate that creatively deals with the aforementioned trade-off can reap growth and employment dividends.

The thesis that open capital accounts are a highly desirable institutional arrangement for developing economies has not withstood the test of empirical scrutiny. Indeed, the IMF has significantly modified its stance on this issue. In mid-1990s, on the eve of the Asian financial crisis, the Fund sought an amendment to its acts to promulgate a provision that all IMF member states should have open capital accounts as an eventual goal. It now argues that, under a variety of circumstances, prudently managed capital controls are desirable (Ostry *et al.*, 2011). This change in thinking reflects the state-of-the-art evidence on the long-run impact of capital mobility on growth and employment. There is a large literature on this topic and the evidence seems to be sparse – at least at the aggregate level – that open capital accounts unambiguously foster better growth outcomes.[16] A lot depends on enabling conditions – such as the maturity of domestic financial markets and the institutional quality of governance – that enable a country to lock in the benefits of capital account liberalization. It seems quite clear that countries that lack such enabling conditions – which is the case for many countries in the developing world – suggesting that an open capital account and fixed exchange rate regimes is not an 'auspicious combination'.[17] Indeed, even well endowed emerging economies (such as Brazil) have been forced to re-enact capital controls on a transitional basis in a bid to cope with the volatility of short-term capital flows that have characterized contemporary developments. Such policy actions are in line with the theoretical case for prudential capital control. There is recognition that counter-cyclical taxes on short-term capital inflows during a boom can reduce the severity of busts.

What about fiscal rules and the benefits that they are supposed to engender? There is some evidence that fiscal rules are associated with better fiscal performance, but even their proponents are careful not to conflate correlation with causation.[18] It is entirely plausible that countries attain better fiscal performance through a variety of means and methods and then use fiscal rules as ex-post validation of such means and methods.

The link between fiscal rules and growth is based on the premise that beyond certain thresholds debts and deficits harm growth. These threshold effects have been contested, with much of the literature now claiming that such thresholds are not based on robust evidence.[19]

For the purpose of this chapter, an attempt was made to estimate cross-country regressions in standard growth equations with the inclusion of fiscal rules as an additional explanatory variable. The results, for what they are worth, suggest that fiscal rules do not add to the explanatory power of cross-country growth regressions (see Table 3.3).

An issue that is highly germane to the chapter is the extent to which developing countries that implement fiscal rules exhibit better performance in terms of selected labour market indicators. The evidence is mixed as shown in Table 3.4. Countries that have fiscal rules are associated with lower unemployment and higher employment rates than countries that do not have fiscal rules. On the other hand, the incidence of in-work poverty is significantly lower in countries without fiscal rules.

While the evidence in favour of the growth promoting properties of fiscal rules is not robust, one does not have to adopt the nihilistic stance that fiscal rules are irrelevant or even undesirable. The challenge is to design fiscal policy, rather than fiscal rules per se, that are development friendly and flexible enough to cope with changing economic circumstances.[20]

Perhaps the central concern among critics of the conventional framework is that the benefits of macroeconomic stability might have been oversold. This has been famously acknowledged by a well-known 2005 World Bank Report on the lessons of the 1990s when developing economies were subjected to structural adjustments programmes led by international financial institutions in the quest to enhance and sustain the goal of macroeconomic stability.[21] Others have endorsed such a view.[22]

A recent study (Srimaneetham and Temple, 2009) has sought to counter such pessimism concerning the role that macroeconomic stability plays in fostering

Table 3.3 Fiscal rules and per capita GDP growth: illustrations from cross-country regressions based on a standard growth equation

Explanatory variables	*Statistically significant at least at 5% level (yes/no)?* Regressions with time effects	*Statistically significant at least at 5% level (yes/no)?* Regressions without time effects
Initial per capita GDP (to test for convergence)	Yes	Yes
Investment	Yes	Yes
Years of schooling	Yes	Yes
Population growth	Yes	Yes
Balanced budget rule (BBR)	Yes, but with wrong sign (suggesting BBR associated with negative growth)	No
Debt limits	No	No

Sources: Authors' estimates based on IMF, *Fiscal Rules Database* (2012), available at: www.imf.org/external/datamapper/fiscalrules/map/map.htm, and World Bank, *World Development Indicators* (2014), available at: http://data.worldbank.org/products/wdi.

Note
Sample size: 732 observations, with 35 countries having fiscal rules.

Table 3.4 Fiscal rules and labour market indicators

Fiscal rule (yes/no)	Mean value: employment rate (%)	Mean value: unemployment rate (%)	Mean value: working poor (%) (IPL: US$2 a day)
Yes: Balanced budget rule	61.9	7.2	33.0
No	57.0	10.6	23.5
Yes: ceiling on public debt	61.5	8.3	38.3
No	57.4	9.9	23.4

Source: authors' estimates based on ILO, *KILM* (2014) and IMF, *Fiscal Rules Database* (2012), available at: www.imf.org/external/datamapper/fiscalrules/map/map.htm. IPL stands for 'international poverty line'.

growth. Employing a multidimensional index of macroeconomic stability and applying it to 70 countries over the 1970–99 period, the authors argue that a 'one standard deviation improvement in the index would raise annual growth by roughly 0.5 to 0.7 percentage points over 30 years'. The motivation of this study is to uphold the 'common sense view that some degree of stability is necessary for rapid growth' while questioning the view that 'macroeconomic stability is largely irrelevant' in understanding the process of long-run economic growth'.[23]

While the aforementioned study is noteworthy for its use of robust and state-of-the-art statistical techniques, the use of any multidimensional index always suffers from the lack of operational substance from the perspective of policy makers. One can readily monitor such macroeconomic variables as the inflation rate, but understanding changes in a composite index is more difficult as they are the result of movements in various components within such an index.

One also needs to dig a little deeper into the cross-country results and subject individual cases to greater scrutiny. According to the authors, the countries in their sample can be classified into three distinct groups based on their index. The worst performers in terms of this index are in group 1 (with the value of the index ranging from –2.97 to –.36), the intermediate performers are in group 2 (with the value of the index ranging from –.33 to .102), the best performers are in group 3 (with the value of the index ranging from .83 to 1.83). The five best performers include Togo and the five worst performers include Uganda. Given this large gap in the preferred measure of macroeconomic stability, how has Uganda fared relative to Togo over time?

What is problematic from the perspective of the cross-country study under review is that Uganda does significantly better than Togo in some important respects, while producing outcomes in other areas that are not much different from Togo.[24] Both Uganda and Togo are in the UNDP's low human development category. In terms of values and ranks that one can assign to the human development index (HDI), the two countries are almost indistinguishable. Thus, Uganda has a HDI value of 0.456 with a rank of 159; Togo has a HDI value of 0.459 with a rank of 161. Between 1985 and 2012, Uganda experienced an annual increase of about 1.6 per cent in the value of its HDI, while Togo experienced an annual increase of about 0.8 in the value of its HDI between 1980 and 2012. Furthermore, recent trends suggest that Uganda is on track to meet the poverty reduction goal under the MDGs, but Togo is significantly off-target, with evidence that both inequality and extreme poverty has increased in recent years.

What is striking is the growth differential between the two countries. Contrary to what is predicted by the cross-country results, Togo's per capita gross national income (GNI at 2005 purchasing power parity measured in US dollars) *decreased* by about 19 per cent between 1980 and 2012; Uganda's per capita gross national income (GNI at 2005 purchasing power parity measured in US dollars) *increased* by 125 per cent between 1985 and 2012. The net result is that Uganda's per capita income was 58 per cent of Togo's in 1985, but was 1.26 times higher than Togo's in 2012.

The above examples thus highlight the pitfalls of relying too heavily on cross-country results for establishing the link between macroeconomic stability, growth and other indicators of inclusive development, such as poverty and inequality.[25] Country-specific peculiarities can confound the neat patterns embedded in cross-country studies however well anchored they are in terms of robust statistical techniques.

So far, the discussion has been couched in terms of the relationship between macroeconomic stability and long-term growth. Yet containing economic volatility in the short run by tempering business cycles is at the forefront of macroeconomic policy goals. Furthermore, there is an association between lower economic volatility and higher growth prospects. These important concerns hardly feature in standard discussions of macroeconomic stability. Yet developing countries generally suffer from a pro-cyclical bias that exacerbates boom-bust cycles. Empowering developing countries to reduce the pro-cyclical bias in their macroeconomic policy settings is an important goal, and one that is receiving renewed attention in the wake of the global economic and financial crisis of 2007–09. Any attempt at rethinking macroeconomic policy from a development perspective would need to incorporate initiatives to enhance the capacity of developing policy makers to engage in counter-cyclical policies.

Cross-country analyses of the macroeconomic stability-growth link also overlook the need to offer a more direct test of the transmission channel via which macroeconomic stability is supposed to foster growth. As has been noted above, it is the 'expectations channel' via which macroeconomic stability is assumed to transmit its positive influence on growth. Yet this proposition is often asserted rather than tested. One of the few cases where this is done is with respect to monetary policy. The evidence is quite striking. In response to surveys, monetary authorities reveal that they assign the lowest priority to the expectations channel of monetary policy. For example, 15 central banks in Sub-Saharan Africa were asked by BIS (Bank for International Settlements) to rank the importance of different transmission channels of monetary policy on a scale of 0 to 5, with 5 being the most important, and 0 being the least important. Based on the survey responses, the expectations channel receives a value of only 0.92 which is among the lowest score vis-à-vis other transmission channels.[26] A survey of central banks in South Asia does not even mention the expectations channel in discussions of the effectiveness of monetary policy.[27]

Another way of assessing the importance of macroeconomic stability from a private sector perspective is to ascertain the extent to which the private sector in developing countries regards lack of macroeconomic stability as a binding constraint on its operations. Here, the striking fact is that, if one draws on the World Bank's enterprise surveys, this factor does not even feature in the survey responses. There is a reference to 'political stability', but it is not interpreted as a surrogate for macroeconomic stability. The top two constraints are lack of access to finance and lack of access to reliable supply of electricity (with the latter acting as a proxy for infrastructure deficit).[28] These constraints, and their policy implications, are discussed in greater detail in a subsequent section.

It is worth noting that these survey responses have important ramifications for the validity of the analytical framework adopted by international organizations to identify constraints on private sector-led development. For example, the IFC, which spearhead's the international community's work on private sector-led development, emphasizes lack of macroeconomic and fiscal stability as a key constraint on job creation (IFC, 2013, chapter 1). Yet, it is unable to corroborate this thesis in its analysis of the enterprise surveys. In sum, despite the importance ascribed to the role of private sector expectations in analytical discussions of the macroeconomic stability–growth link, hard evidence is hard to assemble.

Finally, any critique of the conventional macroeconomic policy framework would be incomplete if it did not highlight the role that incentives play in driving the collective behaviour of macroeconomic policy makers in developing countries. A basic economic premise is that both individuals and organizations respond to incentives. If the incentive structure of macroeconomic policy is such that central banks and finance ministries care only, or largely, about attaining key inflation and fiscal targets, then they might retreat into a mind-set where mainstream development concerns become secondary. This runs the risk of turning major policy institutions in developing countries that are typically influential and resourceful into enclave entities. Perhaps such considerations led a former Indian Prime Minister to remind his central bank governor that he had broader obligations than just the conduct of monetary policy in a narrow, technical sense. He reportedly said:

> With your mind ... fully taken up by issues like interest rates and ... monetary policy transmission, it is easy to forget that monetary policy is also about reducing hunger and malnutrition, putting children in school, creating jobs, building roads and bridges and increasing the productivity of our farms and firms.[29]

Connecting macroeconomic policy to core development concerns

How to connect macroeconomic policy to core development concerns is an important challenge that entails the need for policy innovations. The conventional discourse on macroeconomic stability has downplayed the need for such policy innovations. Admittedly, in the wake of the global economic and financial crisis of 2007–09, there has been a 'rethinking macroeconomics' movement led by leading mainstream economists who are affiliated with the IMF, but the focus of such rethinking is on the policy concerns of rich countries rather than their poorer counterparts.[30]

In light of such lacuna in the pertinent literature, the rest of the discussion in this chapter deals with the topic of establishing a closer alignment between macroeconomic policies and key development concerns. What emerges is the need for a significant modification of the conventional approach to macroeconomic policy rather than a radical overhaul. The key principle is that one needs a 'dual mandate' for macroeconomic policy managers in developing countries. The notion of the dual mandate emphasizes the role of macroeconomic policy managers along two dimensions: (a) as a guardian of stability; (b) as an agent of inclusive development.

Being a guardian of stability does not merely mean passively accepting exogenous targets on debts, deficits and inflation derived from a 'one-size-fits-all' approach. It means upholding the principles of price stability, fiscal and financial sustainability using a country-specific approach. It means protecting people from the vagaries of business cycles and other exogenous shocks through sustainable counter-cyclical policies based on a mix of automatic stabilizers and discretionary interventions. This point is particularly important because developing countries, on average, suffer from greater output and inflation volatility than their developed counterparts (Agenor and Montiel, 2008, p. 5).To make matters worse, developing economies are prone to running pro-cyclical macroeconomic policy (Ilzetski and Veigh, 2008), a point that was made earlier.

The notion of macroeconomic policy managers as agents of inclusive development entails various obligations on developing country governments. It entails an emphasis on a sustainable resource mobilization strategy to support the attainment of core development goals. It should also be interpreted to suggest how policy makers can facilitate the process of structural transformation. One way of engaging with this issue is to identify binding constraints on sectors with the most potential for productive job creation. As will be argued later, promoting financial inclusion and attenuating infrastructure deficits can enhance the job creating potential of various sectors. This is best done by using standard macroeconomic policy instruments, such as giving priority to raising adequate domestic revenue, incentive-compatible credit allocation schemes and appropriate regulatory changes by monetary and financial authorities.

The exchange rate regime can also be used to forge closer links between macroeconomic policy, structural transformation and inclusive development.

This can happen when the exchange rate is kept at a stable and competitive level that is consistent with economic fundamentals. It can stimulate growth and effectively operate as a tool of industry policy that supports structural transformation by shifting resources from the non-traded to the traded goods sector. On the other hand, the use of exchange rate policy to promote structural transformation and employment creation requires prudent capital account management. These issues are explored in greater depth at a later juncture.

The subsequent sections will elucidate some practical policy implications arising from the above assessment in a developing country context. The analysis will start with monetary and financial policies, turn to exchange rate policies and capital account management and conclude with some observations on the design of fiscal policy. The primary conclusion is that one should move beyond inflation targeting, the so-called binary choice between fixed and flexible exchange rate regimes, as well as the preoccupation with capital mobility and fiscal rules.

Beyond inflation targeting: the role of central banks in fostering an inclusive financial system

Central banks in developing countries certainly have the primary obligation to promote price stability. As argued at a previous juncture, this would entail setting an inflation target without necessarily subscribing to the tenets of inflation targeting. Beyond setting an appropriate inflation target, what should central banks in developing country do?

Central banks and financial authorities can support structural transformation and job creation by promoting financial inclusion. This might also engender the collateral benefit of strengthening the transmission mechanism of conventional monetary policy. The lack of a competitive and inclusive financial system is often one of the impediments to an expeditious and reliable monetary transmission mechanism, especially in low income countries. Hence, central banks and financial authorities can justify greater engagement with the agenda of financial inclusion on the ground that there will be spill-over effects that will allow them to perform their traditional functions more effectively.

It has to be said that, despite the growing awareness of the importance of building an inclusive financial system, central banks in developing countries still pay relatively limited attention to it. A content analysis of key speeches delivered either by central bank governors or the next most senior official in 51 low and middle income countries suggests that approximately 27 per cent of such speeches refer to financial inclusion. Such speeches are typically dominated by concerns about macroeconomic and price stability.[31]

The view that developing country central banks should regard promotion of financial inclusion as a key obligation can be justified on the ground that lack of access to finance has been found to constitute a major hindrance to business operations and expansion. According to the World Economic Forum (2012), access to finance is among the five most problematic factors for businesses in 76.5 per cent of the sample of low and middle income countries and 79.9 per cent of the sample that cuts across all income groups. Similarly, the World Bank (2012a) shows that lack of access to finance is an obstacle for firms in low and middle income countries, across all regions of the world. In Sub-Saharan Africa, the Middle East and North Africa and Latin America and the Caribbean, more than 30 per cent of the surveyed firms have cited access to finance as a major constraint (Figure 3.2).[32]

At the household level, more than 2.5 billion people around the world, corresponding to roughly half of the world's adults, remain unbanked. Among those who are adults earning less than US$2 a day, 75 per cent are without a bank account (Demirgüç-Kunt and Klapper, 2012; World Bank, 2013a). Yet, the poorer a household, the greater their need for protection against vulnerabilities – such as illness or unemployment – and for investment in education and health, and thus their need for financial services, such as savings, credit, insurance and remittances. Financial inclusion can also contribute to increasing people's livelihood through enabling them to engage in entrepreneurial activities (Allen *et al.*, 2012; McKinsey, 2012; World Bank, 2012b).

Overcoming barriers to financial inclusion requires a variety of comprehensive actions, including appropriate changes in the design of monetary and financial policies. Developing country central banks should promote an inclusive financial sector, most notably through steering the allocation of credit to underserved areas and targeted sectors. Possible measures include lowering interest

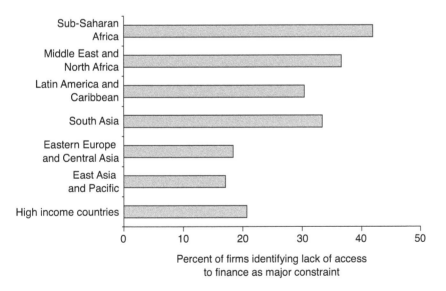

Figure 3.2 Lack of access to finance as a major constraint for firms in low and middle income countries across regions of the world (source: authors' compilation based on World Bank (2012a)).

Note
Regional averages were calculated by taking the mean of country-level indicators, including only those country surveys for which the global methodology has been used.

rates, and providing credit guarantees and subsidized credit to sectors that can contribute to productivity and employment growth, such as small and medium-sized enterprises and export-oriented sectors.

Some country-specific examples can be used to illustrate the importance of financial inclusion as a key part of a central bank's mandate. In Nigeria, for instance, an agricultural lending facility provides loan guarantees that cover up to half of financial institutions' losses incurred from loans to both small farmers and large enterprises in the agricultural sector. The facility also provides incentives to banks to allocate a large share of their credit to agribusiness. Besides, it provides assistance in credit risk assessment for banks as well as in financial management for borrowers. The programme aims at raising lending to the agribusiness from 1 to 7–10 per cent of total loans by 2020 (McKinsey, 2012).

In Rwanda, a donor-supported credit guarantee scheme played an important role in enabling the country to become a significant exporter of specialty coffee in the 2000s. The credit guarantee scheme was able to overcome the risk aversion of traditional lenders who focused on the seasonal financing of large traders and exporters and eschewed support for the investment needs of the specialty coffee sector (ILO, 2011b, pp. 174–177).

Public ownership of parts of the banking system can be a vehicle to realize measures aimed at increasing financial inclusion and supporting employment. In some developing countries, for example Argentina, Brazil, Malaysia, South Korea and Taiwan, investment banks have played a central role in directing credit to targeted sectors (Epstein, 2007).

Can developing countries promote financial inclusion effectively within a reasonable time-period? A good example is Ecuador. Following the 1998–2000 financial and economic crisis, policy makers embraced the opportunity to face the downturn through a set of financial, economic and social policies, including policies to boost financial inclusion. Major changes to the country's institutional arrangements were undertaken, including to the orientation and functions of the Ecuadorian Central Bank which has incorporated financial inclusion into its strategic goals. The institutional capacity of the bank to orchestrate the government's financial inclusion policy is grounded in (1) its responsibility for financial regulation, (2) its participation in financial supervisory bodies, (3) the incorporation of financial inclusion projects in its organizational structure, and (4) the National Payment System, one of the bank's principal instruments to conduct monetary policy.

These policy initiatives appeared to have borne fruit. Over 2005 to 2011, the percentage of the population with a bank account in the national financial system increased from 28.9 to 83.2 per cent, which is quite a dramatic transformation. The share of the population with a bank account in private banks and credit holdings doubled during the same period. Together, private banks and credit unions provided more than 70 per cent of all bank accounts in 2011. Public banks recorded the largest relative increase, up from 1.3 per cent in 2005 to 9.6 per cent in 2011. Besides, regulatory reforms have led to a decline in both real interest rates and consumers' cost for financial transactions (Banco Central del Ecuador, 2012).

In addition to these measures, modern technology can be harnessed to promote financial inclusion. The successful cases of M-PESA in Kenya and Easypaisa in Pakistan, among others, show how mobile phone technology can be deployed to reach the unbanked. M-PESA is a small-value money transfer system that was first launched in Kenya in 2007. The reach of M-PESA is extensive, offering a large share of the population basic financial services. In 2012 – five years after its launch – the number of active users reached the 15 million mark, corresponding to more than 60 per cent of the country's adults and roughly 35 per cent of its total population (Safaricom, 2012, 2013). Likewise, Easypaisa, launched in 2009, has contributed to addressing some of the principal reasons for lack of financial inclusion in Pakistan, including high perceived cost, unsuitable product features, lack of access, insufficient income and high risk associated with traditional banking services (Easypaisa, 2012). Monetary and financial authorities can be a driving force behind the spread of mobile money systems through their role in providing appropriate regulatory leeway.

Exchange rate policy and capital account management: implications for employment creation

Concerns about real exchange rate misalignments have become central to the debate on how to achieve sustained growth. In general, an overvaluation of the real exchange rate is expected to impede economic growth; it can harm domestic firms' competitiveness in international markets and lead to an unsustainably high current account deficit. Beyond that, it has been argued, among others by Freund and Pierola (2008), Rodrik (2008) and Steinberg (2011), that currency undervaluation can facilitate growth and employment. The rationale is that it delivers cost competitiveness in a way that avoids the cumbersome and contentious nature of other policy instruments, such as selective taxes and subsidies, geared towards specific sectoral activities.

A number of studies have analysed the effect of real exchange rate movements on employment. In an open economy, currency appreciations can have negative employment effects through three major channels. First, an appreciation of the real exchange rate can lead to a contraction in employment in the traded goods sector caused by the deterioration of the economy's competitiveness and thus lower net exports. Second, currency appreciation translates into higher real wages (measured in international currency) resulting from a reduction in the cost of imported goods. This can lead to a shift from labour to capital goods, particularly if the latter have a significant import component. The change in relative prices of labour to capital goods affects both the traded and non-traded sectors. Third, the exchange rate can affect employment through the development channel. Given that an appreciation can lead to lower profitability in the traded goods sector, it prevents a shift in resources from the non-traded to the traded sector (a process which effectively can act as an industrial policy). Since the expansion of the traded goods sector is commonly believed to bring about growth and modernization in the economy, real exchange rate appreciation can hinder structural transformation (Frenkel and Ros, 2006). Although not exhaustive, Table 3.5 provides an overview of empirical studies, which have found positive effects of real exchange rate depreciations.

As illustrated in Table 3.5, there is considerable evidence that real exchange rate depreciations have an employment-enhancing effect. These findings are contingent on the absence of the potentially adverse impact that currency depreciations can have in economies with high liability dollarization, i.e. when private sector debt is denominated in foreign currency while assets are denominated in domestic currency. This renders the private sector sensitive to balance sheet effects (that is, the increased indebtedness of firms through a currency mismatch of assets and liabilities) through real exchange rate depreciations. Such negative effects can exceed the positive effects of domestic firms' increased competitiveness (Islam, 2011).

A study by Galindo *et al.* (2006) analyses the impact of real exchange rate movements on employment, with varying degrees of trade openness and debt dollarization. Based on a panel dataset for nine Latin American countries, the authors show that the positive effect of real exchange rate depreciations is reversed, and can be negative, with increasing liability dollarization. Similarly, for Mexico, Lobato *et al.* (2003) find that the balance sheet effect outweighs the competitiveness effect engendered by currency depreciations. While the balance sheet effect is not undisputed (see, for instance, Bleakley and Cowan, 2002; Luengnaruemitchai, 2003), liability dollarization poses a risk to contractionary depreciation and thus a decline in employment.

It is thus clear that there seems to be consensus that currency appreciations have a negative impact on employment whereas depreciations support growth and employment. Does this imply that governments should pursue a policy of deliberate exchange rate undervaluation? Some countries have indeed maintained an undervalued currency over a long period of time, such as China whose currency has been undervalued for a substantial part of the last two decades.[33] Such policy can facilitate growth-enhancing structural transformation, ultimately leading to employment creation (McMillan and Rodrik, 2011). Yet, as emphasized by Rodrik (2008) himself and the IMF (2013b), sustained undervaluation of the exchange rate can lead to global current account imbalances and produce 'beggar-thy-neighbour' effects.

Hence, a more reasonable policy to avoid the adverse effect of overvaluation could consist in keeping the real exchange rate at a stable and competitive level that is consistent with economic fundamentals. However, the presence of liability dollarization acts as a constraint on the central bank's ability to influence the path of the exchange rate through reluctance towards depreciation because it leads to potentially negative balance sheet effects. It is thus crucial to attenuate high levels of liability dollarization through active capital account management and prudential regulation of the financial system (Islam, 2011). This enables the central bank to counteract appreciations that move the currency away from its stable and competitive level and thus support employment.

Country-specific examples can be given of successful cases of prudent capital account management, such as Chile, but what is needed are transparent and

Table 3.5 Effects of real exchange rate movements on employment

Source	Effect on employment	Sample of countries
Bahamani-Oskooee *et al.* (2007)	RER depreciation has a significant employment-enhancing effect in the short run, but not in the long run.	USA
Burgess and Knetter (1998)	Appreciation leads to a decline in manufacturing employment.	G-7 countries
Campa and Goldberg (2001)	Depreciation increases employment in the manufacturing industry (significant for low mark-up industries, but insignificant for high mark-up industries).	USA
Eichengreen (2008)	RER depreciation has a statistically significant positive effect on industry employment.	40 emerging market countries
Faria and León-Ledesma (2005)	In the USA, an appreciation leads to a decrease in employment. In the UK, the employment effect is positive, albeit not statistically significant.	UK, USA
Filiztekin (2004)	Depreciation has a negative employment effect in the manufacturing industry.[a]	Turkey
Frenkel and Ros (2006)	RER appreciation is associated with an increase in the unemployment rate.	Argentina, Brazil, Chile, Mexico
Gourinchas (1999)	RER appreciation leads to job reduction.	France
Hua (2007)	Statistically significant negative effect of RER appreciation on manufacturing employment.	China
Kandil and Mirzaie (2003)	Decrease in employment growth in several industries in response to dollar appreciation, but increase in employment growth in the mining sector.	USA
Klein *et al.* (2003)	RER appreciation significantly affects net employment through job destruction and reduction of net employment growth rate in the manufacturing industry.	USA
Ngandu (2009)	Appreciation can have a negative employment effect in the traded sector, but not in the non-traded sector.	South Africa

Source: adapted from Islam and Kucera (2014, Chapter 1).

Note
a This finding can be ascribed to the high dependency on foreign inputs of production.

widely agreed international rules for capital controls. These controls include price-based measures, such as counter-cyclical taxes on certain types of capital flows. The international community could agree on the type, composition and ceiling on price-based measures pertaining to capital mobility in order to limit any possible harmful side-effects of such measures on economic growth. These codes of conduct could be developed under the auspices of the IMF. The lack of such a global framework means that 'capital controls are still marked by a certain stigma' leading to less than optimal outcomes, with some countries, such as China, pursuing capital controls with vigour, while others are much more ambivalent about it.[34]

From fiscal rules to development-friendly fiscal policy: reinforcing the redistributive capacity of the state, supporting structural transformation and coping with economic volatility

The role of macroeconomic policy makers as agents of both economic stabilization and development entails the pursuit of counter-cyclical policies on the one hand and the implementation of policies that support structural transformation and core development goals on the other hand. At the same time, promoting inclusive development means empowering the redistributive capacity of the state to address existing inequalities using growth-friendly measures. These issues are unlikely to be the centre of attention of the current genre of fiscal rules which are preoccupied with containing debts and deficits. Hence, one has to move beyond fiscal rules as currently conceived.

Fiscal policy as conducted by finance ministries can shape secondary income distribution in a positive direction. Yet, redistribution through fiscal instruments (defined as direct taxes, mandatory social security contributions and transfer payments) across the developing world is limited. Redistribution based on fiscal interventions is considerably lower in low and middle income countries than in high income countries. As shown in Figure 3.3, in high income countries, on average between 1992 and 2012, the maximum reduction in inequality through fiscal instruments amounted to 51.5 per cent (Denmark), compared to a maximum reduction of 3.0 per cent (Trinidad and Tobago). In low and middle income countries, gross income inequality was reduced by a maximum of 33.2 per cent, on average, between 1992 and 2012 (Romania). In the country with the lowest level of redistribution, net income inequality was 6.2 per cent higher than gross income inequality (Peru), implying that redistribution was regressive. While the range of redistribution through fiscal instruments is quite wide both for high income and middle and low income countries, a significant difference is revealed when looking at the median value (as depicted by the black horizontal line). In high income countries, median redistribution amounted to 28.0 per cent, on average between 1992 and 2012, as opposed to 4.9 per cent in low and middle income countries, thus showing that the role of fiscal policy in income redistribution has been limited across the developing world.

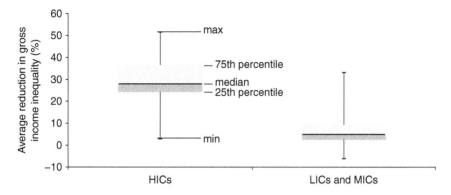

Figure 3.3 Average reduction (per cent) in gross income inequality through taxes and transfers, 1992–2012 (source: authors' own calculations based on Solt (2009): SWIID, version 3.1).

Note
Redistribution was calculated by averaging the differences between gross and net income inequality, over gross income inequality, times 100, over 1992 to 2012 for each country. Subsequently, the values were averaged across income classes.

Perhaps the major reasons behind these results are low tax-to-GDP ratios and insufficiently progressive, or even regressive, tax structures in low and middle income countries. Low tax-to-GDP ratios can either reflect low tax rates or narrow tax bases that can result from a number of factors, including a large informal sector, a high degree of tax evasion, and weak tax administration. Tax ratios tend to be lower in low and middle income countries than in high income countries. Over 1992 to 2010, for instance, the average tax ratio in OECD countries amounted to 34.5 per cent of GDP compared to 12.4 per cent for a sample of 13 Latin American non-OECD countries.[35] The Asia-Pacific region has the lowest tax burden across the developing regions of the world, despite rapid economic growth (UN-ESCAP, 2013).

Low tax revenues limit governments' fiscal space, and consequently their capacity to foster structural transformation and support core development goals. An important aspect pertaining to the relevance of fiscal policy as an instrument to promote structural transformation relates to the role that infrastructure deficits play in inhibiting growth and employment in developing countries.

Evidence suggests that lack of adequate infrastructure undermines growth and employment creation (ADB, 2012; McKinsey, 2012; World Bank, 2012a; World Economic Forum, 2012). For instance, enterprise surveys undertaken by the World Bank (2012a) show that inadequate infrastructure, as proxied by the supply of electricity and transport, is a major hindrance to doing business in low and middle income countries across all regions of the world. Roughly 50 per cent of the surveyed firms in Sub-Saharan Africa, South Asia and the MENA region identified major constraints related to the supply of electricity. Lack of transport is a major constraint for more than one-fifth of the surveyed enterprises in Sub-Saharan Africa, the Middle East and North Africa and Latin America and the Caribbean (Figure 3.4). Further studies have provided similar findings. The Global Competitiveness Report by the World Economic Forum (2012) shows that inadequate supply of infrastructure is among the top five problematic factors for doing business in more than half of the surveyed low and middle income countries.[36]

Estimates suggest that the infrastructure spending gaps are vast. In Sub-Saharan Africa, for instance, infrastructure spending needs are estimated to amount to US$94 billion a year, corresponding to approximately 9 per cent of GDP (Yepes, 2008 as cited in Lin and Doemeland, 2012). CEPAL (2011) estimates that Latin America and the Caribbean needs to invest roughly 5.2 per cent of the region's GDP per year to meet the infrastructure requirements of firms and individuals between 2006 and 2020. If the region aimed at closing the spending gap to a group of East Asian economies, annual spending would have to increase to 7.9 per cent of GDP. Most countries face large infrastructure requirements across a wide range of sectors on the one hand and resource constraints on the other hand. In view of this situation, investment could be allocated to targeted sectors and geographic regions based on its job creation potential.

In highlighting the role of fiscal policy to support core development goals, one can draw on a recent study for the Asia-Pacific region by UN-ESCAP

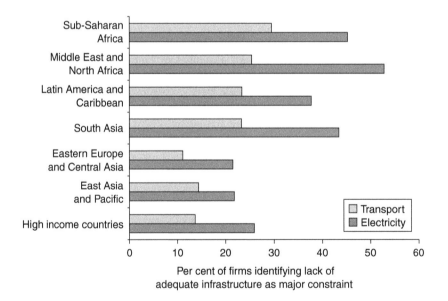

Figure 3.4 Inadequate infrastructure as a major constraint for firms in low and middle income countries across regions of the world (source: authors' compilation based on World Bank (2012a)).

Note
Regional averages were calculated by taking the mean of country level indicators, including only those country surveys for which the global methodology has been used.

(2013). The study finds a negative association between the tax ratio and inequality as well as between social spending and inequality. It stresses that inequality has been exacerbated by the lack of progressivity of tax systems and a low tax burden, which is reflected in lack of public spending. UN-ESCAP also quantifies the fiscal implications of supporting core development goals. The study – influenced by similar exercises conducted by other UN agencies (such as ILO, 2010b) – specifies six elements of a policy package that cuts across the provision of job guarantee schemes, social protection and environmental sustainability. Developing countries in the Asia-Pacific region would need public expenditures ranging between 5 and 8 per cent of GDP to meet the resource requirements of such a policy package at the national level. How to implement such public expenditure programmes in an efficient and fiscally sustainable fashion through tax and other revenue mobilization measures then becomes a core issue for macroeconomic policy makers.

Finally, the need for a stable macroeconomic environment to foster growth and job creation requires the adoption of counter-cyclical fiscal policies that can smooth out economic volatility. Counter-cyclical fiscal policies entail both automatic stabilizers and discretionary interventions. Automatic stabilizers can be linked to social protection, such as unemployment benefits. Yet, due to large informal sectors in the developing world, automatic stabilizers might not reach the poorest (Ocampo, 2011). Policy measures designed to suit developing country conditions, such as job guarantees and conditional cash transfers, might thus be useful to alleviate the employment consequences of economic downturns. The experiences of some Latin American countries, such as Brazil with conditional cash transfers (*Bolsa Familia*), and the case of India with the world's largest rural employment guarantee scheme, suggest that it is possible for developing countries to engage in policy innovations with respect to counter-cyclical measures.[37] Vegh and Vuletin (2014) have revisited the issue and demonstrate, using the experience of eight Latin American countries, that counter-cyclical fiscal policy improve social indicators pertaining to both income and non-income dimensions of poverty.

Getting out of the pro-cyclical trap also requires an ability to build up fiscal space during boom periods and normal periods of growth. A dedicated 'stabilization fund' that is activated during recessions might be an instrument to achieve this (Ocampo, 2011, p. 15). There are successful examples of such initiatives. One can draw attention to Chile's experience with respect to the prudent and counter-cyclical management of revenues from natural resources.[38]

Concluding observations

This chapter commenced with an acknowledgement of the pervasive influence of the conventional approach to macroeconomic policy. The approach is preoccupied with macroeconomic stability and the fundamental role that it is supposed to play in fostering growth and employment creation. The key idea is a so-called 'expectations channel' in which a durably stable macroeconomic environment anchors private sector expectations. The result is a boost in investor confidence, a higher rate of capital accumulation that feeds into higher growth and more jobs. This in turn requires the adoption and maintenance of targets pertaining to inflation, debts, deficits and the external account which can then act as anchors for private sector expectations.

The foremost concern among critics of the conventional framework is that the benefits of macroeconomic stability might have been oversold. This was indeed acknowledged by a well-known publication of the World Bank that was released in the mid-2000s and endorsed by others. Since then, an influential cross-country study has sought to establish a strong statistical link between macroeconomic stability and growth. While such a study rests on state-of-the-art statistical and econometric techniques, greater scrutiny of individual country experiences suggest that they are at variance with the cross-country predictions. This does not mean that macroeconomic stability is irrelevant for understanding the process of long-run growth, but a heavy reliance on cross-country studies, however statistically robust, can be misleading.

The chapter also raised concerns about the incentives facing macroeconomic policy managers in developing countries if they rely solely, or largely, on attaining and maintaining inflation and fiscal targets as the sine qua non of their obligations. They can rest on their laurels and, by default, become disconnected from mainstream development concerns. This would be a pity because macroeconomic policy managers reside in institutions – most notably central banks and finance ministries – that are both powerful and resourceful. They need to play a more active role as agents of development while preserving their role as guardians of stability.

The chapter argued that an objective reading of the evidence pertaining to various components of the conventional framework entitles critics to question the empirical robustness of this framework. Developing countries should certainly avoid double digit inflation, but the rationale to aim for low, single digit inflation does not necessarily rest on hard evidence. Furthermore, developing countries do not face a binary choice between fixed and flexible exchange rates, nor should they be seduced by the promise of significant growth and employment dividends of an open capital account.

The chapter noted that similar caveats apply to the case of fiscal rules that have become so fashionable in recent years. Regardless of whether they improve fiscal performance, fiscal rules as currently conceived are not development-friendly. Such evidence, combined with the ones pertaining to inflation targeting, the choice of exchange rate regimes and capital mobility suggest why eclecticism with respect to institutional arrangements that underpin macroeconomic policy is warranted. One can certainly uphold basic principles – such as the need to make a commitment to price stability – but translating those principles into practice can take a variety of institutional forms. Indeed, one can readily discern a range of institutions pertaining to macroeconomic management in developing countries, whether it pertains to the monetary policy framework or the choice of exchange rates.

The chapter proceeded to suggest how significant modifications can be made to the conventional macroeconomic policy framework that builds on its existing strengths while making a closer connection with core development concerns. The key principle is the need to adopt a dual mandate for low and middle income countries. This means that governments should seek to be (a) guardians of stability and (b) agents of inclusive development. Translated to specific policy actions, this means having the capacity to conduct counter-cyclical policies to smooth business cycles and promoting financial inclusion. It also means the use of exchange rate policy and prudent capital account management to promote an agenda of employment creation and structural transformation.

Fiscal policy should go beyond the preoccupation with fiscal rules that target debts and deficits. It should be primarily assigned to strengthen the redistributive capacity of the state to promote equity using growth-friendly measures, mobilizing domestic revenue to meet core development goals and attenuating infrastructure deficits.

The chapter argued that the specific policy actions proposed above are not merely hypothetical in nature. They are rooted in concrete cross-country evidence and country-specific experiences. Most importantly, these proposals do not represent a radical overhaul of the conventional framework but represent incremental changes to it. The net impact is likely to be a framework that promotes growth, employment and inclusive development.

Notes

 1 Taylor (1993).
 2 Mishkin (2000, p. 2).
 3 This fiscal treaty now has a reinforced version under a 'fiscal compact'. See Fitoussi and Saraceno (2013) for a description and an evaluation.
 4 OECD (2014) spells out this framework explicitly and the discussion here draws on that version of the conventional macroeconomic policy framework complemented by structural and labour market reforms.
 5 IMF (2013b, p. 43).
 6 Schaechter *et al.* (2012).
 7 Mishra *et al.* (2012, 2014).
 8 Anwar and Islam (2011).
 9 Mohanty (2010).
10 Reserve Bank of India (2014).
11 Anwar and Islam (2011).
12 See the collection of essays in Reichlin and Baldwin (2013). The consensus among the contributors is that inflation targeting in a narrow sense might be 'dead', but one should aim to rectify the regime rather than replace it.
13 These issues are reviewed in Reichlin and Baldwin (2013).
14 Oakova (2007).
15 Ghosh *et al.* (2013).
16 Williamson *et al.* (2013).
17 Kose *et al.* (2007).
18 Schaechter *et al.* (2012).
19 Chowdhury and Islam (2012a) review the evidence. Herndon *et al.* (2013) highlight anomalies in empirical studies of the debt-growth relationship.

20 Chowdhury and Islam (2012b) review these issues in some detail.
21 World Bank (2005).
22 Montiel and Serven (2006).
23 Srimaneetham and Temple (2009, p. 475).
24 See http://hdr.undp.org/sites/default/files/Country-Profiles/TGO.pdf and http://hdr. undp.org/sites/default/files/Country-Profiles/UGA.pdf, both accessed on 1 August 2014.
25 This is in line with Rodrik's (2012) thesis that one should not rely on cross-country regressions to make strong inferences.
26 Christensen (2011).
27 State Bank of Pakistan (2014).
28 IFC (2013, p. 38) uses the enterprise surveys to identify the key constraints facing 45,000 firms in 106 developing countries.
29 As reported in Subbarao (2013).
30 Blanchard *et al.* (2010, 2013b).
31 ILO (2014a).
32 In its survey on Africa, McKinsey (2012) finds that access to finance is among the top three barriers to private sector growth. The Asian Development Bank (2012) points out that small and medium-sized enterprise frequently face constraints related to accessing finance in Asia. The IFC (2013) highlights lack of access to finance as the most important constraint for a sample of 45,000 firms in 106 developing countries. As was pointed out at an earlier juncture, the IFC study draws on the World Bank's enterprise surveys.
33 For an overview on China's currency policy, see Morrison and Labonte (2011).
34 Williamson *et al.* (2013) drawing on Jeanne *et al.* (2012).
35 Calculations based on OECD (2013).
36 Likewise, a survey across five African countries by McKinsey (2012) identifies infrastructure shortcomings, including transport and electricity, among highly cited barriers to job growth.
37 For a detailed discussion, see Chapter 9.
38 Frankel (2012).

Bibliography

ADB (Asian Development Bank) (2012) *Outlook 2012: Confronting Rising Inequality in Asia*, Mandaluyong City.

Agenor, P. and Montiel, P. (2008) *Development Macroeconomics*, Princeton University Press, New Haven.

Allen, F., Demirgüç-Kunt, A., Klapper, L. and Martinez Peria, M.S. (2012) *The Foundations of Financial Inclusion: Understanding Ownership and Use of Formal Accounts*, Policy Research Working Paper No. 6290, World Bank, Washington, D.C.

Anwar, A. and Islam, I. (2011) *Should Developing Countries Target Low, Single Digit Inflation to Promote Growth and Employment?* Employment Working Paper No. 87, ILO, Geneva, available at: www.ilo.org/wcmsp5/groups/public/@ed_emp/@emp_ policy/documents/publication/wcms_160448.pdf (accessed 27 October 2014).

Bahamani-Oskooee, M., Mirzaie, I.A. and Miteza, I. (2007) 'Sectoral Employment, Wages and the Exchange Rate', *Eastern Economic Journal*, vol. 33, no. 1, pp. 125–136.

Banco Central del Ecuador (2012) *De la Definición de la Política a la Práctica: Haciendo Inclusión Financiera* [in Spanish], available at: www.afi-global.org/library/publications/de-la-definicion-de-la-politica-la-practica-haciendo-inclusion-financiera (accessed 4 March 2013).

Bastagli, F., Coady, D. and Gupta, S. (2012) *Income Inequality and Fiscal Policy*, SDN/12/08, IMF, Washington, D.C.

Blanchard, O., Dell'Ariccia, G. and Mauro, P. (2010) 'Rethinking Macroeconomic Policy', *Journal of Money, Credit and Banking*, vol. 42 (supplement), 199–215.

Blanchard, O., Dell'Ariccia, G. and Mauro, P. (2013a) *Rethinking Macroeconomic Policy: Getting Granular*, Staff Discussion Note 13/03, IMF, Washington, D.C.

Blanchard, O., Florence, J. and Loungani, P. (2013b) *Labour Market Policies and IMF Advice in Advanced Economies during the Great Recession*, Staff Discussion Note 13/02, IMF, Washington, D.C.

Bleakley, H. and Cowan, K.N. (2002) *Corporate Dollar Debt and Depreciations: Much Ado About Nothing?* Working Paper 02–5, Federal Reserve Bank of Boston.

Burgess, S. and Knetter, M.M. (1998) *An International Comparison of Employment Adjustment to Exchange Rate Fluctuations*, NBER Working Paper No. 5861, Cambridge, MA.

Campa, J.M. and Goldberg, L.S. (2001) 'Employment versus Wage Adjustment and the U.S. Dollar', *Review of Economics and Statistics*, vol. 83, no. 3, pp. 477–489.

CEPAL (2011) *The Economic Infrastructure Gap in Latin America and the Caribbean*, FAL Bulletin, Issue 293, no. 1.

Chowdhury, A. and Islam, I. (2012a) 'The Debate on Expansionary Fiscal Consolidation: How Robust is the Evidence?', *The Economic and Labour Relations Review*, vol. 23, no. 2, pp. 13–38.

Chowdhury, A. and Islam, I. (2012b) 'Fiscal Rules: Help or Hindrance?', 4 October, available at http://voxeu.org/debates/commentaries/fiscal-rules-help-or-hindrance (accessed 1 August 2014).

Christensen, B.V. (2011) 'Have Monetary Transmission Mechanisms in Africa Changed?', in Mihaljek, D. (ed.) *Central Banking in Africa: Prospects in a Changing World*, BIS Papers No. 56, Bank for International Settlements, Basel.

Demirgüç-Kunt, A. and Klapper, L. (2012) *Measuring Financial Inclusion: The Global Findex Database*, Policy Research Working Paper No. 6025, World Bank, Washington, D.C.

Easterly, W. (2001) 'The Lost Decades: Developing Countries' Stagnation in Spite of Policy Reform 1980–1998', *Journal of Economic Growth*, vol. 6, no. 2, pp. 135–157.

Easypaisa (2012) *Branchless Banking: The Easypaisa Way*. Online, available at: www.icap.org.pk/userfiles/conference/Shahid-Mustafa-isb-CFO2012.pdf (accessed 8 March 2013).

Eichengreen, B. (2008) *The Real Exchange Rate and Economic Growth*, International Bank for Reconstruction and Development/World Bank on behalf of the Commission on Growth and Development, Washington, D.C.

Epstein, G. (2007) *Central Banks as Agents of Employment Creation*, Working Paper No. 38, United Nations Department of Economic and Social Affairs.

Faria, J.R. and León-Ledesma, M.A. (2005) 'Real Exchange Rate and Employment Performance in an Open Economy', *Research in Economics*, vol. 59, no. 1, pp. 67–80.

Filiztekin, A. (2004) *Exchange Rate and Employment in Turkish Manufacturing*, Faculty of Arts and Social Sciences, Sabanci University, Istanbul.

Fitoussi, J.-P. and Saraceno, F. (2013) 'European Economic Governance: The Berlin-Washington Consensus', *Cambridge Journal of Economics*, vol. 37, no. 3, pp. 479–496.

Frankel, J. (2012) 'Chile's Counter-cyclical Triumph', *Foreign Policy*, 27 June, available at www.foreignpolicy.com/articles/2012/06/27/chile_s_countercyclical_triumph (accessed 27 October 2014).

Frenkel, R. and Ros, J. (2006) 'Unemployment and the Real Exchange Rate in Latin America' *World Development*, vol. 34, no. 4, pp. 631–646.

Freund, C.L. and Pierola, M.D. (2008) *Export Surges: The Power of a Competitive Currency*, World Bank Policy Research Working Paper No. 4750, Washington, D.C.

Galindo, A., Izquierdo, A. and Montero, J.M. (2006) *Real Exchange Rates, Dollarization and Industrial Employment in Latin America*, Working Paper No. 575, Inter-American Development Bank, Washington, D.C.

Ghosh, A.R., Ostry, J.D. and Qureshi, M. (2013) *Exchange Rate Management and Crisis Susceptibility: A Reassessment*, Paper presented at 14th Jaques Polak Annual Conference, 7–8 November, IMF, Washington, D.C.

Gourinchas, P. (1999) 'Exchange Rates do Matter: French Job Reallocation and Exchange Rate Turbulence, 1984–1992', *European Economic Review*, vol. 43, no. 7, pp. 1279–1316.

Herndon, T., Ash, M. and Pollin, R. (2013) *Does High Public Debt Consistently Stifle Economic Growth? A Critique of Reinhart and Rogoff*, April 15, PERI, University of Massachusetts, Amherst.

Hua, P. (2007) 'Real Exchange Rate and Manufacturing Employment in China', *China Economic Review*, vol. 18, no. 3, pp. 335–353.

IFC (International Finance Corporation) (2013) *IFC Jobs Study: Assessing Private Sector Contribution to Poverty Reduction and Job Creation*, Washington, D.C.

ILO (International Labour Organization) (2010a) *Global Wage Report 2010/11: Wage Policies in Times of Crisis*, Geneva.

ILO (International Labour Organization) (2010b) *World Social Security Report 2010/2011: Providing Coverage in Times of Crisis and beyond*, Geneva.

ILO (International Labour Organization) (2011a) *Key Indicators of the Labour Market (KILM)*, 7th edition, Geneva.

ILO (International Labour Organization) (2011b) *Efficient Growth, Employment and Decent Work in Africa: Time for a New Vision*, Geneva.

ILO (International Labour Organization) (2014a) *How Much do Central Banks Care about Growth and Employment?* Policy Brief, 4 July, available at: www.ilo.org/wcmsp5/groups/public/–ed_emp/documents/publication/wcms_249061.pdf (accessed 1 August 2014).

ILO (International Labour Organization) (2014b) *Key Indicators of Labour Markets (KILM)*, 8th edition, Geneva.

Ilzetski, E. and Veigh, C. (2008) *Procyclical Fiscal Policy in Developing Countries: Truth or Fiction?* NBER Working Paper No. 14191, Cambridge, MA.

IMF (International Monetary Fund) (2013a) *Jobs and Growth: Analytical and Operational Considerations for the Fund*, Washington, D.C.

IMF (International Monetary Fund) (2013b) *Annual Report on Exchange Arrangements and Exchange Restrictions*, Washington, D.C.

Islam, I. (2011) 'The Perennial Quest for Fiscal and Policy Space in Developing Countries', in Islam, I. and Verick, S. (eds) *From the Great Recession to Labour Market Recovery: Issues, Evidence and Policy Options*, ILO, Geneva and Palgrave Macmillan, Basingstoke.

Islam, I. and Chowdhury, A. (2012) *Full Employment and the Global Development Agenda: Going Beyond Lip Service*, 19 January, available at: www.voxeu.org/debates/commentaries/full-employment-and-global-development-agenda-going-beyond-lip-service (accessed 27 October 2014).

Islam, I. and Chowdhury, A. (2014) *Promoting Employment and Structural Change in Developing Countries: A Dual Mandate for Macroeconomic Policy Managers*, 18 June, available at: http://voxeu.org/debates/commentaries/promoting-employment-and-structural-change-developing-countries-dual-mandate-macroeconomic-policy-managers (accessed 27 October 2014).

Islam, I. and Kucera, D. (eds) (2014) *Beyond Macroeconomic Stability: Structural Transformation and Inclusive Development*, MacMillan and ILO: Geneva and UK.

Jeanne, O., Williamson, J. and Subramanian, A. (2012) *Who Needs to Open the Capital Account?* Peterson Institute for International Economics, Washington, D.C.

Jolly, R. (1991) 'Adjustment with a Human Face: A UNICEF Record and Perspective on the 1980s', *World Development*, vol. 19, no. 12, pp. 1807–1821.

Kandil, M. and Mirzaie, I.A. (2003) 'The Effects of Dollar Appreciation on Sectoral Labour Market Adjustments: Theory and Evidence', *Quarterly Review of Economics and Finance*, vol. 43, no. 1, pp. 89–117.

Klein, M.W., Schuh, S. and Triest, R.K. (2003) 'Job Creation, Job Destruction, and the Real Exchange Rate', *Journal of International Economics*, vol. 59, no. 2, pp. 239–265.

Kose, M.A, Prasad, E., Rogoff, K. and Wei, S.-J. (2007) 'Financial Globalization: Beyond the Blame Game', *Finance and Development*, Vol. 44, No. 1, available at: www.imf.org/external/pubs/ft/fandd/2007/03/kose.htm (accessed 27 October 2014).

Lin, J.Y. and Doemeland, D. (2012) *Beyond Keynesianism: Global Infrastructure Investments in Times of Crisis*, Policy Research Working Paper No. 5940, World Bank, Washington, D.C.

Lobato, I., Pratap, S. and Somuano, A. (2003) *Debt Composition and Balance Sheet Effects of Exchange Rates and Interest Rate Volatility in Mexico: A Firm Level Analysis*, available at: www.iadb.org/res/laresnetwork/projects/pr197finaldraft.pdf (accessed 17 April 2013).

Luengnaruemitchai, P. (2003) *The Asian Crisis and the Mystery of the Missing Balance Sheet Effect*, Economics Department, University of California, Berkeley.

McKinsey (2012) *Africa at Work: Job Creation and Inclusive Growth*, Report, McKinsey Global Institute.

McMillan, M.S. and Rodrik, D. (2011) *Globalization, Structural Change and Productivity Growth*, NBER Working Paper No. 17143, Cambridge, MA.

Mishkin, F. (2000) *What Should Central Banks Do?*, Federal Reserve Bank of St. Louis, November/December.

Mishra, P., Montiel, P. and Spilimbergo, A. (2012) 'Monetary Transmission Mechanism in Low Income Countries: Effectiveness and Policy Implications', *IMF Economic Review*, vol. 60, no. 2, pp. 270–302.

Mishra, P., Montiel, P., Pedroni, P. and Spilimbergo, A. (2014) 'Monetary Policy and Bank Lending Rates in Low Income Countries: Heterogeneous Panel Estimates', mimeo, March, IMF and Williams College.

Mohanty, D. (2010) 'Monetary Policy Framework in India: Experience with Multiple Indicators Approach', Speech of the Executive Director of the Reserve Bank of India, Orissa Economic Association, Badipada, Orissa, 21 February, available at: www.bis.org/review/r100304e.pdf (accessed 27 October 2014).

Montiel, P. and Serven, L. (2006) 'Macroeconomic Stability in Developing Countries: How Much is Enough?', *World Bank Research Observer*, vol. 21, no. 2, pp. 151–178.

Morrison, W.M. and Labonte, M. (2011) *China's Currency Policy: An Analysis of the Economic Issues*, Congressional Research Service, Washington, D.C.

Ngandu, S.N. (2009) 'The Impact of Exchange Rate Movements on Employment: The Economy-Wide Effect of a Rand Appreciation, *Development Southern Africa*, vol. 26, no. 1, pp. 111–129.

Oakova, D. (2007) *Flattening of the Phillips Curve: Implications for Monetary Policy*, IMF Working Paper No. 76, Washington, D.C.

Ocampo, J.A. (2011) 'Macroeconomy for Development: Counter-Cyclical Policies and Production Sector Transformation', *CEPAL Review*, 104, August, pp. 7–35.

OECD (Organisation for Economic Co-operation and Development) (1994) *The OECD Jobs Study: Facts, Analysis, Strategies*, Paris.

OECD (Organisation for Economic Co-operation and Development) (1996) *Shaping the 21st Century: The Contribution of Development Co-operation*, Paris.

OECD (Organisation for Economic Co-operation and Development) (2011) 'An Overview of Growing Income Inequalities in OECD Countries: Main Findings', in *Divided We Stand: Why Inequality Keeps Rising*, Paris.

OECD (Organisation for Economic Co-operation and Development) (2013) *OECD. Stat Extracts*, available at: http://stats.oecd.org (accessed 28 May 2013).

OECD (Organisation for Economic Co-operation and Development) (2014) *Growth Policies and Macroeconomic Stability*, OECD Economic Policy Paper, February.

Ostry, J. *et al.* (2011) *Managing Capital Inflows: What Tools to Use?* IMF Staff Discussion Note 11/06, Washington, D.C.

Reichlin, L. and Baldwin, R. (eds) (2013) *Is Inflation Targeting Dead? Central Banking after the Crisis*, Centre for Economic Policy Research, London.

Reserve Bank of India (2014) *Report of the Expert Committee to Revise and Strengthen the Monetary Policy Framework*, 21 January, available at: www.rbi.org.in/scripts/PublicationReportDetails.aspx?UrlPage=&ID=743 (accessed 27 October 2014).

Rodrik, D. (2008) *The Real Exchange Rate and Economic Growth*, John F. Kennedy School of Government, Harvard University, Cambridge, MA.

Rodrik, D. (2012) 'Why We Learn Nothing from Regressing Economic Growth on Policies', *Seoul Journal of Economics*, vol. 25, no. 2, pp. 137–151.

Safaricom (2012) *Celebrating 5 Years of M-PESA*, available at: www.squaddigital.com/beta/safaricom/facebook/saftimelineiframe/pdf/infograph.pdf (accessed 6 March 2013).

Safaricom (2013) online, available at: www.safaricom.co.ke (accessed 10 April 2013).

Schaechter, A., Budina, N., Weber, A. and Kinda, T. (2012) *Fiscal Rules in Response to the Crisis: Toward the 'Next-Generation' Rules. A New Dataset*, IMF Working Paper, WP/12/187, Washington, D.C.

Solt, F. (2009) 'Standardizing the World Income Inequality Database', *Social Science Quarterly*, vol. 90, no. 2, pp. 231–242 (SWIID Version 3.1, December 2011).

Srimaneetham, V. and Temple, J. (2009) 'Macroeconomic Stability and the Distribution of Growth Rates', *The World Bank Economic Review*, vol. 23, no. 3, pp. 443–479.

State Bank of Pakistan (2014) 'Monetary Policy Frameworks in the SAARC Region', April, Karachi, Pakistan.

Steinberg, J. (2011) *Real Exchange Rate Undervaluation, Financial Development and Growth*, available at: www.econ.umn.edu/~stein781/files/rerpaper.pdf (accessed 17 April 2013).

Subbarao, D. (2013) 'Five Years of Leading the Reserve Bank: Looking ahead by Looking back', 10th Nani A. Palkhiwala Memorial Lecture, 29 August, Mumbai, available at: www.bis.org/review/r130830e.pdf (accessed 27 October 2014).

Taylor, J.B. (1993) 'Discretion versus Policy Rules in Practice,' *Carnegie-Rochester Conference Series on Public Policy*, 39, pp. 195–214.

UN-ESCAP (2013) *Economic and Social Survey of Asia and the Pacific: Forward-Looking Macroeconomic Policies for Inclusive and Sustainable Development*, United Nations, Bangkok.

United Nations (1995) *World Summit for Social Development*, Copenhagen.

Vegh, C.A. and Vuletin, G. (2014) 'The Social Impact of Fiscal Policy Responses to Crises', 12 June, available at: http://voxeu.org/article/fiscal-policy-responses-crises-social-impacts (accessed 27 October 2014).

Williamson, J., Jeanne, O. and Subramanian, A. (2013) International Rules for Capital Controls, 11 June, available at: http://voxeu.org/article/international-rules-capital-controls (accessed 27 October 2014).

World Bank (2005) *Economic Growth in the 1990s: Learning from a Decade of Reforms*, Washington, D.C.

World Bank (2012a) *Enterprise Surveys*, available at: www.enterprisesurveys.org (accessed 14 January 2013).

World Bank (2012b) *The Little Data Book on Financial Inclusion*, Washington, D.C.

World Bank (2012c) *World Development Report 2013: Jobs*, Washington, D.C.

World Bank (2013a) *Three Quarters of the World's Poor are Unbanked*, available at: www.econ.worldbank.org/WBSITE/EXTERNAL/EXTDEC/0,,contentMDK:23173842~pagePK:64165401~piPK:64165026~theSitePK:469372~isCURL:Y,00.html (accessed 24 April 2013).

World Bank (2013b) *World Development Indicators*, available at: www.data.worldbank.org/data-catalog/world-development-indicators (accessed 18 April 2013).

World Economic Forum (2012) *The Global Competitiveness Report 2012–2013*, Geneva.

Yepes, T. (2008) *Investment Needs for Infrastructure in Developing Countries, 2008–15*, mimeo, World Bank, Washington, D.C.

4 Structural transformation and productive employment creation
Alternative pathways

Introduction

In standard development discourse, the assumption is that the essence of a job creation strategy is to transfer low-productivity, 'surplus' labour from rural areas to urban-based manufacturing activities geared towards labour intensive exports. This transition of labour from rural to urban-based export-oriented activities is thus seen as a hallmark of both industrial development and structural transformation that promote durable employment. The success of East Asia in general and China in particular is regarded as a vindication of the effectiveness of this development strategy.

In many parts of the developing world, and most notably Sub-Saharan Africa, the evolution of national economies does not necessarily fit the predictions of standard development theory. The much-awaited transition and productive transformation from rural to an urban-based manufacturing export sector has not taken place.

In tandem with these structural realities, many developing economies have seen the persistence of a moderately sized manufacturing sector that has not managed to play the role of a leading sector in terms of productive employment generation.[1] Instead, the service sector has played a major role in employment creation. Past policies have also entailed benign neglect of the agricultural sector. Rather than bemoaning the phenomenon of 'premature de-industrialization', one needs to find pathways to durable and productive job creation in the developing world that do not necessarily conform to standard models of industrial development and structural transformation.

The chapter will argue that it is fruitless to aim for a 'one size fits all' approach. Many developing countries will need to consider a multi-faceted strategy that emphasizes agricultural diversification and service sector driven growth. The chapter will note that there is growing international evidence that the expansion of the productive segments of the service sector, rather than being seen as a retrograde step, can have a significant impact on aggregate GDP growth and thus spur both employment expansion and sustainable poverty reduction. In any case, the policy choice is not between either manufacturing or services, but a symbiotic relationship between the two. Modern services can provide intermediate inputs that can propel the expansion of the manufacturing sector.

The chapter will also highlight the case of the non-renewable natural resources sector that has played a significant role in many countries in Sub-Saharan Africa and elsewhere. It is customary to regard the natural resources sector as a 'curse' that brings the 'Dutch disease' in its wake and 'crowds out' manufacturing sector activities through the appreciation of the real exchange rate. In addition, the windfall gains emanating from the natural resource sector can be a source of fiscal malfeasance and corruption. The chapter takes a less pessimistic, but pragmatic, view. It notes that the natural sector cannot, given its characteristics, be a major source of employment creation. However, with the necessary political commitment and appropriate policies, the natural resource sector can support growth and employment-promoting structural transformation.

The messages embodied in this chapter are consistent with a revisionist view of the role of industrial policies in economic development. Such policies are no longer seen as a sterile debate on whether governments could pick 'winners' while supporting declining industries or whether market forces should drive the process of resource allocation both within and between sectors. Developing countries – especially in the 2000s – are increasingly committing themselves to a holistic vision of industrial policies, ranging from Brazil to Morocco.[2] Admittedly, some countries, such as India, have expressed the aspiration to re-industrialize, but even here a broader approach to sectoral policies is evident.[3] Such policies are guided by a mix of institutions (such as development banks, technology funds, etc.) and instruments (such as credit allocation and procurement policies). They encompass state-led investments in health, education and infrastructure, as well as tailored interventions that promote high-value added activities across agriculture, industry and services.

Premature de-industrialization?

One of the stylized facts of the process of development is that, as countries become affluent, there is a steady decline in the share of output and employment that can be attributed to low productivity, rural-based agricultural activities. Urban-based manufacturing/industrial activities experience an inverted-U pattern, with both output and the share of employment in such activities rising over time, reaching a peak and then experiencing a steady decline. Consistent with this inverted-U pattern, one witnesses a post-industrial phase associated with the expansion of the service sector. This is the essence of 'structural transformation' in which there is a shift of labour and relevant resources from low productivity to high productivity sectors. Such structural transformation is the source of both sustainable growth and good quality employment. It lies at the core of the classic Lewisian model of development and has been empirically substantiated by a number of important studies.[4]

A key aspect of the contemporary debate on structural transformation is that this process no longer holds for many developing countries. One of the salient intellectual influences in this debate is the Harris–Todaro model in which the benign and smooth process of structural transformation envisaged in the Lewisian framework is supplanted by a process in which workers in the rural-based, low productivity agricultural sector move to urban areas in search of better opportunities but end up swelling the ranks of the unemployed because of labour market rigidities.[5] Nevertheless, rural–urban migration is individually optimal, as long as prospective migrants have a significant probability of being productively employed in the urban economy. One of the suggested policy interventions in the original version of the Harris–Todaro model was a policy package of wage subsidies and restraints on rural–urban migration because it was not politically feasible to remove labour market rigidities.

The contemporary variant of the Harris–Todaro view of the developing world emerges as a thesis of 'premature de-industrialization' despite the fact that the proponents of this thesis do not necessarily recognize its pedigree.[6] As one study puts it, 'de-industrialization ... refer(s) to changes in the share of the manufacturing sector in GDP and/or employment'. Using this criterion, a decline in the share of manufacturing in employment 'has been characterized as de-industrialization'.[7] Of course, as noted above, this is a seemingly natural phenomenon as societies become more affluent. The advanced economies of today acquired prosperity through the route of manufacturing-led growth. In the United Kingdom, the first country to develop manufacturing, 'factory jobs grew from around 22 per cent of total employment in 1841 to 35 per cent in 1960'. Those that followed in the footsteps of the United Kingdom experienced major structural transformation. Thus, in the 'United States ... manufacturing employment grew from around 6 per cent of total employment in 1800 to around 36 per cent in 1960'.[8] Since then, manufacturing employment in these two countries and in other advanced economies has experienced an inexorable downward trend.

To some scholars, this seemingly natural phenomenon of 'de-industrialization' has affected developing countries at a much earlier stage than is the case with the advanced economies of today. Hence, one encounters the notion of 'premature de-industrialization'. As Dani Rodrik (2013a) puts it, 'the developing world's pattern of industrialization has been different. Not only has the process been slow, but de-industrialization has begun to set in much sooner'. How 'much sooner'? Rodrik provides some estimates:

> When US, Britain, Germany, and Sweden began to deindustrialize, their per capita incomes had reached US$9,000–11,000 (at 1990 prices). In developing countries, by contrast, manufacturing has begun to shrink while per capita incomes have been a fraction of that level: Brazil's deindustrialization began at US$5,000, China's at US$3,000 and India's at US$2,000.[9]

In a related, and subsequent contribution, Rodrik (2014) bemoans the fact that in developing countries structural change has become increasingly perverse: from manufacturing to services (prematurely), tradable to non-tradable activities, organized sectors to informality, modern to traditional firms, and medium-size and large firms to small firms. Quantitative studies show that such patterns of structural change are exerting a substantial drag on growth in Latin America, Africa, and in many Latin American countries.

What are these 'quantitative studies'? There is a reference to one of Rodrik's co-authored study (McMillan and Rodrik, 2011) which has turned out to be quite influential. It relies heavily on a decomposition framework that seeks to isolate the sectoral sources of labour productivity growth. The purpose of such a framework is to decompose overall labour productivity growth – in a strictly accounting sense – into a 'reallocation effect' and a 'within sector' effect. This reflects the fact that structural change promotes productivity growth – and hence overall economic growth – through two channels: (a) labour moves from low to high productivity sectors; (b) there is an improvement in productivity within sectors. If (a) is significantly positive, for any given level of (b), one can conclude – *à la* McMillan and Rodrik (2011) – that structural change is growth-promoting. On the other hand, if (a) is significantly negative for any given level of (b), one can infer that structural change is growth-inhibiting. Based on a sample of 38 developing countries for the 1990 to 2005 period and a classification of nine sectors, the authors conclude:

> [S]ince 1990 structural change has been growth reducing in both Africa and Latin America, with the most striking changes taking place in Latin America. The bulk of the difference between these countries' performance and that of Asia is accounted for by differences in the pattern of structural change – with labour moving from low to high productivity sectors in Asia, but in the opposite direction in Latin America and sub-Saharan Africa.
>
> (McMillan and Rodrik, 2011, pp. 78–79)

How well have the 'premature de-industrialization' thesis and the associated notion that structural change can be growth-inhibiting stood up to empirical scrutiny by others? Arvind Subramanian (2014) approves of this thesis. He finds that:

> [I]n 1998, for the world as a whole, the peak (employment) share of manufacturing … was 30.5 per cent and attained at a per capita income of US\$21,700. By 2010, the peak share of manufacturing was 21 per cent (a drop of nearly one-third) and attained at a level of US\$12,200 (a drop of nearly 45 per cent).

Note that, unlike Rodrik and the ADB, Subramanian relies on the employment share of the industrial sector rather than manufacturing. Nevertheless, the fact is that the inverted-U curve depicting the relationship between the employment share of manufacturing/industry and per capita GDP has shifted *down* and to the *left* is corroborated (see Figure 4.1).

The ADB (2013: 17) also examines the notion of de-industrialization and finds, for a sample of 16 Asian countries that, on average, the employment share of manufacturing peaked at 20.8 per cent between 1976 and 2007 relative to the OECD average of 27.5 per cent. However, within these averages, there are several cases where the employment share of manufacturing peaked in the Asian region at rates well above the OECD norm. These cases are: Hong King, China (45.3 per cent, 1976), Malaysia (27.6 per cent, 1997), Republic of Korea (28.7 per cent, 1989), Singapore (30.4 per cent, 1981), Taipei, China (35.4 per cent, 1987).

De-industrialization per se is not problematic, as Rowthorn and Wells (1987) emphasized. It can be 'positive' if workers displaced from manufacturing are productively absorbed in other sectors, such as services. It is, however, a major concern if it is associated with what McMillan and Rodrik (2011) regard as growth-reducing structural change. Here, the evidence is not as unambiguous as it seems. Indeed, in a subsequent update, McMillan acknowledges that there has been a turnaround in the case of Sub-Saharan Africa based on a sample of 19 countries and post-2000 data.[10] Yet, there has been 'premature de-industrialization' in the sense that the bulk of the growth-promoting structural change has taken place through the route of the service sector and the share of employment manufacturing has changed only marginally in the 2000s.

As if to contradict the findings of McMillan and uphold the thesis of the negative aspects of de-industrialization, another study on Sub-Saharan Africa – based on 11 countries and the 1960–2010 period – also uses a decomposition

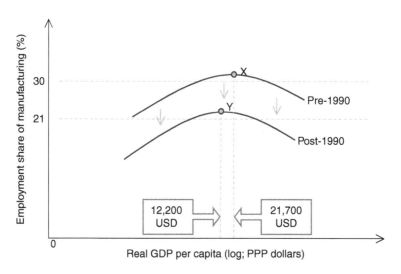

Figure 4.1 Premature de-industrialization: suggested relationship between employment share in manufacturing and GDP per capita (source: authors' compilation based on Subramanian (2014)).

framework to conclude on a much more pessimistic note. The authors of the study (de Vries *et al.*, 2013) make a distinction between 'static' and 'dynamic' productivity gains. Structural change promotes 'static' productivity gains if labour moves from low to high productivity sectors; such change translates into 'dynamic' gains if labour is re-allocated to sectors with high productivity growth regardless of their initial levels. The authors maintain that the nature of structural transformation in Sub-Saharan Africa has been characterized by 'static' gains but 'dynamic' losses, although such losses were not large enough to offset the 'static' gains (encompassing both within sector and re-allocation components).[11] The net result is that aggregate labour productivity growth is still positive (1.4 per cent per annum) for the 1960–2010 period. Of course, it would have been higher in the presence of 'dynamic' gains.

The aforementioned study claims to support the deleterious impact of 'de-industrialization' in Africa, but several anomalous features stand out. First, the relative productivity levels in services and manufacturing are virtually identical for the reported period (1960–2010) and the secular trends are similar, with both experiencing a decline in the productivity premium over time.[12] Second, when the authors replicated the estimates of McMillan and Rodrik (2011) and compared them with their results, rather sharp differences emerged. In the McMillan-Rodrik version, the re-allocation component is significantly negative (–1.27), while the authors' findings reveal a significantly positive re-allocation component (0.51).[13] Third, McMillan and Harttgen (2014) point out that the interpretation of 'dynamic losses' is problematic.

The 2011 McMillan and Rodrik study on the notion of growth-inhibiting structural change in Latin America and elsewhere has been questioned by others. Kucera and Roncolato (2014) and Roncolato and Kucera (2014) also use a decomposition framework to identify the sources of aggregate productivity growth for a sample of 81 developed and developing countries for two periods: 1984–98 and 1999–2008. They conclude that both manufacturing and services have contributed to productivity growth. Unlike McMillan and Rodrik (2011), the authors find that for all regions of the developing world, the 'within sector' component is more significant than the 'between sector' component in terms of contributing to overall labour productivity growth. More importantly, the 'between sector' component is *positive* (albeit to a moderate degree) rather than *negative* in both Latin America and Sub-Saharan Africa as highlighted in the McMillan-Rodrik study. They also note that the results reported in the influential McMillan-Rodrik study is sensitive to the methodological procedures that have been constructed, most notably whether weighted or unweighted estimates are used.[14]

In sum, the thesis of 'premature de-industrialization' is a valid description of statistical regularities pertaining to the relationship between changes in the employment share of manufacturing and per capita GDP. It is worth pointing out that, despite premature de-industrialization, eight of the top 20 countries in the world in manufacturing are represented by developing and emerging economies (OECD, 2013, p. 7).[15] Furthermore, whether premature de-industrialization connotes growth-reducing structural change is less clear. One needs a holistic approach to sectoral changes as economic development proceeds rather than suggesting that the mere expansion of employment in non-manufacturing sectors is undesirable. This means that due recognition should be given to the role that other sectors – most notably services – can play in supporting a process of structural transformation that promotes both growth and employment. At the same time, the agricultural sector should not merely be seen as a residual sector serving the needs of the manufacturing sector. It is still a major source of livelihood in many developing countries. Not surprisingly, agricultural diversification is regarded as a major plank of development strategy in a number of low and middle income countries. Finally, the particular circumstances of natural resource rich countries should not be dismissed as victims of the dreaded 'Dutch disease'. These are the issues that explored and expanded in the rest of the chapter.

Going beyond premature de-industrialization: the role of the services sector

It should by now be clear that structural transformation should not be narrowly conceptualized as a movement of labour from agriculture to the manufacturing sector. The harsh reality is that the manufacturing sector is unlikely to be a major source of employment for workers across the world in the foreseeable future. Globally, UNIDO estimates suggest that the employment share of manufacturing is around 16 per cent.[16] Even in the fast growing East Asian economies – such as China and Vietnam – the employment share of manufacturing does not exceed the global norm. In contrast, services account for a significant share of employment ranging from 29 per cent in low and lower middle income countries to 53 per cent in upper middle income countries. As expected, the agricultural sector is the major source of employment in low and lower middle income countries, while its importance diminishes sharply once countries move into the upper middle income range. (See Table 4.1.)

Given that the service sector is going to be a major source of employment for workers in low and middle income countries, what is the way forward? To start

Table 4.1 Sectoral employment shares (%), 1991–2010

GDP per capita (PPP, real: US$)	AGR	NMI	MANF	SER
Low and lower middle income countries (less than US$6,000)	50	7	14	29
Upper middle income countries (less than US$15,000)	23	9	16	53
High income countries	4	9	18	69

Source: adapted from UNIDO (2013, Table 1.2: 25). Based on a sample of 108 countries, excluding natural resource rich countries.

Note
AGR = agriculture; NMI = non-manufacturing industry; MANF = manufacturing; SER = services.

with, one should dispel the notion that the service sector entails a preponderance of low productivity activities.

Admittedly, this is the popular image invoked by a Harris–Todaro view of the developing world, but the statistical realities are quite different. One study shows relative productivity levels by broad sectors for 11 African countries for the 1960–2010 periods. While, as expected, the agricultural sector has the lowest productivity, the service sector is as productive as the manufacturing sector. What one can say at least is that the increase in the employment share of services between 1960 and 2010 in the sample of African countries under review does not, as is popularly assumed, entail a movement from low productivity agriculture to low productivity services.[17]

Noland *et al.* (2012, p. 65) summarize the nature of the productivity differential between services and industry for the late 2000s for 20 Asian economies ranging across different income levels. The industrial sector (which includes mining and other capital intensive activities) enjoys a productivity premium (relative to services) in nine out of the 20 countries. Hence, even allowing for non-manufacturing capital intensive activities, the industrial sector is not universally more productive than the service sector in Asian economies.

A global view – based on the aforementioned UNIDO study (2013) – suggests that the service sector is a lot more productive than agriculture. The manufacturing sector certainly enjoys a productivity premium (relative to services) in low and middle income countries, but it is not large. Furthermore, as Ghani (2012, p. 45) emphasizes, 'In 58 out of 94 countries for which we have data, productivity growth in services exceeded that in industry'.

In sum, it would be fair to say that the popular notion that the service sector entails a preponderance of low productivity activities in developing economies is not supported by the available evidence. This is simply because the service sector is diverse entailing a mix of modern and traditional activities.

There is also the popular notion that the service sector is essentially non-tradable in nature. Hence, if developing countries need to raise living standards through the route of labour intensive exports, they need to rely heavily on manufactured exports.

The available evidence suggests that this popular notion needs to be revisited (Ghani, 2010). This is because modern services can be transported internationally through satellite and telecommunications networks. Modern service exports include: call centres; desktop publishing; remote management and maintenance of IT networks; compiling audits; completing tax returns and processing insurance claims; transcribing medical and health records; financial research and analysis. Indeed, the evidence suggests that developing country service sector exports have grown in sophistication over time (Ghani *et al.*, 2012).[18]

One study (Goswami *et al.*, 2012, p. 25) notes that:

> The lower middle income countries have seen service exports grow at an average of 24 per cent since 2001, compared with the world average growth

rate of 15 per cent during the same period. Their share of world exports in services has increased from 5 per cent in 1982 to 11 per cent in 2008.

The study (Goswami *et al.*, 2012, p. 26) then proceeds to highlight some country-specific success stories. These include: India (software and business process services which, in recent years have amounted to 33 per cent of India's exports); Brazil, Costa Rica, Uruguay (export of professional and IT related technology services); Mexico (communication and distribution services); Kenya, Morocco, South Africa, Morocco and Tunisia (professional services); Egypt (endowed with a world-class call centre sector); India and Thailand (health services).

Service sector exports from the developing world – as a 2005 UNCTAD Report has highlighted – are diversified both in terms of activities and export markets, with the average developing country serving 33 export markets. South–south trade is also important because developing countries account for two-thirds of the service export markets of other developing countries. It would also be fair to claim that service exports are less prone to protectionist sentiments and less prone to allegations of 'sweat shop' conditions from the advanced countries relative to manufactured exports. This, together with greater scope to make inroads in world trade – given recent trends – means that developing countries do not have to rely exclusively on manufactured exports as pathways to global economic integration.

There is also the issue of linkages between the service sector and manufacturing. The cross-country evidence suggests a strong positive correlation in productivity growth between services and manufacturing (Ghani, 2010; Noland *et al.*, 2012). This suggests that modern services can provide intermediate inputs – through IT and business processing services – that can boost the productivity of the manufacturing sector and lead its expansion. Dasgupta and Singh (2005) argue that this is the role that the service sector has played – and continues to play – in the case of India.

What is perhaps most germane to the contemporary discourse on the role of the service sector in economic development is the extent to which it can affect the goal of sustainable reductions in poverty. The cross-country evidence – based on multivariate regressions – suggests that, as an explanatory variable, service sector growth outperforms manufacturing and agriculture sector growth in understanding cross-country variations in poverty reduction in Asia (Ghani, 2010; Noland *et al.*, 2012). In the case of Sub-Saharan Africa, cross-country regression, based on a sample of more than 30 Sub-Saharan African countries, suggests that growth in both agriculture and services (but not manufacturing) has a strong, negative impact on poverty reduction (IMF, 2014, p. 37).

There are some additional – and desirable – features of the role of the service sector in the development process. These include: gender dimensions of development and the environmental aspects of structural change. In developing countries, services accounted for a higher share of female employment relative to manufacturing (World Development Report, 2012). This suggests that the expansion of service sector might contribute to the goal of gender equity.

It is well known that the expansion of manufacturing activities can be resource intensive – such as land, water and fuel. This is not necessarily the case with modern services. For example, the expansion of financial services and the ICT sector relies on skilled labour and electricity rather than land, water and fuel. Of course, there are service sector activities – such as tourism – that are also resource intensive, but to the extent that a developing country seeks to expand particular types of modern services, such expansion might place less of a burden on the environment.

Beyond premature de-industrialization: the role of agricultural diversification

In conventional models of development, the agricultural sector plays a residual role serving as a source of cheap inputs, most notably labour, for a burgeoning, urban-based manufacturing sector. Yet, as noted, for low and lower middle income countries, the agricultural sector remains a major source of livelihood for at least 50 per cent of the population. In such a situation, agricultural sector diversification can play an important role in improving productivity and livelihoods in the rural economy. Diversification in the agricultural sector can also act as a brake on excessive rural–urban migration by improving rural-based employment opportunities. From a structural transformation perspective, the focus on agricultural diversification is appropriate, given the evidence reviewed earlier from decomposition exercises, that the 'within sector' (in this case agriculture) component is a major source of aggregate labour productivity growth.

Various studies have shown that 'diversification will, in most instances, increase employment for the rural poor' (Barghouti *et al.*, 2004, p. 12). This happens because '(s)ubstantial employment opportunities are generated in seed and seedling production, precision land preparation … irrigation, harvesting, cleaning, grading, and packaging of high-value crops' (Barghouti *et al.*, 2004, p. 12). It is not quantitative expansion employment as a result of the expansion of high-value crops that matters. The quality of employment – in terms of higher wages – is also likely to be high. Average labour use is significantly higher in vegetables for a sample of four Asian countries. Similarly, the returns to labour are higher for non-cereal production.

It is also worth noting that multiplier effects of agricultural diversification are higher than agricultural specialization in cereal production. This is the consequence of the fact that 'high-value crops, compared to cereals, are more strongly interlinked with other sectors of the economy' (Barghouti, 2004, p. 13).

Exporting 'high value crops' or – as is more commonly known – high value added (HVA) agricultural commodities is a lucrative and inclusive growth strategy for developing countries.[19] There are several reasons behind this thesis. To start with, the demand for HVA agricultural commodities is rising rapidly (in relation to the demand for other agricultural commodities). The former represent a dominant and growing proportion of world trade. For example, the share of HVA agricultural commodities in world trade went up from 60.8 per cent of world trade in 1980/81 to 87.3 per cent in 2000/01 with a corresponding decline in the trade share of traditional tropical products. In 2000/01, the share of such products was a minuscule 12.7 per cent of world trade.[20] More recent statistics by the Food and Agriculture Organization (FAO) for the 2000s corroborate these robust trends. For example, '(o)ver the 2000–2010 decade, the fruit and vegetable sector has grown by 11 per cent per year at the global level, by almost 20 per cent in Africa and by 17 per cent in Asia' (FAO, 2013, p. 154). It is also noteworthy that HVA agricultural products garner higher prices (especially in the developed markets) than traditional commodities.

While the focus on the export of HVA agricultural commodities is a desirable goal, it is possible, even within traditional commodities, such as coffee, to engage in diversification and upgrading. This is illustrated by the subsequent discussion of Rwanda's success in diversifying into specialty coffee. Indeed, export growth of coffee has been quite robust in the 2000s, as FAO has pointed, with this sector accounting for 30 per cent of tripling in value of coffee, tea, cocoa and spices.

Floriculture, and especially cut flowers, is a sub-set of HVA agriculture. Cut flowers are a lucrative trade prospect for many African countries given their agro-climatic conditions, abundant availability of land around urban centres, ready supply of unskilled and low cost labour as well counter-cyclical seasonality to the European markets. The African pioneers in international trade in cut flowers include Kenya which successfully organised institutions and facilities to promote their produce in this field and subsequently entered European and other markets. The discussion that follows documents the rise of Ethiopia as an export success story in the global business in cut flowers. The cases of Ethiopia and Rwanda are supplemented by the experiences of Peru and Vietnam. Peru is the world's leading exporter of asparagus, while Vietnam, usually regarded as a successful industrializing country, is the world's leading exporter of processed cashews.

Agricultural diversification: the case of Ethiopian cut flower exports[21]

Ethiopian export of cut flowers is not new, dating back to 1980, but export activity languished for a long period and declined sharply between 1992 and 1999. The value (in US$) of cut flower exports in 1999 was a mere 21 per cent of the levels attained in 1992. One could detect a slow turnaround at the turn of the new millennium, but between 2004 and 2008, the rise was truly extraordinary with cut flower exports increasing by 52 times. By 2009, Ethiopian cut flowers accounted for 2 per cent of the world exports and 13 per cent of African exports. In 2009, it also ranked as the second largest exporter to the EU among all African countries and the fifth largest non-EU exporter to the EU. The growth of exports of cut flowers appears to have been sustained despite the global recession of 2009. In the first ten months of 2010, Ethiopia exported US$250 million of cut flowers.

How did such a dramatic transformation take place? Many forces, factors and actors were involved, but proactive government policy played a significant role. To start with, initial comparative advantage helped: favourable growing conditions, availability of cultivable land around the capital city, proximity to EU markets, ready supply of low-cost, unskilled labour. These initial endowments were always there, but one needs to understand why there was such a take-off in cut flower exports in the mid-2000s and not earlier.

Luck and timing played a role. Kenya, Africa's largest and most established exporter, was beginning to lose its primacy at the turn of the twenty-first century as a result of environmental concerns pertaining to the cultivation of cut flowers, concerns about labour issues, rising labour costs and its loss of trade privileges in EU markets. Political violence in the late 2000s also added to an uncertain business climate. Some established businesses decided to relocate offshore.

Ethiopian cut flower exports emerged in such a context. There were so-called 'first movers' who established the export business in its current form. Initially, in its industry and sectoral policy design that was unveiled in 1998, the Ethiopian government did not include cut flowers exports as worthy of promotion, but by 2003 a revamped industry policy framework clearly identified it as a major new export activity. The driving principles of this policy framework were (1) creating a conducive business environment and (2) providing direct support to selected sectors that were deemed to be competitive in international markets. A plethora of sector-specific support to the cut flower industry emerged after 2003: (a) access to land under very cost-effective leasing arrangements; (b) access to cheap, long-term credit; (c) exemption of import duties and taxes on export earnings; (d) infrastructure and airport transport coordination. All of these were geared towards alleviating binding constraints on the growth of the private sector in a nascent industry that is land intensive as well as capital intensive requiring up-front investment in greenhouse facilities, irrigation systems and refrigeration facilities to store and transport a highly perishable product. Furthermore, the profitability and viability of the industry as a major supplier to EU markets depended heavily on efficient and cost-effective cargo facilities.

It would be naïve to suggest that in Ethiopia only the government played a leadership role. Private actors and donors made significant contributions as well. Cut flower producers successfully lobbied the government for sector-specific support while donors provided assistance in capacity building through training programmes for farm managers and supervisors and showcased the quality of Ethiopian cut flowers. The cut flower business has gained from agglomeration economies that have been engendered by industrial clusters. Private foreign direct investment (FDI) and global value chains provided some degree of technology transfer.

The cut flower industry, while requiring high start-up costs, entails at planting, harvesting and post-harvesting stages labour intensive processes that require relatively simple skills. Hence, in principle the expansion of cut flower exports should enhance the demand for unskilled labour. Unfortunately, the employment consequences of the cut flower trade in Ethiopia has been insufficiently analysed.

The available studies suggest direct employment creation that ranges between 35,000 and 50,000 workers in 81 farms. Hardly any evidence is provided on indirect job creation through the expansion of ancillary services, although one study claims that the industry as a whole has created 250,000 direct and indirect jobs. Taking these and estimated labour coefficients per hectare at the farm level into account yields a back-of-the-envelope estimate that a doubling of cut flower exports over the next five years (plausible given recent growth) would yield about 500,000 direct and indirect jobs.

There are nagging concerns that cut flower exports respond to the tight just-in-time deadlines of buyer-driven value chains that often result in feminization and flexibilization of production processes. The business is characterized by regular peaks and troughs in demand which entail a tight control over labour utilization rates. The sketchy data from Ethiopia corresponds rather well to this syndrome. The bulk of the jobs (60 to 70 per cent) are part-time and seasonal and there is a preponderance of female workers (around 70 per cent). There is the risk of injury (particularly in the harvesting of roses) and exposure to hazardous substances entailed in the application of pesticides. On the other hand, one of the few studies that have analysed the characteristics of workers at the farm level using a purpose-built survey provides some encouraging developments. The average worker has between seven to eight years of mean schooling, receives on-the-job training and earns wages that are 1.5 times higher than agricultural wages.

There are also significant environmental concerns. The cut flower trade requires the use of farms that are intensive in water usage and pesticides. Kenya became the object of considerable international attention as a result of pollution of Lake Naivasha around which many of the farms were established. Hence, the Ethiopian cut flower industry is also subject to these environmental risks.

How does one create a 'win–win' situation in which the benefits of job creation through the expansion of cut flower exports are combined with efforts that make the industry ecologically friendly and measures that promote decent working conditions? One encouraging sign is that the buyer-driven supply chains in the cut flower trade have developed codes of conduct that seek to uphold environmental and labour standards. Global value chains have learnt over the years that there can be considerable damage to brand reputation if a combination of media campaigns, civic activism of labour NGOs and discerning customers in rich countries lead to exposure of 'sweatshop conditions' in export-oriented industries in developing countries from which they source their products. Admittedly, these codes of conduct are by no means adequate to guard against abuse of labour standards in the absence of a well functioning collective bargaining system. Hence, the Ethiopian government will have to find means of reinforcing self-governing codes of conduct by the cut flower business owners through improvements in the labour inspection system and by encouraging proper representation of the interests and rights of workers. The private sector, workers' representatives and civil society associations have a collective responsibility to work with governments on this critical issue.

Agricultural diversification: the case of the specialty coffee sector in Rwanda[22]

As a land-locked, low income resource-poor SSA economy, the majority (around 80 per cent) of Rwandans rely on agriculture for their livelihoods. Within agriculture, coffee is a major export item. For nearly a century, 'Rwanda was an exporter of largely ordinary coffee'. In the early 2000s, 'it ... emerged on to the world stage as a producer of high quality specialty coffee', marketed in the UK by a major retailer (Sainsbury's) and supported in the United States by Starbuck's. In terms of value, specialty coffee exports increased 128 times between 2002 and 2009 and 101.5 times in volume over the same period.

In 2002, the Rwandan government issued a National Coffee Sector Strategy within the framework of its long-term development plan that envisioned a goal to capture a large share of the specialty coffee market. This strategy was preceded by donor-supported technical assistance that studied the feasibility of adding value to Rwandan coffee through the production of higher grade, washed and fermented specialty coffee.

The export of specialty coffee fetches a premium price in international markets. This requires moving into the fully washed coffee (FWC) segment at the core of which lies the installation and operation of washing stations. The government set ambitious production targets. By 2012, it was envisaged that more than 80 per cent of coffee produced would be from the FWC segment. Today, the attained targets stand at a little over 20 per cent. Although well below target, this is a significant achievement. In 2002, there was only one washing station. By 2009, it had risen to 112 and by 2010 it had risen to 188, although utilization rates are less than optimal.

What explains the sharp rise in washing stations after 2001? It turns out that donor-supported policy intervention alleviated a binding constraint in the production of specialty coffee, namely, access to finance. Prior to 2001, there was no need to invest in washing stations. Banks provided seasonal financing to traders and middlemen who procured the coffee directly from small-holders or cooperatives, 'dry milled' the coffee using traditional methods and exported it. As a result of large losses in 2001 incurred by banks, even this seasonal financing was targeted towards large traders and exporters. When it became evident that the installation and operation of washing stations was a prerequisite for the transition to the specialty coffee sector, the investment needs of the sector shot up, given that it required substantial start-up costs and working capital. Conventional seasonal financing could not meet such investment needs. The implementation of a loan guarantee scheme through the Development Credit Authority (DCA) and the provision of donor-supported credit lines appeared to break the barrier to the financing of washing stations.

What have been the employment and social consequences of Rwanda's transition to the specialty coffee sector? Here, the evidence is even patchier than in the case of the case of Ethiopia's cut flower exports. A 2006 evaluation suggests that 2,000 direct jobs have been created in washing stations. There is no indication of indirect job creation and no references to wages and working conditions. Using labour coefficients per washing station, back-of-the envelope estimates suggest that nearly 5,000 jobs would have been directly created by 2010. These estimates appear like the proverbial drop in the ocean given Rwanda's immense need for creating durable and productive employment for its workforce.

The focus on direct job creation underestimates the more indirect impact of the transition to the specialty coffee sector on the lives of approximately 500,000 coffee growers. Because owners of coffee stations (both cooperatives and the private sector) receive a premium price in international markets compared with the export of low-grade coffee, they are able to offer a better price to farmers. The procurement price appears to have gone up 2.3 times between 2004 and 2008. One study finds that farmers who sell coffee cherries to washing stations experienced a 17 per cent increase in expenditure (on a per adult equivalent basis) than their counterparts who still sell ordinary coffee to exporters.

Agricultural diversification: the case of Peruvian asparagus exports[23]

Asparagus is a high-value, labour intensive vegetable crop that can be grown throughout the year with suitable agro-climatic conditions. Asparagus can sold in three forms: canned, frozen and fresh. Green asparagus is typically sold as a fresh product, while white asparagus is available as a processed product.

Peru is the world's leading exporter of asparagus and the second largest producer of the crop after China. It has acquired a reputation as a major producer of green asparagus which is mainly exported to the United States and the European Union. In recent years, Peruvian exported green asparagus has grown rapidly in the Chinese market. Peru is also the world's most productive producer of asparagus which, combined with labour costs and farm prices that are lower than its competitors, gives it a distinctive competitive advantage in world markets.

The 2000s saw a 40 per cent increase in harvested areas devoted to asparagus cultivation. Asparagus cultivation is concentrated in the coastal strip encompassing La Libertad, Ancash, Lima and Ica. Although asparagus production can be traced to the 1950s, it really emerged as a major export item in the 1990s. Even then, canned asparagus dominated exports. It was only in 2002 that green asparagus surpassed the exports of canned asparagus. How did that happen?

As in the case of the cut flower industry, multiple actors and factors are at work, encompassing the private sector, donors and the government, that built on the natural comparative advantage of agro-climatic conditions favouring year round cultivation. Legal changes in the 1990s ushered in significant changes in land ownership structures and encouraged the growth of large-scale commercial farming that could build on the drip-irrigation technology that is otherwise too costly for small-holders to adopt. Such technology drives large-scale asparagus production. Today, the asparagus industry is characterized by vertically integrated farms together with contract farming. Large farms dominate the production clusters. Still, there is significant entry and exit of firms.

The contribution of the private sector to the development of asparagus exports is reflected in the fact that a producer's association (Ica Farmers Association) investigated options to replace traditional farm products with export crops. They received funding and technical support from a donor (the US agency for International Development) that enabled their collective quest for product discovery to become a reality. Furthermore, as in the case of cut flowers, complementary investments are needed in cold storage and cargo facilities to export fresh produce that required access to credit as well as public investment in relevant infrastructure. The Peruvian government was also instrumental in the formation of an agency which promotes exports and helps the industry to sustain the competitiveness of the asparagus sector as well as other non-traditional exports.

The growth of Peruvian exports of asparagus and other non-traditional agricultural exports faces a favourable international trade environment with the implementation of the USA–Peru Free Trade Agreement in 2009 and the EU–Peru Free trade agreement in 2010. Both have led to complete reduction of tariffs of Peruvian exports to the USA and European Union. On the other hand, the dividends from favourable changes in the international trade environment can only be reaped if enabling domestic factors as documented above are in place.

The available evidence suggests that the asparagus industry is directly responsible for the employment of 50,000 to 60,000 workers, of which 60 per cent are women. Given various linkages – such as packaging, cold storage facilities and cargo facilities – there is also a boost to indirect job creation. The employment rates in the main asparagus growing regions are some of the highest in Peru. Since 2003, employment rates in these regions have increased at an average rate of 9 per cent with commensurate increases in real wages which are usually around US$5 per day and thus notably above the US$2 a day poverty line.

It would be naïve to argue that the Peruvian asparagus industry is a story of unqualified success and that there are no challenges worth highlighting. As in the case of the cut flower industry, critics have highlighted environmental concerns and express considerable disquiet about wages and working conditions. Environmental constraints are likely to threaten the continued development of the asparagus industry, given that the main asparagus growing area is supplied by ground water. Hence, fresh water availability through over-exploitation is a major concern.

Critics also allege that women workers endure hazardous working conditions, while pregnant women usually face considerable discrimination in terms of employment contracts. The government appears to have failed in its obligation to implement comprehensive labour laws, while judicial procedures seem to favour business owners. As a result, any momentum to bring about improvement in wages and working conditions in the asparagus industry relies heavily on the activism of civil society associations.

The appropriate response to the aforementioned concerns about the asparagus industry is not to campaign for clamping down on the growth of the industry, but to continue advocacy for better wages and working conditions through appropriate legislation and cooperation with the private sector. At the same time, both the private sector and the government would have to take the environmental concerns seriously. Otherwise, benign neglect can end up derailing the future of the asparagus industry and the lives of many thousands whose economic fortunes are closely tethered to sustainable asparagus production and exports.

Agricultural diversification: the case of Vietnamese cashew exports[24]

The cashew tree is a native of Brazil, but the agro-climatic conditions for its cultivation are such that they are now grown in tropical countries. Cashews have historically been largely grown by subsistence farmers; they can be cultivated in soil which is too poor for other crops. Cashew trees take three to four years to bear fruit with a life span of 25 years. While serving as a source of supplementary income for poor farmers, cashews are consumed mainly by middle-class people as party or 'between meal' snacks. It is in this important sense that cashews are regarded as non-traditional agricultural exports. Cashews are sold mainly as kernels ranging from 'natural' to various concoctions (roasted, deep fried, spiced and sweetened, etc.). They are used for cooking, confectionery and baking, but this is largely limited to India. World prices for cashews are volatile, but there has been a strong upward trend, with world prices rising by 150 per cent over the 2000s. Recent trends in the USA and Europe suggest that cashew consumption is seen as part of a healthy life-style and has turned out to be recession-proof.

The world's major producers and exporters are India, Vietnam and Brazil, representing a high degree of consolidation of the global cashew industry following the sharp decline of African producers. Since 2007, Vietnam has maintained its position as the world's leading exporter of processed cashews. It has come a long way since the 1980s when cashews were grown on a small scale by poor farmers. The cashew industry – both in terms of farming and processing – is regionally concentrated in a few provinces (Dong Nai, Binh Duong, Long An and Binh Phuoc). From a cashew planting country, Vietnam has emerged as a major processing country and is now responsible for 24 per cent of the world's processed cashews. Vietnamese cashews have penetrated markets in 30 countries across the world, but a major share (76 per cent) can be attributed to three countries (USA, China and Netherlands).

With the exception of Brazil, the processing of cashews is still highly labour intensive requiring application of manual skills in roasting/steaming, drying and shelling. Because of the laborious and hazardous nature of these operations, efforts have been underway for many years in Vietnam and elsewhere to engage in mechanization through the use of shelling machines, but they were hampered by unacceptably high breakage rates of cashew kernels. In 2009, Vietnamese manufacturers unveiled new processing equipment which they claim could peel cashews equivalent to the amount peeled by 30 workers per day while maintaining acceptably low breakage rates. Fifty per cent of Vietnam's 225 shelling factories now use this equipment and early indications are that this equipment is likely to become an important export item in its own right. Thus, the cashew industry in Vietnam appears to have spawned a positive spill-over effect (production and export of processing equipment).

Relatively little information is available on employment, wages and working conditions in the cashew industry. Tentative estimates suggest that 500,000 workers are employed, with a large majority being women. Indirect employment effects are likely to be significant. Tentative estimates also suggest that an average farmer who plants and sells raw cashews to others (mostly independent 'collectors')[25] was able in the mid-2000s to earn above the average income of the country.

Multiple factors have played a role in the emergence of the Vietnamese cashew industry. Although some claim that the cashew industry has grown largely on the basis of private initiative, the role of the government, especially in a country like Vietnam which identifies itself as a 'socialist market economy', cannot be discounted. The economic reforms of the mid-1980s that paved the way for the emergence of the private sector are the primary conduit via which the export-oriented cashew industry, like all other industries, emerged.[26] In addition, the Vietnamese government supported the development of a business association (the Vietnamese cashew association or Vinacas) that has represented the collective interest of the industry. Vinacas, together with the Vietnamese trade promotion agency (Vietrade), is playing an important role in charting the future of the industry. Vinacas, with the support of the government, will work with the Global Cashew Council to support research that will promote the nutritional aspects of Vietnamese cashews globally. It has also embarked on a well-funded national programme to build a national brand that can be protected through a trade mark in key export markets and to produce new products that are suitable for local tastes.

Like all non-traditional exports, the Vietnamese cashew industry is not immune to various concerns. Wages and working conditions are still considered unsatisfactory, exposing workers to various physical hazards that afflict the processing of cashews. Gender discrimination is an ever-present challenge. These unpleasant aspects of the industry are perhaps one reason why labour shortages are rife. Allegations have also been made that Vietnam uses forced labour in the production of cashews. As in the case of the cut flower industry, the appropriate response is not to clamp down on the growth of the industry, but to find ways to strengthen incentives for the private sector to implement improved wages and working conditions. At the same time, supporting civil society associations and public sector capacities to demand and enforce basic labour standards and gender equity is critical.

One redeeming feature of the cashew industry is that, unlike cut flowers and asparagus, it is less prone to environmental hazards. The cashew tree prevents soil erosion. Hence, planting cashew trees promotes sustainable farming. Furthermore, some of its by-products, such as the discarded seed coat (or testa) can used for poultry and ruminant feed.

The four case studies presented here suggest the returns from a strategy of agricultural diversification can pay dividends in more and better jobs. Indeed, even within traditional cash crops, such as coffee, diversification is feasible and desirable. Developing countries that seek to engage in a strategy of agricultural diversification face buoyant export prospects. Successful agricultural diversification requires the implementation of a multi-pronged strategy.

One cannot overlook the prevailing concerns about unsatisfactory wages and working conditions as well as the challenge of environmental sustainability that have been raised by the critics of these agro-based industries. Admittedly, these concerns are not unique to the cases covered. Allegations have been made of the large-scale use of forced labour in the thriving Thai sea-food industry, while the 2013 Rana Plaza disaster in Bangladesh, in which more than 1,000 mostly women workers perished in a garments factory, suggests that manufacturing industries too have their share of tragedies.[27] These concerns and calamities suggest that the private sector, the government and civil society will have to work together to make the most of the new opportunities for promoting the cause of inclusive development that would otherwise remain neglected if policy makers remain preoccupied with the notion of manufacturing-led industrialization as the sole route to economic prosperity.

Beyond premature de-industrialization: the role of non-renewable natural resources sector

Low income countries that are blessed with non-renewal natural resources are often considered to be the victims of a 'natural resource curse'. Faced with a windfall gain as a result of commodity price booms, they can end up contracting the so-called 'Dutch disease' in which the real exchange appreciates and crowds out both import-competing sectors and prospective manufactured exports. Furthermore, windfall gains from the natural resource sector can easily become a source of fiscal malfeasance and poor governance. There is, in short, a tragic proclivity among policy makers in developing countries to squander natural wealth. Discovery of oil and other precious resources can lead to destructive boom-bust cycles.[28]

Take the case of Africa. Here is a continent that has the largest share of least developed countries (LDCs) and also a significant share of natural resource-rich economies. Fifteen per cent of Sub-Saharan Africa's major annual output can be attributed to non-renewable natural resources. Fifty per cent of its exports are engendered by the natural resource sector. Twenty out of 45 Sub-Saharan African countries are major exporters of natural resources. Of these, ten are fiscally dependent on revenues from the natural resource sector.[29]

Given such statistics, it is not surprising that one might succumb to the tendency to regard Sub-Saharan Africa's recent robust growth, after the 'lost decades' of the 1980s and 1990s, as the ephemeral product of the recent boom in natural resource prices. Of course, prices of minerals and energy have doubled or tripled in the 2000s, but it would be a mistake to attribute the growth performance merely to a resource price boom. First, growth accounting exercises suggest that this is, at best, a partial interpretation. The major source of growth (about 70 per cent) has come from the diversified range of sectors, rather than just mining activities. Second, and more importantly, a natural resource curse is not inevitable. Managed well, the natural resource sector can play a 'crucial role in transforming economies' (Rielaender, 2013, p. 1). Hence, the appropriate question is: how can a low income country make the most of its natural resources? This depends critically upon a range of factors. They range from the fiscal management of resource, building of domestic capabilities through a regulatory regime and redistribution of the largesse provided by the natural resources sector.[30]

In an effort to mitigate the resource curse, a growing number of developing countries are using a 'savings regime' in the form of special savings funds which are often called 'sovereign wealth fund' (SWF). While this is a fiscally prudent move, a 'savings regime' does not respond to the imperatives to support structural transformation. It is possible to be fiscally prudent while using the proceeds from the natural resource sector to support the expansion of new activities and industries.

Consider the case of Chile which used its copper proceeds to promote the expansion of its new agricultural commodities. Particularly noteworthy is the development of the salmon industry that was financed by revenues from copper exports. The industry has its roots in the 1970s, but production on a commercial scale began in 1991. By the mid-2000s, Chile was the fastest-growing salmon producer in the world, and second only to Norway. In 2007, the industry 'provided around 25,000 direct jobs and 20,000 indirect jobs associated with a nucleus of approximately 40 companies and more than 1,200 affiliates suppliers' (Alvial *et al.*, 2012, p. 14).

Other examples include Malaysia which invested its oil revenues to pursue an agenda of structural transformation, including diversification within agriculture. The result was the emergence of a buoyant export crop sector (such as palm oil). Indonesia used oil revenues to support the agricultural sector. Oil resources were used to develop deposits of natural gas for export and as an input to fertilizer production. Fertilizers were used at subsidized prices to farmers that led to increased yields in the agricultural sector. Furthermore, Indonesia, especially after the end of the oil boom in 1981, began to counter the potential consequences of the 'Dutch disease' by tempering real exchange rate appreciations. This enabled manufacturing exports to flourish.[31]

Perhaps the biggest potential dividend that revenues from the natural resources sector can provide is by enhancing the fiscal space for developing countries to invest in health, education and infrastructure as well as to support conditional or even universal cash transfer programmes.[32] This promotes human development and employability. By alleviating binding constraints, such a strategy – funded by revenues from the natural resources sector – can enable the private sector to grow which in turn contributes to overall growth and employment.

Concluding observations

This chapter adopted a generic definition of structural transformation, describing it as a process in which labour and related resources move from low productivity sectors to high productivity sectors. Such a process promotes both growth and productive employment. Using a decomposition framework, one can say that structural change has a 'within sector' component (when there are productivity improvements within a sector) and a 'between sector' or 're-allocation' component (when there are productivity improvements as a result of movement of resources between low and high productivity sectors).

The chapter proceeded to highlight the debate on the pros and cons of structural transformation as it has evolved in developing countries. The essence of this debate can be captured in the notion of 'premature de-industrialization'. This thesis, the chapter noted, had two dimensions: (a) a descriptive statement on the changing relationship between employment shares of manufacturing and per capita income; (b) a normative statement that developing economies in many parts of the world experienced growth-reducing structural change. This meant that labour and resources moved into low productivity non-manufacturing activities from low productivity agriculture. In the language of decomposition of aggregate productivity, this meant that, for any given level of changes in within-sector productivity, changes in between-sector productivity were negative. The effect was as a drag on growth and employment. More importantly, this deleterious outcome can be attributed to (a), which demonstrated that developed countries have de-industrialized at a rate that was faster than the historical norm. Hence, the manufacturing sector was unable to absorb the growing labour force in developing countries entailing a concomitant expansion of low productivity activities in the non-manufacturing sector. The chapter noted that this evoked a Harris–Todaro view of the world which can be contrasted with the optimism of a Lewisian framework of structural transformation.

The chapter assessed the relevant evidence on premature de-industrialization and concluded that while (a) as stated above was largely valid, the veracity of (b) was less clear. Admittedly, one influential study upheld (b); others have produced estimates that were contrary to the notion of premature de-industrialization. The chapter built on this argument to suggest that one should not adopt the view that manufacturing-led industrialization is the only route to economic prosperity. Certainly, this route led to unprecedented prosperity in the post-industrial societies in the Western world as well as to a distinctive group of East Asian economies in the 1960s and 1970s. On the other hand, one cannot ignore the structural reality that, in the developing world of today, non-manufacturing activities are the primary sources of livelihood and will remain so in the long term. Furthermore, in low and lower middle income economies the agricultural sector will continue to be a major source of livelihood for decades. At the same time, the chapter noted that the non-renewable natural resources sector played a crucial role in many low income countries, especially in Sub-Saharan Africa. These structural realities needed to be addressed in a way that went beyond the pessimism of premature de-industrialization.

The chapter then drew on cross-country data and country-specific examples to demonstrate that service sector-led structural transformation was feasible and desirable, while agricultural diversification was an integral part of inclusive development. At the same time, the chapter drew on practical examples to suggest how low income economies can make the most of their natural resources.

The chapter recognized that there are prevailing concerns about unsatisfactory wages and working conditions, as well as problems of environmental sustainability, impairing the employment dividends that flow from a strategy of agricultural diversification. Governments, the private sector, workers' representatives and civil society associations will have to work together to develop an appropriate strategy to deal with these concerns and thus make inclusive development through agricultural diversification a reality.

The messages embodied in this chapter were consistent with a re-interpretation of the role of industrial policies in economic development. Such policies were no longer seen as a sterile debate on whether governments should support industrial development or whether market forces should be allowed to prevail. Developing countries were increasingly committing themselves to a holistic vision of industrial policies. Such policies encompassed state-led investments in health, education and infrastructure as well as tailored interventions that promoted high-value added activities across all sectors – agriculture, industry, services. Thus, one needs to recognize that there are multiple and diverse pathways to structural transformation.

Notes

1 See Chapter 2 for a discussion of this topic.
2 OECD (2013, p. 10).
3 ILO (2013, p. 3).
4 Lewis (1954). This is among the most cited articles (more than 8,500 citations) in development economics. Other iconic contributions that focus on structural change include Chenery (1960) and Kuznets (1966). There has recently been a revival of interest in the topic on structural transformation (Lin, 2011). In 2013 alone, major reports on this theme were produced by several international organizations: ADB (2013); African Development Bank *et al.* (2013); UNIDO (2013). Good examples of formal model-based accounts of structural transformation include Herrendorf *et al.* (2013) and Duarte and Restuccia (2010).
5 Harris and Todaro (1970, p. 126) refer to a 'politically determined minimum urban wage at levels substantially higher than agricultural earnings'. In retrospect, this much cited paper (more than 5,500 citations), exaggerated the binding nature of minimum wages and the seriousness of urban unemployment and also its relevance as a measure of labour market slack in developing economies. Nevertheless, one could argue that the Harris–Todaro model served as the precursor to the literature on the informal sector in developing economies in which rural–urban migrants eke out an existence in low productivity urban informal activities because they cannot afford to stay unemployed. Early examples of this genre include ILO (1972), Hart (1973) and Sethuraman (1981).
6 In a much-noted paper, discussed at some length in the chapter, McMillan and Rodrik (2011) argue that labour market rigidities represent one of the salient factors behind what they call 'growth-reducing' structural change.

 7 Tregenna (2011, p. 5). Note that, in another contribution, Tregenna (2009) argues that one should also focus on the changing share of manufacturing in output. The author contends that much of the decline in the employment share of manufacturing globally is due to a decline in labour intensity or a rise in labour productivity.
 8 UNDO (2013, p. 15).
 9 This may happen at even lower levels of income. For example, in Nepal, a low income country, the carpet weaving and ready-made-garments industry simply collapsed because of a multiplicity of factors. See Islam (2012).
10 As cited and discussed in Rodrik (2013b, p. 15). This is also reported in AfDB *et al.* (2013). An updated version is McMillan and Harttgen (2014).
11 de Vries *et al.*, 2013, Table 4:17.
12 de Vries *et al.*, 2013, Table 2:11.
13 de Vries *et al.*, 2013, Table b1, appendix: 33.
14 Roncolato and Kucera, 2014 (Table 6: 418).
15 These are: Brazil, China, India, Indonesia, Mexico, Thailand, Turkey.
16 UNIDO (2013, Table 1.2: 25). This is an unweighted average of employment shares in manufacturing distributed across low and lower middle-income, upper-middle income and high-income countries for the 1991 to 2010 period.
17 de Vries *et al.*, 2013, Table 2:11. The employment share of the service sector in the 11 African countries expanded from 18 per cent in 1960 to 36.8 per cent in 2010. Over the same period, the employment share of manufacturing expanded from 4.3 per cent in 1960 to 8.3 per cent in 2010, but it was 8.9 per cent in 1990.
18 Of course, traditional services, such as tourism, can be a major source of export revenue. See, for example, the experience of Nepal (Islam, 2012).
19 The 'traditional' agricultural commodities include: sugar, cotton, jute, tobacco, coffee, cocoa, tea, bananas, cereals, roots and tubers, oilseeds. The HVA agricultural commodities include: dairy products, meat products, vegetables, fruit, fish, nuts, spices and essential oils, herbs, floriculture. See Davis (2006, p. 5).
20 Davis (2006, p. 6).
21 This section draws on ILO (2011, chapter 6, pp. 169–173). See Hidalgo (2011) for a broader discussion of opportunities for agricultural diversification in Southern and Eastern Africa based on an export-led strategy.
22 This section draws on ILO (2011, chapter 6, pp. 173–176).
23 The Peruvian case study is based on: Cannock (2011); Ferm (2008); Freund and Pierola (2010); Rios (2007); Shimizu (2006); US Foreign Agricultural Service (2013).
24 The Vietnamese case study is based on: EDE Consulting (2005); IFC (2010); International Labour Rights Forum (2014); Kanji (2004); Ministry of Trade and Industry of the Socialist Republic of Vietnam (2014); Vietnam News (2014); Vietnam Trade Promotion Agency (2014).
25 These collectors – who operate on motor bikes and can penetrate remote parts of the Vietnamese countryside – are an important part of the cashew industry. They are responsible for collecting 95 per cent of the raw cashew nuts from farmers. They then sell it to agents who in turn sell them to medium- and large-scale processors and exporters. Note that the domestic supply of raw cashews is inadequate to meet the demands of the cashew processing industry. Hence, Vietnam relies significantly on imports of raw cashews, mainly from African countries.
26 Lim (2014).
27 See Lawrence (2014) on the Thai sea-food industry. See Siegle and Burke (2014) on the Rana Plaza disaster in Bangladesh.
28 As Moss (2011, p. 2) puts it: 'After more than twenty years of research, the 'resource curse' ... has come to be widely accepted by political scientists, economists, journalists and policymakers'.
29 IMF (2012, p. 61).

30 See the collection of studies in Hujo (2012) for a comprehensive discussion of how mineral rents can be used to finance social policy.
31 The Indonesian and Malaysian case are discussed in Gelb and Grassman (2010).
32 Moss (2011) is a leading advocate of the view that one of the best ways of sharing the benefits of revenues from the natural resources sector is to use them to finance universal income transfer schemes. The Mongolian child transfer scheme, funded from such revenues, is an example that illustrates the relevance of the Moss thesis.

Bibliography

ADB (Asian Development Bank) (2013) *Special Chapter, Asia's Economic Transformation: Where to, How and How Fast? In Key Indicators for Asia and the Pacific*, Manila: ADB, available at: www.adb.org/sites/default/files/pub/2013/ki2013-special-chapter.pdf.

African Development Bank, Development Centre, OECD, UNDP and UNECA (2013) *Special Thematic Edition: Structural Transformation and Natural resources, African Economic Outlook*, available at: www.africaneconomicoutlook.org/fileadmin/uploads/aeo/PDF/Regional_Edition/AEO_2013_THEMATIC_EDITIONS_WEB.pdf.

Alvial, A., Kibenge, F., Forster, J., Burgos, J.M., Ibarra, R. and St-Hilaire, S. (2012) *The Recovery of the Chilean Salmon Industry: The ISA Crisis and its Consequences and Lessons*, 23 February, Puerto Montt, Chile.

Barghouti, S., Kane, S., Sorby, K. and Ali, M. (2004) *Agricultural Diversification for the Poor: Guidelines for Practitioners*, World Bank Agricultural and Rural Development Discussion Paper No. 1, Washington, D.C.

Cannock, G. (2011) 'Peru and China as Competitors in World Markets: The Asparagus Case', Workshop on Agricultural Trade Linkages between Latin America and China, FAO, Rome, September.

Chenery, H.B. (1960) 'Patterns of Industrial Growth', *American Economic Review*, vol. 50, pp. 624–654.

Dasgupta, S. and Singh, A. (2005) 'Will Services be the New Engine of Indian Economic Growth?', *Development and Change*, vol. 36, no. 6, pp. 1035–1057.

Davis, J. (2006) *How can the Poor Benefit from the Growing Markets for High Value Added Agricultural Products?* Natural Resource Institute, January.

de Vries, G., Timmer, M. and de Vries, K. (2013) 'Structural Transformation in Africa: Static Gains, Dynamic Losses', October, available at: www.ggdc.net/publications/memorandum/gd136.pdf.

Duarte, D. and Restuccia, D. (2010) 'The Role of Structural Transformation in Aggregate Productivity', *The Quarterly Journal of Economics*, vol. 125, no. 1, pp. 129–173.

EDE Consulting (2005) *Sustainability Aspects in the Vietnamese Cashew Industry*, June, Hanoi.

FAO (Food and Agriculture Organization) (2013) *Statistical Yearbook*, Rome.

Ferm, N. (2008) 'Non-traditional Agricultural Export Industries: Conditions for Women Workers in Colombia and Peru', *Gender and Development*, vol. 16, no. 1, pp. 13–26.

Freund, C. and Pierola, M. (2010) *Export Entrepreneurs: Evidence from Peru*, Policy Research Paper No. 5407, World Bank, Washington, D.C.

Gelb, A. and Grassman, S. (2010) *How Should Oil Exporters Spend their Rents?* Center for Global Development, Working Paper No. 237, August, available at: www.cgdev.org/publication/how-should-oil-exporters-spend-their-rents-working-paper-221.

Ghani, E. (ed.) (2010) *The Service Revolution in South Asia*, Oxford University Press, New Delhi.

Ghani, E. (2012) 'Service Revolution', in ILO: *The Global Development Agenda after the Great Recession of 2008–2009: Revisiting the Seoul Development Consensus*, Papers and Proceedings of a Conference, 21 November 2011, available at: www.ilo.org/public/libdoc/ilo/2012/112B09_46_engl.pdf.

Ghani, E., Goswami, A. and Kharas, H. (2012) 'Service with a Smile', *Economic Premise*, November, No. 96, The World Bank, available at: http://siteresources.worldbank.org/EXTPREMNET/Resources/EP96.pdf.

Goswami, A.G., Mattoo, A. and Saez, S. (eds) (2012) *Exporting Services: A Developing Country Perspective*, World Bank, Washington, D.C.

Harris, J.R. and Todaro, M.P. (1970) 'Migration, Unemployment and Development: A Two-Sector Analysis', *American Economic Review*, vol. 60, no. 1, pp. 126–142.

Hart, K. (1973) 'Informal Income Opportunities and Urban Employment in Ghana', *Journal of Modern African Studies*, vol. 11, no. 1, pp. 61–89.

Herrendorf, B., Rogerson, R. and Valentinyi, A. (2013) *Growth and Structural Transformation*, 17 February, available at: www.imf.org/external/np/seminars/eng/2013/SPR/pdf/rrog2.pdf.

Hidalgo, C. (2011) *Discovering Southern and East Africa's Industrial Opportunities*, Economic Policy Paper Series, German Marshall Fund of the United States, Washington, D.C.

Hujo, K. (2012) *Mineral Rents and the Financing of Social Policy: Opportunities and Challenges*, Palgrave Macmillan, London.

IMF (International Monetary Fund) (2012) *Regional Economic Outlook: Sub-Saharan Africa – Maintaining Growth amid Global Uncertainty*, Washington, D.C., available at: www.imf.org/external/pubs/ft/reo/2012/afr/eng/sreo1012.pdf.

IMF (International Monetary Fund) (2014) *Regional Economic Outlook: Sub-Saharan Africa – Fostering Durable and Inclusive Growth*, Washington, D.C., available at: https://www.imf.org/external/pubs/ft/reo/2014/afr/eng/sreo0414.pdf.

IFC (International Finance Corporation) (2010) *Prospects for Cambodia's Cashew Sub-Sector*, Cambodia Agribusiness Series No. 1, Washington, D.C.

ILO (International Labour Organization) (1972) *Employment, Income and Equality: A Strategy for Increasing Productivity in Kenya*, Geneva.

ILO (International Labour Organization) (2011) *Efficient Growth, Employment and Decent Work in Africa: Time for a New Vision*, Geneva.

ILO (International Labour Organization) (2013) *India Labour Market update*, ILO Country Office for India, December.

International Labour Rights Forum (2014) 'Forced Labour in Vietnam', 7 September, available at: www.laborrights.org/blog/201109/forced-labor-vietnam-violation-ilo-convention-29 (accessed 27 October 2014).

Islam, R. (2012) *Nepal: Addressing the Employment Challenge through the Sectoral Pattern of Growth*, mimeo, Geneva and New Delhi.

Kanji, N. (2004) 'Corporate Responsibility and Women's Employment: The Cashew Nut Case', *Perspectives*, no. 2, March, International Institute for Environment and Development.

Kucera, D. and Roncolato, L. (2014) 'Structure Matters: Sectoral Drivers of Growth and the Labour Productivity_Employment Relationship', in Islam, I. and Kucera, D. (eds) *Beyond Macroeconomic Stability: Structural Transformation and Inclusive Development*, ILO and Palgrave Macmillan, Geneva and London.

Kuznets, S. (1966) *Modern Economic Growth: Rate, Structure and Spread*, Yale University Press, New Haven and London.

Lawrence, F. (2014) 'Thailand's Seafood Industry: A Case of State-Sanctioned Slavery', *Guardian*, 10 July, available at: www.theguardian.com/global-development/2014/jun/10/thailand-seafood-industry-state-sanctioned-slavery.

Lewis, W.A. (1954) 'Economic Development with Unlimited Supplies of Labour', *The Manchester School*, no. 22, pp. 139–191.

Lim, D. (2014) *Economic Growth and Employment in Vietnam*, Routledge, London and New York.

Lin, J. (2011) *New Structural Economics: A Framework for Rethinking Development*, World Bank Policy Research Working Paper No. 5197, Washington, D.C.

McKinsey Global Institute (2012) *Africa at Work: Job Creation and Inclusive Growth*, August.

McMillan, M. and Harttgen, K. (2014) *What is Driving the 'African Growth Miracle'?*, National Bureau of Economic Research, Working Paper, No. 20077, available at: www.nber.org/papers/w20077.

McMillan, M. and Rodrik, D. (2011) 'Globalization, Structural Change and Productivity Growth', in Bachetta, M. and Jansen, M. (eds): *Making Globalization Socially Sustainable*, ILO and WTO, Geneva.

Ministry of Industry and Trade of the Socialist Republic of Vitenam (2014) *In 2013 Vietnam Cashew Export Increased Both in Volume and Value*, Hanoi, 28 February.

Moss, T. (2011) *Oil to Cash: Fighting the Resource Curse through Cash Transfers*, Center for Global Development, Working Paper No. 237, available at: www.cgdev.org/files/1424714_file_Oil2Cash_primer_FINAL.pdf.

Noland, M., Park, D. and Estrada, G.A. (2012) 'Developing the Service Sector as an Engine of Growth in Asia', mimeo, Peterson Institute for International Economics, the East–West Center and the Asian Development Bank.

OECD Development Centre and European Development Finance Institutions (2013) *Perspectives on Global Development: Industrial Policies in a Changing World*, OECD, Paris, available at: www.oecd.org/dev/pgd/COMPLETE-%20Pocket%20EditionPGD2013.pdf.

Prigent, A.-L. (2013) 'Industrial Policies for Development: It's More than you Think', *OECD Insights*, 24 June.

Rielander, J. (2013) 'Africa: Making the Most of its Natural Resources', *OECD Observer*, no. 296, Q3.

Rios, L.D. (2007) *Agro-Industry Characterization and Appraisal: Asparagus in Peru*, Agricultural Management, Marketing and Finance Working Document No. 23, FAO.

Rodrik, D. (2013a) *The Perils of Premature Deindustrialization*, Project Syndicate, 11 October, available at: www.project-syndicate.org/commentary/dani-rodrikdeveloping-economies–missing-manufacturing.

Rodrik, D. (2013b) *Structural Change, Fundamentals and Growth: An Overview*, mimeo, Institute for Advanced Study, September, available at: www.sss.ias.edu/files/pdfs/Rodrik/Research/Structural-Change-Fundamentals-and-Growth-An-Overview_revised.pdf.

Rodrik, D. (2014) *The Growing Divide within Developing Economies*, Project Syndicate, 11 April, available at: www.project-syndicate.org/commentary/dani-rodrik-examines-why-informal-and-traditional-sectors-are-expanding–rather-than-shrinking.

Roncolato, L. and Kucera, D. (2014) 'Structural Drivers of Productivity and Employment Growth: A Decomposition Analysis for 81 Countries', *Cambridge Journal of Economics*, vol. 38, no. 2, pp. 399–424.

Rowthorn, R. and Wells, J. (1987) *De-industrialization and Foreign Trade*, Cambridge University Press, Cambridge.

Sethuraman, S.V. (1981) *The Urban Informal Sector in Developing Countries: Employment, Poverty and Environment*, ILO, Geneva.

Shimizu, T. (2006) 'Expansion of Asparagus Production and Exports in Peru', Discussion Paper No. 73, Institute of Developing Economies, Tokyo.

Siegle, L. and Burke, J. (2014) *We Are What We Wear*, *Guardian*, available at: http://guardianshorts.co.uk/wearewhatwewear/.

Subramanian, A. (2014) *Premature Deindustrialization*, 22 April, available at: www.cgdev.org/blog/premature-de-industrialization.

Tregenna, F. (2009) 'Characterising Deindustrialisation: An Analysis of Changes in Manufacturing Employment and Output Internationally, *Cambridge Journal of Economics* 33(3), 433–466.

Tregenna, F. (2011) 'Manufacturing Productivity, Deindustrialization, and Reindustrialization', UNU-*WIDER Working Paper*, no. 2011/57, available at: www.wider.unu.edu/publications/working-papers/2011/en_GB/wp2011–057.

UNCTAD (United Nations Conference on Trade and Development) (2014) *Natural Resources Sector: Review and Identification of Opportunities for Commodity-Based Trade and Development*, Trade and Development Board, Trade and Development Commission, Multi-year Expert Meeting on Commodities and Development, 9–10 April, Geneva.

UNIDO (United Nations Industrial Development Organization) (2013) *Industrial Development Report, Sustaining Employment Growth: The Role of Manufacturing and Structural Change*, Vienna, available at: www.unido.org/fileadmin/user_media/Research_and_Statistics/UNIDO_IDR_2013_main_report.pdf.

US Foreign Agricultural Service (2013) *Peru: Annual Aspagarus Report*, 8 February, Washington, D.C.

Vietnam News (2014) 'Cashew exports to reach US$2.2b in 2014', 7 May, available at: www.vietnamnews.vn.

Vietnam Trade Promotion Agency (2014) 'Cashews', 29 June, available at: www.vietrade.gov.vn.

World Bank (2012) *Gender Equality and Development*, World Development Report, Washington, D.C., available at: http://siteresources.worldbank.org/INTWDR2012/Resources/7778105–1299699968583/7786210–1315936222006/Complete-Report.pdf.

5 Rights-based approach to employment

Introduction

The contemporary discussion on human rights is increasingly going beyond civil and political rights to cover economic and social dimensions. A rights-based approach to employment and development has its roots in economic and social rights. If one considers various declarations and agreements at the international level, a rights-based approach to development and employment can be seen to have a history. But discussion on this in the development literature is of relatively recent origin. It is, therefore, important to understand the major issues underlying the approach itself and those that may emerge in the process of its operationalization. The purpose of the present chapter is to address some of these issues.

A basic question that may be useful to address is whether employment (or right to work) can be regarded as a human right. That, in turn, would require one to look at what constitutes the basic criteria for a right to be regarded as a human right and to see if the right to work also qualifies as one.

In any discussion of rights, an issue that comes naturally is that of 'right holder' and 'duty bearer'. In the case of employment, and development in general, right holders are not difficult to identify, but an answer to the question of duty bearer may not be so obvious.[1] In a predominantly market-based economy, much of employment is growth-mediated, although the practice of public provisioning also exists, albeit in varying degrees. Who, in such a situation, can be regarded as the duty bearer? More fundamentally, is it essential to have one clearly specified duty bearer, or could there be multiple agents who could hold the responsibility?

Third, it is important to understand the scope of the right to work. Irrespective of the level of development of a country, work can take a variety of forms, e.g. wage-based employment, self-employment, etc. In a rights-based approach to employment, does one talk about only the former and not the latter? If not, how would one capture issues relating to self-employment?

Fourth, efforts to operationalize the rights-based approach to employment would involve identification of the roles and responsibilities of various agents in implementing the right, formulation of relevant policies and monitoring the process of their implementation. An important question in that respect is whether legal frameworks are needed in order to formalize such procedures or whether it would be adequate to put in place governing procedures that clearly define and articulate the required steps. Mention may be made in this respect of employment related conventions and recommendations adopted by the ILO for application and monitoring of which there are various mechanisms. It would be useful to see how the system works and whether that may be regarded as a possible mechanism for operationalizing the rights-based approach to employment.

The present chapter attempts to address the issues and questions raised above with respect to the rights-based approach to employment. It starts with a brief description of the historical background and how the right to work has been enshrined in various international protocols. In the third section, the conceptual underpinnings of the rights-based approach to employment are discussed with a focus on whether it can be regarded as a human right, who the rights holders and duty bearers are, what could be their relative roles and responsibilities. The fourth section is devoted to a delineation of the scope of the right to work. In doing so, the difference between right *to* work and rights *at* work will be brought out. Issues relating to the operationalization of the rights-based approach to employment and the role of relevant instruments of the ILO will be discussed in the last section.

Right to work in international declarations and agreements

International recognition of the right to work dates back to 1948 when the Universal Declaration of Human Rights (UDHR) was proclaimed and adopted by the United Nations General Assembly. The first paragraph of Article 23 of the Declaration states: 'Everyone has the right to work, to free choice of employment, to just and favourable conditions of work and to protection against unemployment'.

Likewise, Article 6 of the International Covenant on Economic, Social and Cultural Rights which was adopted by the UN General Assembly on 16 December 1966 and put into force from 3 January 1976 makes provision for right to work. The Covenant defined right to work 'as the opportunity of everyone to gain their living by freely chosen or accepted work'. Significantly, the description goes on to add: 'Parties are required to take appropriate steps to safeguard this right, including technical and vocational training and economic policies aimed at steady economic development and ultimately full employment'. As we shall point out later, such policies can be critical in operationalizing the rights-based approach to employment.

While adopting the Employment Policy Convention, 1964 (No. 122), the ILO took note of the right to work enshrined in the UN's UDHR and called upon member states to 'declare and pursue, as a major goal, an active policy designed to promote full, productive and freely chosen employment'. Paragraph 2 of Article 1 of the Convention states:

The said policy shall aim at ensuring that:

(a) There is work for all who are available for and seeking work;
(b) Such work is as productive as possible;
(c) There is freedom of choice of employment and the fullest possible opportunity for each worker to qualify for, and to use his skills and endowments in, a job for which he is well suited, irrespective of race, colour, sex, religion, political opinion, national extraction or social origin.

Of course, C122 does not explicitly incorporate right to work as one of its articles; and like other ILO Conventions, it is also not binding on all member states. However, the preamble to this Convention makes explicit reference to right to work as enshrined in the UDHR, thus indicating that the instrument can be looked at as emanating from a rights-based approach to employment. Moreover, as with other ILO Conventions, there is a standard procedure for supervising the application of the convention in countries that ratify it.[2]

Another international effort that recognizes the importance of right to work, especially in a human rights approach to poverty reduction strategies, is that of the Office of the United Nations High Commissioner for Human Rights. In the 'Principles and Guidelines for a Human Rights Approach to Poverty Reduction Strategies' prepared by that Office, right to work has been incorporated as one of the guidelines. The importance of productive and decent work has been recognized there as an important means of poverty reduction and 'instrumental in securing other rights such as food, health, and housing'.[3] The set of guidelines mentioned above incorporates a set of targets and indicators relating to employment, income from employment, financial support during spells of unemployment, elimination of gender discrimination in employment, and of child and bonded labour, and conditions of work. The guidelines go on to outline some basic features of a strategy for realizing the right to work.[4]

Conceptual underpinnings of the rights-based approach to employment

Recognition of the right to work in international declarations does not mean that the debate around the issue of work as a human right has been settled. In fact, one view interprets right to work in a narrow sense of individuals holding the right to get a job and states as the duty bearer having a legal obligation to provide them with jobs that are sought. In the world today, a very small proportion of total employment in an economy are within the purview of the states, of course, with the exception of former socialist economies where that proportion may be higher. In such situations, states may not be willing to concede to its citizens a legal right to claim jobs. One could, therefore, argue that the right to acquire a job is not legally enforceable.[5]

In order to provide legal cover to the provisions of the Universal Declaration of Human Rights and the International Covenant on Economic, Social and Cultural Rights (that recognize the right to work) it would be necessary to incorporate them into a country's legal system. In that sense, right to work may not stand the test of a legal right unless and until it is enacted through the legislative procedure at the country level.[6] However, this can still be regarded as a human right because such rights are derived not from law but from the concept of human dignity (Sengupta, 2000). As Amartya Sen (2004, p. 319) points out, 'human rights can be seen as primarily ethical demands. They are not principally "legal", "proto-legal", or "ideal-legal" commands'. He goes on to argue: 'The implementation of human rights can go well beyond legislation, and a theory of human rights cannot be sensibly confined within the juridical model in which it is frequently incarcerated' (Sen, 2004, p. 319). Looked at this way, even without legal backing, employment can be regarded as a human right.

Employment is not only a critical element in safeguarding human dignity but also an important factor enabling individuals to participate in the process of development. The importance of employment as a human right becomes clear when development is looked at as the process of expanding human freedoms and lack of gainful employment is regarded as one of the 'varieties of unfreedom' (Sen, 1999). In order to place 'the perspective of freedom at the centre of the stage' (Sen, 1999, p. 53), lack of employment as one type of unfreedom would need to be addressed. In fact, employment could be regarded as one of the 'instrumental' types of freedom that are necessary to promote human freedom and development.[7] In that sense, employment should be regarded both as a means and an end of development, and the right to work looked at in a similar manner as the right to development.

How could the right to work be realized in practice if there is no legal back-up for its realization? Is it possible (or even necessary) to clearly define duty bearers who would have to be responsible to rights holders and/or for ensuring that the right to work is safeguarded in reality? While addressing such questions, it is important to note the basic concept and nature of human rights. In that respect, it may be useful to quote from Sengupta (2000, p. 557):

> In the final analysis, human rights are those rights which are given by people to themselves. They are not granted by any authority, nor are they derived from some overriding natural or divine principle. They are human rights because they are recognized as such by a community of people, flowing from their own conception of dignity, in which these rights are supposed to be inherent. Once they are accepted through a process of consensus building, they become binding at least on those who are party to that process of acceptance.

Several elements of this characterization would be relevant for employment. First is recognition by a community of people and flowing from their own conception of dignity. It would be difficult to imagine a community that would not recognize employment as a critical factor in self-esteem and dignity. If employment is indeed important in safeguarding one's dignity, there should be no question about its being recognized as a human right. The second issue is whether a community of people recognizes this through a process of consensus, which is the case with the various declarations and the ILO conventions mentioned in section 2. The third important issue that comes out of the above quote is that once a declaration is adopted through a process of consultation and consensus, its contents become binding on the part of those who were involved in that process. By implication, the responsibility for applying them then rests on all the parties that were involved in the process. And that brings one to the issue of duty bearers in the case of right to work.

A basic perception about human rights (especially those concerning political and social rights) is that the state is the ultimate duty bearer and is responsible for ensuring that individuals enjoy the rights. Could one apply the same principle, or is it even necessary to apply it to the case of right to work? Since employment results from and involves the action of different parties, viz., the government, employers and workers, realization of the right to work should also be the joint responsibility of these various parties. In order to appreciate this, it is necessary to start from the basic premise that in most situations, the government is not the employer. In such situations, the government can only influence the magnitude and pattern of the demand for labour and the behaviour of employers (existing as well as potential) through its policies. The employers, on the other hand, play a critical role in generating demand for labour and in creating the jobs that are needed for the members of labour force. Likewise, prospective job seekers have to prepare themselves through acquiring necessary qualifications (often with support from the government) for the jobs that are available in the labour market. Thus, all three parties have responsibility to ensure that the right to work is realized in practice. But the critical question in this respect would be how to ensure that all parties are playing their respective roles and carrying out their responsibilities.

When the realization of a right depends on collective action by different parties, democratic behaviour in the form of persuasion and peer pressure assumes an important role in ensuring that this happens in reality. At the country level, this can happen through a participatory process involving social dialogue, while at the international level, it can happen through the formal mechanisms that exist in different organizations for monitoring the behaviour of the involved parties. In other words, it should be possible to realize the right to work even without setting up formal legal frameworks. This of course presupposes the existence of two things: (1) a functioning democracy and commitment on the part of the government at the country level, and (2) various forms of accountability mechanisms through which the duty bearers – in particular, the government – can be challenged if they fail in their duty. This is especially true when the right has not been formally incorporated in the legal system.

An example of how a rights-based approach to employment can function through joint work at national and international levels is provided by the supervisory and reporting mechanism that exists within the ILO with respect to the application of its various conventions that include those relating to employment policy. Although application of ILO conventions is not binding on the part its member states, those who have ratified the convention are required to adopt policies aimed at promoting 'full, productive and freely chosen employment'. It may be noted in addition that the first of the four strategic objectives highlighted in the *ILO Declaration on Social Justice for Fair Globalization*, adopted by the International Labour Conference (ILC) at its 97th Session, Geneva, 10 June, 2008 (ILO, 2008), is the promotion of employment. The employment related conventions[8] and recommendations and the Social Justice Declaration taken together should provide a framework to realize the right to work. Even if a country has not ratified the relevant conventions, by adopting the Social Justice Declaration, all member states have expressed their commitment to various goals including that of promoting full, productive and freely chosen employment. It would, therefore, be incumbent on them to undertake necessary measures in pursuance of this goal. Thus, even without a legally assigned responsibility as the duty bearer, member states are expected to make the best possible efforts to attain the goal of full employment. And in that respect, governments have a particular responsibility (in terms of formulating and implementing relevant policies). But the other partners, i.e. workers (and prospective members of the labour force) and employers, also have some responsibilities. Even if right to work is not included in the formal legal framework of a country, it should not imply that a rights-based approach to employment cannot be adopted.[9]

As for the role of governments as duty bearers, two points are worth noting. First, even if there are multiple duty bearers for any particular right, the nation states (i.e. their legitimate governments) remain the principal duty bearer. And this is true for the right to work as well.

Second, being the principal duty bearer does not, however, entail the responsibility that the government must *provide* the work. As a principal duty bearer it first of all has the responsibility of ensuring a conducive environment for fulfilling the right and, second, to ensure that other duty bearers do play their roles properly.

It is possible to classify the principal duty bearer's role in three parts: to protect, to promote and to fulfil. 'To provide' is a component of the third part – 'to fulfil'. This means that if the other parts suffice to realize a right satisfactorily there is no need to take on the responsibility 'to provide'. One could argue that the state should act to 'provide' as a last resort, but this demand would be valid only if it can be established that the state has done its best to discharge the other parts of its responsibility, so that direct provision indeed becomes a matter of last resort.

China provides a good example of how the government of a country can perform the above-mentioned functions of a duty bearer. In 2007, the country adopted an Employment Promotion Law (which became effective from 1 January 2008) which changed the role of the government from taking care of employment for all to fostering an accelerated role for the market-oriented mechanism for employment generation. Under the Law,[10] the government is responsible for 'promoting' employment largely through the mechanism of a development strategy and by establishing a macroeconomic environment that would be conducive to employment generation. The provisions of the Law focus on placing employment generation at the heart of policy making and on formulation and implementation of proactive employment policy. The emphasis, thus, is not on 'providing' work but on creating a conducive environment and on performing the role of facilitating job creation.

Governments may formally assume the responsibility of employment provider if it acts as the employer of last resort (ELR)[11] and institutes a legal framework within which it takes this responsibility upon itself. Employment guarantee programmes are examples of such legal frameworks within which governments underwrite the right to work and agree to provide jobs when the alternative is unemployment. In developing countries, such programmes usually take the form of public works programmes that are implemented with the twin objective of job creation and infrastructure development. In some cases (e.g. in Bangladesh, India, South Africa) they are undertaken to address the problems of chronic unemployment, underemployment and poverty, and seasonal unemployment, while there have been instances where job creation programmes in infrastructure were undertaken in response to economic crisis (e.g. in Argentina during the economic crisis of 2001, in Indonesia, Malaysia, Republic of Korea during the Asian economic crisis if 1997–98). In the case of the National Rural Employment Guarantee Programme of India, the programme has been given legal backing by enacting a legislation in the parliament in 2005. Thus, the government acts as the duty bearer and is obliged by law to provide employment to job-seekers who request jobs of the type (i.e. physical labour in infrastructure construction) stipulated under the law. Hence, this programme is often cited as one that has adopted a rights-based approach. In other countries, even though the public works programmes are not backed up by legislative frameworks, they are nevertheless indicative of the respective governments taking responsibility to provide jobs to those who seek work and are willing to work in construction.

Scope of the right to work

There are two issues that need to be addressed with regard to the scope and content of the rights-based approach to employment. First, when one talks about the right to work, does it imply work of a particular type like paid jobs? Such an approach would be very restrictive and unrealistic because a large proportion of employment in a typical developing country is actually outside the framework of wage payment. Many are self-employed in various sectors, and may indeed prefer to continue to remain so. If right to work focuses only on wage employment, the possibility of using this important route to work will be overlooked. Hence, the purview of the right to work should include both types of employment. An important question, of course, is how can the right to self-employment be handled in reality? The answer to this question should not be difficult if one notes that realizing the right to work would need a variety of policies and programmes, and some of those could be geared towards providing support in starting or strengthening enterprises. Such measures may range from credit, to assistance in design and marketing, business counselling, etc.

The second issue that needs to be addressed with regard to the scope of the rights-based approach to employment is that of rights at work. This is a vast area that includes the rights of those who are already at work. The rights that one can talk about include (but are not limited to) the freedom to form associations, the right to bargain collectively through their associations, non-discrimination in place of work, child labour and forced labour. These are important aspects of workers' rights in a democratic society, and there are core ILO instruments in these areas that have been ratified by a large number of countries.[12] However, when one talks about right *to* work, one should distinguish that from these rights *at* places of work. In fact, the subsequent discussion on realizing the right to work would confine itself to the former.

Realization of the right to work

Although the realization of the right to work depends on collective action by different parties and hence should be the joint responsibility of the relevant parties, namely the government, employers and workers, governments will have to take the lead role in this regard. Three steps would have to be taken in that regard: (1) making a political commitment towards achieving the goal of full employment; (2) building institutions and establishing procedures for formulating and implementing necessary policies for employment generation; (3) adoption and implementation of policies with respect to job creation and skill development.

Political commitment

Political commitment towards full employment, or at least towards the pursuit of employment as major objective of development policy, is the first important step that is needed for realizing the right to work. Such commitment can be expressed through a variety of means, and some examples may be provided for illustrative purposes.[13]

- There are countries whose constitution recognizes the right to work in some form; they include Benin, Brazil, China, Nepal, Nicaragua, Panama, Rwanda and the United Arab Emirates.
- In China, Employment Promotion Law was adopted by the government in 2007 and came into effect from 1 January 2008.[14] The Central Committee of the Communist Party of China and the State Council attach importance to employment as a priority objective of the country, and the government adopts annual targets for (1) new jobs to be created, (2) the rate of registered urban unemployment, (3) the number of laid-off workers to be re-employed, and (4) the number of disadvantaged persons to be employed.

- Some countries adopt a target rate of employment, e.g. 70 per cent by Republic of Korea, 80 per cent by U.K. The 'Employment Guidelines' of the European Union target 75 per cent employment rate by the year 2020.
- South Africa's National Development Plan of 2011 targets lowering the unemployment rate by 6 per cent which implies a target job growth of 5.4 per cent per year.
- Argentina aimed at reducing the unemployment rate to 10 per cent by 2015.

It is clear from the above examples that there is a variety of ways in which countries articulate their commitment towards recognizing the right to work. The highest form for doing so is to make it a constitutional obligation. But there are countries, e.g. China and India, where employment is not a constitutional obligation, and yet legislative frameworks have been established to promote/create employment. And there are others where employment promotion is neither a constitutional obligation nor required under law, but governments nevertheless attach priority to the goal of job creation and express them in the form of various targets. What is important is to make a political commitment towards pursuing employment promotion as a goal and recognizing the right to work as a human right.

Building institutions and establishing procedures for formulating and implementing necessary policies for employment generation

The type of institutions that will need to be built and strengthened depends on the kind of policies that are required to realize the right to work. Policies needed to promote employment operate from both demand and supply factors. While some policies help augment demand for labour, others operate on the supply side. Employment policies at the national level should ideally combine both kinds of policies and should include elements ranging from macroeconomic and sectoral policies to education, training and other active labour market policies (more on this to follow).

At the international level, the importance of economic policies in the context of employment has been recognized in both the Philadelphia Declaration and the Employment Policy Convention (C.122) of the ILO. According to the terms of the former, it is the responsibility of the ILO to examine and consider the bearing of economic and financial policies upon employment policy. The text of C.122 mentions that measures to be adopted for attaining the goal of full, productive and freely chosen employment (the subject of the Convention) are to be reviewed within the framework of coordinated economic and social policy.

Such wide-ranging policies also require action from a similar range of institutions. For example, since the responsibility for monetary policy of a country lies with the central bank, its involvement would be critical in giving an employment orientation to this policy. Likewise, the ministry of finance and its affiliated institutions would have to play a key role in ensuring that the fiscal policy framework of the country supports the goal of employment. Similarly, ministries dealing with important sectors like agriculture, manufacturing, construction, trade, etc. would have to take into account possible impact of their respective policies. On the supply side, ministries of education and labour have the responsibility for human capital development and preparing the labour force in such a way that they can access the employment opportunities created through the process of economic activities.

It should be clear from the above description that a large number of institutions would have to be involved if the goal of full employment and realizing the right to work were to be achieved. Coordination of the work of such institutions would be important from the point of view of ensuring that their acts are orchestrated well and towards achieving the same goal. Compartmentalization of roles and responsibilities of various institutions and fragmented views in this regard often stand in the way of attaining the goal of employment. For example, central banks typically consider fighting inflation to be their main (or often only) task, and they tend to pursue that goal without much regard to other objectives. Likewise, in formulating budgets, the finance ministry would typically try to balance the accounts and keep budgetary deficits to a minimum without much regard to the employment implications of allocations. In operationalizing a rights-based approach to development in general and to employment in particular, such traditional approaches would need to be revisited and necessary modifications introduced. Hence, what is important is not only building and strengthening necessary institutions but also bringing about new orientation in their approaches and functioning where employment will be an important consideration.

Adoption and implementation of employment policies: mainstreaming employment into policy making

Mention has already been made of the importance of policies ranging from those who work on the demand side to those that operate on the side of labour market. Some illustrations of both types of policies are provided in Table 5.1. Demand side measures include macroeconomic and sectoral policies and policies aimed at direct job creation. Expansionary macroeconomic policies help increase demand for labour by raising the rate of economic growth. On the other hand, carefully formulated monetary and fiscal policies may be helpful in influencing the pattern of growth to make it more employment friendly. Likewise, sectoral policies are important for promoting the growth of sectors that are more employment intensive. Similarly, direct job creation programmes (e.g. public works) are often used to create jobs.

On the supply side, policies relating to education may have both quantitative and qualitative effect on labour force. Policies aimed at raising the rate of enrolment and encouraging young people to continue with education/training can reduce the supply of labour in the market. Education and skill training can also improve the quality of labour force and help by reducing the mismatch between demand for and supply of labour. Active labour market policies (e.g. training and retraining of workers, employment services, etc.) play an important role in

Table 5.1 Possible types and areas of employment policies

Type of policy	Areas of policy
Demand side	*Macroeconomic policy* (i) Growth inducing expansionary macroeconomic policy (ii) Fiscal and monetary policies to support employment intensive sectors (iii) Subsidies for supporting job creation or for preserving jobs *Sector level policies* (i) Policies in support of SMEs (ii) Policies in support of labour intensive manufacturing industries *Direct job creation* (i) Programmes for creating jobs directly, e.g. through infrastructure (ii) Programmes targeted at specific groups, e.g. youth, older workers, women
Supply side	(i) Policies relating to education and training (ii) Active labour market policies (including training and retraining, employment services, etc.)

Source: author's elaborations.

bringing about needed adjustments in the labour market and preventing unemployment.

In order to operationalize the rights-based approach to employment, especially where the legal framework of a country does not formally include this right, it would be necessary for the government to make all efforts towards attaining the goal of full employment and ensuring that every member of the labour force has access to productive employment of his/her choice. One critical element in such efforts would be to mainstream employment in the country's growth and development strategy. The latter would imply going beyond labour market policies and special employment programmes and integrating employment concerns into policy making at various levels, macroeconomic as well as sectoral (as outlined above). One can think of several tasks in such an approach. The first would follow from the finding from various studies (e.g. Islam, 2010) that one way of increasing the employment intensity of economic growth is to identify sectors that are more employment friendly and pursue policies and programmes conducive to their growth. This approach would be relevant especially for developing countries that still have surplus labour to be absorbed through the growth of employment intensive modern sectors (e.g. labour intensive manufacturing, trade and services). Second, at the levels of policy making – both macroeconomic and sector level – it is possible for policies to have an impact on the employment outcome of output growth. In developed countries and in developing countries that no longer have surplus labour, the approach outlined above may not be needed. But macroeconomic policies should be geared to the pursuit of stability and growth as well as employment objectives. Moreover, during economic downturns, countercyclical policies are needed in order to ensure that the unemployment situation does not aggravate. An important question in that regard would be whether such possibilities are taken into account while formulating policies.[15]

Actual translation of the concept of mainstreaming of employment will, however, depend on the extent to which sectors with high employment potential are given importance in the overall growth strategy and how they are sought to be encouraged to grow faster. In other words, mainstreaming of employment, in the first place, would require that the pattern of economic growth has greater weight of sectors with high employment potential. In developing countries where planning is still used as a mechanism to determine the rate and pattern of economic growth, the state can play a direct role in this respect through the allocation of public investment which continues to be a significant part of total investment. In market economies, the incentive structure through market prices can be used to influence the direction of private investment.

The next level at which mainstreaming of employment can take place is in the framing of macroeconomic, i.e. fiscal, monetary (credit) and trade-policies. Of course, these policies have their own objectives, but employment generation could also be one of them. At least, it could be ensured that they do not militate against the objective of employment generation. For example, tax policy would have increased revenue as its main objective, but it could also include a structure of incentives for employment intensive sectors or technologies. It could also ensure that taxation structure does not discourage employment generation by levying higher tax rates on establishments employing more people per se. Subsidy policy could be used for employment creation.

How can ILO instruments be used in operationalizing a rights-based approach to employment?

It has already been argued that ILO's employment related instruments (i.e. the Conventions and Recommendations) along with the *Declaration on Social Justice* should provide a framework for realizing the right to work. It would be useful to look at how it can work in practice.

Take, for example, Convention 122 on employment policy (which is the basic instrument on employment). Like any ILO Convention, countries who have ratified this Convention are required to submit an annual report on measures taken by them to give effect to the provisions of the Convention. For purposes of preparing such reports, there is a standard 'Report Form' (ILO, 1986) which asks questions specifically on each Article of the Convention. For example, with regard to Article 1 that stipulates adoption of policies towards stimulating growth and development and ensuring that there is work for all that is as productive as possible and can be chosen freely, the report form asks for information on what kind of policies have been pursued under three broad categories: (1) overall and sectoral development policies; (2) labour market policies; (3) educational and training policies. The form also asks for information, among other aspects, on the situation regarding employment, unemployment and underemployment in the country, with particular focus on gender, young people and the disabled.

The ILO's Report Form recognizes that many aspects of the employment policy mentioned above go beyond the Ministry of Labour (who has the responsibility to respond to the ILO questionnaire), and hence other ministries will need to be consulted in preparing the report. Moreover, the form also asks for information on consultations that have been undertaken with employers' and workers' organizations. It is thus clear that the reporting mechanism of the ILO has provision for broad based participation.

The Report Form for ILO's Employment Policy Convention also provides practical guidelines for drawing up reports by the countries. These guidelines specifically mention that the first report (i.e. after a country has ratified the Convention) should contain detailed information based on the form while in subsequent reports, replies should be given to any questions that may have been raised by supervisory bodies.

ILO's reporting and supervisory procedure is not limited to countries that have ratified a particular convention. The General Survey of Employment Instruments that is carried out periodically[16] provides a mechanism to cover the situation in countries that have not ratified the employment related conventions. In accordance with Article 19 of the ILO Constitution, a questionnaire is sent to all countries, and a question is asked to provide information on law and practice in the country regarding the non-ratified Conventions and Recommendations. They are also asked to identify obstacles to ratification. The second part of the questionnaire (though that is optional) asks for information on trends, policies and developments with respect to employment in the country. A specific question asks whether the country has (1) adopted an active policy to promote full, productive and freely chosen employment for all, (2) taken measures to promote employment within the framework of coordinated economic and social policies, (3) established mechanisms to monitor progress towards full productive and freely chosen employment, and (4) consulted social partners on matters relating to employment policy.

Concluding observations

To sum up, ILO's employment related instruments do provide a basis and a framework which can be used to operationalize a rights-based approach to employment. There can be two types of situations in this respect. One is in countries that have ratified the Conventions: they are required to bring their legal and administrative frameworks in line with the requirements of the Conventions. Even in those situations, the system is not entirely legalistic; much is done through the ILO's system of monitoring and reporting. The second situation obtains in countries that have not ratified the relevant Convention(s). They also are brought within the purview of ILO's monitoring mechanism. Hence, if this system is applied in spirit, all countries would be obliged to not only declare employment for all as a goal but also adopt appropriate measures to move towards that goal. In terms of responsibilities, although governments have the primary responsibility, others in the society including employers, workers and the society as a whole have to regard this as something they need to pursue together. The ILO's system provides for a participatory approach, and it is incumbent on all in the society to adopt it in order to realize the right to work for everybody.

Before this discussion is concluded, a few words may be in order about the effectiveness of the ILO instruments mentioned above in realizing the right to work. In a framework that is non-binding and is not covered by a country's legal system, the effectiveness of application of its provisions depends primarily on willingness, commitment, as well as the ability of various agents (especially of governments as the principal duty bearers) to formulate and implement the right means of action. The mechanisms for monitoring at various levels also play an important role. But in order to make all these effective, it is also important to raise the level of awareness and capacity of the agents to use democratic means and peer pressure to the extent possible. In fact, national strategies are needed to undertake a real campaign for attaining the goal of full employment and realizing the right to work for everybody.

Notes

1 Of course, it needs to be noted that for human rights in general, the principal duty bearer is the state because it is the community of nation states that together agreed to accept some obligations as human rights of their citizens. The role of state as a duty bearer in the case of right to work will be discussed further in the present chapter.
2 As of June 2014, 108 (out of a total of 185) member countries have ratified C122.
3 Office of the UNHCHR (n.d.).
4 The 'three principles' mentioned in that respect are improving the productive potential of the economy, policies for maximizing the demand for labour and creating conditions to enable the poor to integrate into economic processes. These 'principles' bear strong resemblance to strategies for employment intensive growth outlined in some ILO studies (e.g. Islam, 2006; Khan, 2006; Osmani, 2006).
5 See Elster (2001), for example, for this line of argument.
6 This has been done in the case of the employment guarantee programme in India, about which more will be said later in the present chapter as well as in Chapter 9.
7 Although the list of instrumental freedoms provided by Sen includes economic facilities, and employment is not explicitly mentioned there, it is easy to see that his explanation of economic facilities makes it possible to include employment among them. See Sen (1999, pp. 38–39).
8 They include the employment policy convention C122, training convention C142, the recommendation on cooperatives (No. 193) and the Recommendation No. 189 on promotion of small and medium-sized enterprises. Texts of these conventions and recommendations can be found in ILO (2004).
9 In this context, it may be worthwhile to remember what Amartya Sen (2000, p. 123) says: 'The frameworks of rights-based thinking extends to ethical claims that transcend legal recognition'. He goes on to say that rights-based thinking can be extended from the pure domain of legality to the broader arena of social ethics, and that the realization of rights can be helped by a general societal commitment to work for appropriate functioning of social, political and economic arrangements to facilitate widely recognized rights (Sen, 2000, p. 123). See also Sen (2004) where it is argued

that some human rights are not ideally legislated but are better promoted through other means including public discussion, appraisal and advocacy. Right to work can be said to belong to that category of human rights.

10 More details on the Law can be found in ILO and MOHRSS (2011).

11 For a discussion of this approach and examples from India and Argentina, see Wray (2007).

12 These are known as 'fundamental' conventions. They are: C029 Forced Labour Convention, 1930, 177 ratifications; C087 Freedom of Association and Protection of the Right to Organise and Collective Convention, 1948, 153 ratifications; C098, Right to Organise and Collective Bargaining Convention, 1949, 153 ratifications; C100, Equal Renumeration Conventon, 1951, 171 ratifications; C105, Abolition of Forced Labour Convention, 1957, 174 ratifications; C111, Discrimination Convention, 1958, 172 ratifications; C138, Minimum Age Convention, 1973, 167 ratifications; C182 Worst Forms of Child Labour Convention, 1999, 179 ratifications. Details available from www.ilo.org/dyn/normlex/en/f?p=1000:12001:0::NO:::.

13 The following examples are from ILO (2010) and Islam (2014).

14 For details, see ILO and MOHRSS (2011).

15 For further discussion, see Chapter 3.

16 Recent reports are dated 2004 and 2010. See ILO (2004, 2010).

Bibliography

Elster, J. (2001) 'Is There or Should There Be a Right to Work?' In Schaff, K. (ed.) *Philosophy and the Problems of Work: A Reader*, Rowman and Littlefield, Lanha, Maryland, and Oxford, U.K.

ILO (International Labour Organization) (1986) *Report Form for the Employment Policy Convention, 1964 (No. 122)*, Geneva.

ILO (International Labour Organization) (2004) *Promoting Employment: Policies, Skills, Enterprises*, Report III (Part 1B), International Labour Conference, 92nd Session, Geneva.

ILO (International Labour Organization) (2008) *ILO Declaration on Social Justice for a Fair Globalization*, adopted by the International Labour Conference at its 97th Session, Geneva, 10 June 2008.

ILO (International Labour Organization) (2010) *General Survey concerning Employment Instruments*, Report III (Part 1B), International Labour Conference, 99th Session, Geneva.

ILO (International Labour Organization) and MOHRSS (2011) *From Active Employment Policies to the Employment Promotion Law: Coping with Economic Restructuring and Labour Market Adjustments*, Geneva.

Islam, R. (2006) 'The Nexus of Economic Growth, Employment and Poverty Reduction: An Empirical Analysis', in Islam, R. (ed.) *Fighting Poverty: The Development-Employment Link*, Lynn Rienner, Boulder and London.

Islam, R. (2010) *The Challenge of Jobless Growth in Developing Countries: An Analysis with Cross-Country Data*, Occasional Paper, Bangladesh Institute of Development Studies, Dhaka.

Islam, R. (2014) *Employment Policy Implementation Mechanisms: A Synthesis Based on Country Studies*, Employment Working Paper No. 161, Employment Policy Department, ILO, Geneva.

Khan, A.R. (2006) 'Employment Policies for Poverty Reduction', in Islam, R. (ed.) *Fighting Poverty: The Development-Employment Link*, Lynn Rienner, Boulder and London.

Office of the UNHCR (United Nations High Commissioner for Human Rights) (n.d.) *Principles and Guidelines for a Human Rights Approach to Poverty Reduction Strategies*, Geneva.

Osmani, S.R. (2006) 'Exploring the Employment Nexus: The Analysis of Pro-Poor Growth', in Islam, R. (ed.) *Fighting Poverty: The Development-Employment Link*, Lynn Rienner, Boulder and London.

Sen, A. (1999) *Development as Freedom*, Alfred A. Knopf, New York.

Sen, A. (2000) 'Work and Rights', *International Labour Review*, vol. 139, no. 2, pp. 120–127.

Sen, A. (2004) 'Elements of a Theory of Human Rights', *Philosophy and Public Affairs*, vol. 32, no. 4, pp. 315–356.

Sengupta, A. (2000) 'Realizing the Right to Development', *Development and Change*, vol. 31, pp. 553–578.

Wray, L.R. (2007) *The Employer of Last Resort Programme: Could it Work for Developing Countries?* Economic and Labour Market Papers, ILO, Geneva.

6 Human capital and inclusive development

Introduction

The role of human capital[1] in promoting economic growth is well recognized in the development literature. This has also been borne out by the experience of countries that have been successful in achieving high rates of sustained and broad-based economic growth. The countries of East and South East Asia are particularly notable in this respect.[2]

Theories of economic growth have long acknowledged that the entire growth of output in an economy cannot be explained by the quantities of the factors of production employed,[3] and that technical progress plays an important role in explaining the part that cannot be ascribed to the physical inputs like capital and labour. In trying to understand the process of technical progress, it has been recognized that the intellect and efforts of human beings play an important role. And it is in that context that the idea of human capital emerged.

While labour is regarded as a factor of production along with capital, it is not homogeneous; the quality of labour can vary depending on the levels and types of education and training received by the members of the labour force. Individuals and a country can build up its human capital base by investing their savings in education and training. And human capital can make contributions in production that are different from that made by unskilled labour.[4] Shortage of human capital may emerge as a constraint on the growth of economies in developing countries.

However, from the point of view of inclusive development, it is important to look at the role of human capital not only on the rate of economic growth but also on elements that make growth more inclusive. Following the characterization of inclusive growth presented in Chapter 1, it would be important to ask whether in addition to raising economic growth, education and skill training help reduce poverty and inequality and improve the employability of potential job-seekers.

Another issue that has not yet received detailed analysis in development literature is how the pattern of demand for education and skills changes with the level of economic development. For example, a country with a good base of elementary education may be able to achieve economic growth up to a certain level and yet face constraints arising from the shortage of skilled workers at a higher level of development. If that is the case, countries would need to keep upgrading the level of their human capital as they achieve higher levels of economic development.

The purpose of the present chapter is to provide an overview of the role of human capital in attaining inclusive development combining economic growth with reduction of poverty and inequality and improvement in the employability of the labour force. In doing so, particular attention will be given to differential education and skill requirement at different levels of development. The chapter will deal with the role of education in economic growth, reducing poverty and improving the distribution of income and employability of potential job-seekers. The issue of differential educational and skill requirement at different levels of development will also be addressed.

Education and economic growth

Channels of transmission of the effect of education on economic growth

The contribution that education makes to economic growth can be viewed from both micro and macro perspectives. At the micro level, education is expected to play a positive role in at least two ways. First, by raising the productivity of individuals it can help them increase their earnings. Second, by lowering the fertility of women, education can contribute to an increase in labour force participation. Education can result in a number of externalities that may make an indirect contribution to economic growth. In addition to its impact on fertility, education can contribute to an improvement of health, especially of children. Furthermore, educated parents are more likely to send their children to school, thus raising the overall level of education of the future generation. Education and skills of members of the labour force may also improve the ability of neighbours, since people often learn through observation. This may apply in a wide range of activities, including simple measures leading to an improvement in health and hygiene to the adoption of improved technology and practices in economic activities, especially farming.[5]

At the macro level, higher and better education is expected to contribute to higher growth of labour productivity. Two more channels of interaction between human capital and economic growth include the positive impact of education on both domestic and foreign investment, and its role in fostering higher levels of product variety and innovation (Hawkes and Ugur, 2012).

It needs to be underscored that human capital plays a critical role in raising productivity and growth not only in the relatively more modern sectors of the economy, but also in sectors like agriculture. Even before biotechnology and genetic complexities started playing a role in raising productivity in agriculture, studies demonstrated the role of education of farmers in raising farm productivity (Schultz, 1991). With genetic and environmental considerations becoming increasingly important in agricultural operations, and with the growing importance of diversification, emerging management practices (e.g. contract farming) and commercialization, education has become even more important in achieving the real potential of the agricultural sector (Chadha, 2003). Education has also been found to be important in improving the mobility of the workforce from farm to non-farm activities (Schultz, 1991).

In manufacturing, even in relatively more labour intensive sectors, such as ready-made garment manufacturing, the use of computer-based techniques is becoming increasingly frequent. Likewise, effective and efficient management of micro and small enterprises in an increasingly commercialized and competitive environment would require a minimum level of education that is necessary for applying basic accounting and management practices. And the same goes for services, especially if one goes beyond the rudimentary and traditional type of services.

The analysis of the link between education and productivity has its foundation in the notion of rate of return to education. The basic argument goes as follows. In a competitive situation, wages paid to a worker are expected to be equal to his/her marginal revenue product. On the other hand, the standard wage (or earnings) equation exhibits a positive relationship between wages and education.[6] That, in turn, implies that educated workers have higher marginal revenue product of labour as they are more productive. This positive relationship between education, productivity of labour and higher output is expected to hold at the macroeconomic level as well.

In addition to analysis based on rate of return to investment in education, two other approaches have been adopted in the literature on linkage between education and economic growth: (1) growth accounting where the approach is to split the growth of output into the contributions of various inputs, e.g. capital, labour, quality adjusted labour, and (2) growth regressions where cross-country data are used to estimate the relationship between education and economic growth.[7]

Empirical evidence of the link between education and economic growth

Notwithstanding the difficulties of providing statistical evidence on the role of education and skills in raising productivity, a large number of studies have been undertaken on linkages among education, productivity and development. Studies on rate of return carried out in the 1970s, 1980s, and 1990s (Blaug, 1976; Psacharopoulos, 1985 and 1994, for example) brought out a number of points that have important implications for possible policies on education in relation to economic growth in developing countries. It may, therefore, be useful to recount them:

- Rate of return to education tends to be higher in low income countries;
- Rate of return is usually found to be higher for primary education, and especially so in developing countries;

- Rate of return tends to decline with the level of schooling and the country's per capita income;
- Investment in girls' education tends to yield a higher rate of return than investment in boy's education.

After reviewing a number of such studies, Schultz (1991) concluded that there are strong empirical regularities between educational attainment of populations and their productivity and performance in both market and non-market production activities. Likewise, Behrman (1990) also notes the critical role of schooling in increasing labour productivity. After reviewing a number of growth models that incorporated the human resource factor and empirical studies containing analysis of the contribution of human capital to productivity and economic growth, Behrman (1990, p. xiv) concluded: 'Even though it is difficult to quantify the contribution of human capital to economic growth, there is virtually unanimity regarding its critical role'.

Of course, subsequent studies on rates of return put into question some of the earlier conclusions, especially the one on the relative rates of return of primary versus higher levels of education. For example, the private rate of return to investment in higher education in low income countries is found to be slightly higher than that of primary education (Table 6.1). Likewise, in Ghana, India, Kenya, Rwanda, South Africa and Tanzania, returns to higher education are found to be higher than that of primary education (Table 6.2). In some countries, returns to secondary education are also found to be higher than that of primary education. These results imply that at some stage of development, primary education is no longer adequate for many jobs in the labour market, especially those that yield higher earnings. This has started happening in countries like South Africa (Palmer *et al.* 2007).

Since the 1990s, growth regressions have been used in a large number of studies to examine the impact of education and skills on economic growth at the macroeconomic level. The basic approach is to regard output per worker as a function of capital, unskilled labour and human capital (some indicator of education used as a proxy for the latter). Of course, precise measures of both the dependent variable and of education as well as methods used vary a great deal, and with that vary the results obtained. While most studies show a positive

Table 6.1 International averages of rates of return to education

Regions	Social rate of return			Private rate of return		
	Primary	*Secondary*	*Higher*	*Primary*	*Secondary*	*Higher*
Low income	21.3	15.7	11.2	25.8	19.9	26.0
Sub-Saharan Africa	25.4	18.4	11.3	37.6	24.6	27.8
Asia	16.2	11.1	11.0	20.0	15.8	18.2
World	18.9	13.1	10.8	26.6	17.0	19.0

Source: adapted from data in Psacharopoulos and Patrinos (2004).

Table 6.2 Private rates of return from country studies

Country	Primary	Secondary	Higher
Rwanda	13.2	21.3	46.9
Ghana	19.4	13.5 (Junior)	9.1
		19.5 (Senior)	
Ghana	24.5	17.0	37.0
India	2.6	17.6	18.2
South Africa	2.9	9.7	60
Kenya	25	7	35
Tanzania	3.6	6.9	9.0

Source: adapted from data in Psacharopoulos and Patrinos (2004).

Notes
The figures quoted in this table are from various country studies mentioned in Palmer *et al.* (2007).
The two sets of figures reported for Ghana are from two different studies.

impact of education on economic growth, there are some where the impact is not very strong. Although this is not the place for a comprehensive survey of such studies,[8] it may be useful to look at some of them in order to understand why education is considered to be an important factor influencing economic growth.

One exercise (Stevens and Weale, 2003) based on historical data of primary school enrolment in 1882 and GDP per capita (1985 US$) in 1913 in eight countries (Brazil, France, Germany, Italy, Japan, Korea, Spain and UK) shows the following result (with standard errors in parentheses):

$$\ln \text{GDP per capita} = 0.35 \quad \ln \text{Enrolment Rate} + 5.23$$
$$\quad\quad\quad (0.12) \quad\quad\quad\quad\quad\quad (0.77)$$

$$R^2 = 0.59$$

The above estimate suggests that 1 per cent increase in enrolment rate raises GDP by 0.35 per cent.

Coming to studies that use data from the second half of the twentieth century and cover a much larger number of countries, mention may be made of a few well-known early studies like Barro (1991), Levine and Renelt (1992) and Mankiw *et al.* (1992), and more recent ones like Krueger and Lindahl (2001), Pritchett (2001), Sala-i-Martin *et al.* (2004) and Cohen and Soto (2007). Out of these, only Pritchett (2001) fails to find a significant effect of education on economic growth.

Barro (1991) uses Penn World Tables data and finds that both primary and secondary enrolment rates have significantly positive impacts on the rate of economic growth (represented by the growth rate of per capita GDP during 1960 to 1985). His regressions also show a negative relationship between education and fertility and a positive relationship between enrolment rates and private domestic investment. These imply that education can indirectly contribute to economic growth by reducing fertility and making private investment more productive. Barro's estimates of the impacts of primary and secondary enrolment rates in 1960 on economic growth are about 0.025 and 0.030 respectively. This implies that a country with a primary enrolment rate of 100 per cent (i.e. 1) in 1960 had a rate of economic growth 1.25 percentage points (0.0125) higher than a country that had a primary school enrolment rate of 50 per cent.

Mankiw *et al.* (1992) proxies investment in human capital by the secondary net enrolment rate multiplied by the fraction of the working age population of secondary school age and finds that the coefficient of this variable is statistically significant. In their regression, the dependent variable is log of GDP per worker in 1985 minus the log of GDP per worker in 1960. Apart from education, the other independent variables used include investment in physical capital whose coefficient is also statistically significant. The magnitude of the impact estimated by this study is higher than in Barro's: a 50 percentage point increase in enrolment rate will lead to an increase in economic growth of about 3.1 percentage points.

On the basis of regression analysis using cross-country data, Gemmell (1996) concludes that educated labour raises not only output, but also its rate of growth.[9] Krueger and Lindahl (2001) find that both the initial stock of human capital and the change in this stock have significant impact on economic growth. Sala-i-Martin *et al.* (2004) finds that primary school enrolment is the 'second most robust variable' (in the sense of frequently emerging as statistically significant) amongst the explanatory factors for economic growth. Likewise, Cohen and Soto (2007) also find a highly statistically significant positive effect of education on economic growth.

Levine and Renelt (1992) run a large number of regressions, and in contrast with the studies mentioned above, find that neither primary school enrolment nor secondary enrolment rates have consistently positive and statistically significant impacts on the rate of economic growth. Pritchett (2001) also finds no significant impact of education per worker on economic growth. He regresses growth rates in GDP per worker on growth of human capital (measured by years of schooling), growth of capital stock and the log of initial GDP per worker.

The examples mentioned above show that although most studies show positive and statistically significant impact of education on economic growth, a few fail to show such impact (or show weak impact). One may therefore ask: what explains such differences in results? A variety of answers to this question is possible.

While regression analysis is useful in establishing causality, a number of issues arise in exercises attempting to examine the relationship between education and economic growth. First, there are issues relating to the measurement of both the dependent and independent variables. As for economic growth, while both GDP growth and per capita GDP growth have been used as indicators, there are studies that have used the level of output/income as the dependent variable. Measurement of education is more complex, and a variety of measures ranging from enrolment rates at different levels, through years and levels of education to expenditure on education have been used. Apart from measurement errors, regression analysis may suffer from other problems of econometric nature that include omitted variables and inadequate specification of models, misspecification of models and endogeneity of variables.[10]

Given the different ways in which both the dependent and independent variables are measured in different studies, and differences in model specifications employed, it is not surprising that different results emerge. Even contradictory results are possible when a model specification omits key variables.

Taking into account the different measures of both growth and education that have been used in the literature and the different methods that have been adopted to estimate the effect of education on growth, a very useful synthetic review of the relevant literature has been undertaken in Hawkes and Ugur (2012). They synthesize 33 empirical papers by using a meta-analysis approach. In order to control for different measures of economic growth and education, the review identifies three measures of growth (GDP growth, per capita GDP growth and TFP growth) and nine different measures of education (including enrolment rates, years of schooling and levels of education). Three tools of meta-analysis were applied in synthesizing the results: (1) fixed-effect weighted means of the estimates reported in each study; (2) random-effect weighted means of the estimates reported by a group of studies nested/clustered within consistent measures of education and economic growth; (3) precision-effect test (PET) for testing whether the random effect weighted means can be considered as reliable measures of a statistically significant relationship between education and economic growth.

Applying the above mentioned tools to the 33 studies selected, the Hawkes and Ugur (2012) study concludes that human capital does have a positive and genuine effect on economic growth in low income countries. The estimates of the effect of education and skills on economic growth give an increase varying from 0.4 to 24 per cent per unit of education or skill investment. The variation in the impact is found to be related to the proxy for human capital used with the largest effects found when the measure of education is the proportion of population with a set level of education while the smallest effect found when average years of schooling is used.

In most of the studies mentioned above, education has been measured in terms of quantity, e.g. years of schooling or levels of educational attainment. Not much effort has been made to incorporate the qualitative aspect of education. But in order to make an impact on productivity of workers and on output, it is the quality of education and training that is more important. A study by OECD (2010) attempts to incorporate the quality aspect of education into the analysis of the link between human capital and economic growth by using scores/indices of cognitive skills developed by its Programme for International Student Assessment (PISA).[11] Using the composite measure of cognitive skills obtained from the 2003 survey data on schooling for 1960 and annual growth of GDP per capita during 1960–2000 for 23 OECD countries, the following regression estimate was obtained:

$$G = -3.54 - 0.30 \text{ GDP/cap } (1960) + 1.74\,C + 0.025\,S$$
$$\quad (2.0) \qquad\qquad (5.8) \qquad\qquad (4.2) \quad (0.3)$$

$$R^2 = 0.83$$

where G is average annual growth of GDP per capita during 1960–2000,
GDP/capita is per capita GDP in initial year (1960) to test for convergence,
C is composite measure of cognitive skills,
S is years of schooling in 1960.

The figures within parentheses represent the respective t-values.

The above mentioned regression equation shows that cognitive skills have a statistically significant impact on economic growth. But the impact of years of schooling is not significant, though positive.

OECD (2010) reports a similar exercise covering 50 countries of the world (including countries from the developing regions) and finds that variation in the growth of GDP per capita during 1960–2000 is closely related to differences in cognitive skills. In fact, the plotting of regional growth in real per capita GDP against average test scores shows regional growth rates falling on a straight line. That result shows the importance of the quality of education across countries irrespective of the level of development. However, this should not be interpreted to mean that schooling is not important. In fact, schooling can contribute greatly to the development of cognitive skills and also the ability to absorb higher levels of education and training. What is important to note is that from the point of contributions to economic growth, in addition to years of schooling and certificates obtained, the quality of education is critical.[12]

The empirical evidence on the relationship between cognitive skills and economic growth and the results of studies showing that primary education is not always associated with higher rate of return compared to higher levels of education indicates the importance that needs to be attached to the quality of education as well as higher levels of education. While basic literacy and primary education can be looked at as the minimum required for modern sectors of an economy, as an economy grows and aims at higher levels of development, its labour force must be equipped with better quality and higher levels of education. In this context, one may even question the utility of regarding universal primary education by itself a 'development goal' unless the qualitative aspect is introduced. The question becomes particularly important in view of the wide variation in the quality of education and the spread of low quality education observed in low income countries.

Education and poverty

Channels of transmission

Although the role of education in promoting economic growth does not seem to be in doubt, from the point of view of inclusive development, a number of other issues become important. First, what is the role of education in reducing poverty and inequality? This question would also bring in the issue of access of the poor to good quality education. Second, as will be discussed presently, employment is an important mechanism through which education can contribute to a reduction of poverty and inequality. Hence, it would be important to examine the relationship between education and employment. This issue will be discussed in the next section.

Education can contribute to poverty reduction both directly and indirectly (see Figure 6.1). The most direct channel works at the levels of individuals and households via improvement in the ability and productivity of those in the labour force which, in turn, helps raise incomes of individuals as well as households. As incomes of households increase, they are able to spend more on the education of children which in turn helps raise the productivity and earnings of the future generation of workers and reduce poverty further.

The indirect effects of education on poverty at the individual and household levels work through a variety of channels that include:

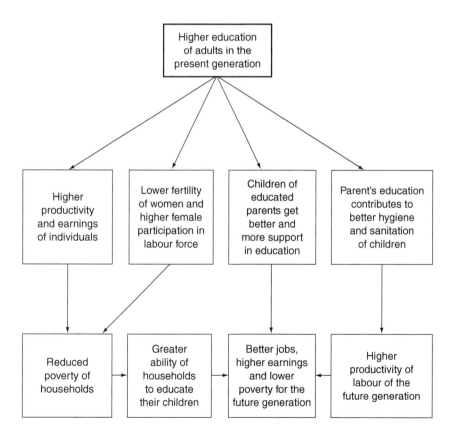

Figure 6.1 Linkage between education and poverty at the individual and household levels.

- Reduction of women's fertility which in turn helps raise female participation in the labour force and increase incomes of households.
- Parental education (especially women's education) leads to greater awareness about and attention to hygiene and nutrition of children, thus contributing to improvements in their health, productivity when they become adults. That enables them to access better jobs and raise incomes for themselves and their households, leading to reduction of poverty amongst the future generation.
- Children of educated parents are likely to get better support from their parents in pursuing their education and thus perform better at school. When they enter the labour force, they are likely to be able to access better jobs with higher earnings compared to children of uneducated parents.

In addition to benefits at the individual and household levels, education can confer benefits at the community and national levels which may contribute indirectly to poverty reduction (Palmer *et al.*, 2007). There are a variety of channels through which this may happen. A community may benefit from educated individuals when they:

- provide services to the community by becoming teachers, doctors, etc.;
- create enterprises that provide employment to others;
- send remittances to family members who have remained behind;
- introduce better technology/practices in farming and other economic activities that may be imitated by neighbours and other members of the community, etc.

Benefits of more educated population at the national level include:

- higher productivity of better educated labour force;
- creation of a conducive environment for investment in activities requiring higher levels of education and skill of the workforce;
- rise in incomes of a larger number of households may broaden the tax base of the country and contribute to an increase in revenues of the government which, in turn, can improve their ability to spend on social services for the poor.

Empirical evidence on the link between education and poverty

The link between education and poverty may work both ways: while education makes an important contribution to poverty reduction (as discussed above), poverty may also affect access to education and the quality of education received. Given this simultaneity, application of econometric methods becomes complicated. There is nevertheless a good deal of empirical evidence from a number of country level and cross-country studies that lend support to the contention that education can have significant positive effect on poverty at the household level.

Notable in this regard are the country studies on Bangladesh, Bolivia, Ethiopia, India, Indonesia and Vietnam presented in Islam, R. (2006b). It may be useful to recount some of the empirical evidence available in those studies.

In Bangladesh (in 1999–2000), nearly 57 per cent of the poor never went to school while the corresponding share of the non-poor was about 29 per cent. At the other end of educational attainment, 3.4 per cent of the poor had secondary and equivalent level of education while 15 per cent of the non-poor had that level. Likewise, amongst the poor, only 1 per cent were graduates while nearly 10 per cent of the non-poor were in this category. Moreover, logistic regression of the probability of being poor carried out in that study showed that education of the head of household as well as of working members has a statistically significant negative effect on the probability of being poor. The result was obtained separately for rural and urban areas (Rahman and Islam, 2006).

In Bolivia (in 2001), strong correlation was found between educational levels of workers and their real earnings, especially in urban areas. Workers with university level education had the highest real income as well as the highest rate of growth of real income, whereas workers with no education had the lowest real income. The incidence of poverty was also found to be closely linked to educational levels: those with no education had the highest level of poverty (over 60 per cent). The corresponding figure for those with university degrees was only 10 per cent. The same result was found for rural areas also, although the earnings differential between workers with various levels of education was lower compared to the urban areas. Regression analysis also showed that educational level of the head of household had a statistically significant effect on the probability of being in poverty (Jemio and Choque, 2006).

In Ethiopia (1999–2000), in rural areas, male adult literacy was found to have a statistically significant positive effect on per capita consumption in rural areas. The effect of adult males who completed primary education was also positive though not statistically significant. In the urban areas, literate adult males, literate adult females and adult females who completed secondary education had statistically significant positive effect on per capita consumption. As in rural areas, adult males with primary education had a positive effect which was not statistically significant (Demeke *et al.* 2006).

In India (1993–94), amongst the poor households in rural areas, nearly 71 per cent were illiterate whereas the corresponding figure for the non-poor households was about 50 per cent. In the urban areas, the figures were 47.5 and 17.5 per cent respectively. The contrast in urban areas was greater for those with above secondary education. Less than 4 per cent of the poor households had above secondary education whereas 27 per cent of the non-poor had that level. Regression exercise for one state (Madhya Pradesh) showed that education of working members of the household had a statistically significant negative effect on the probability of the household being poor. The result showed that a 10 percentage point rise in the proportion of workers with secondary or higher level of education would lower the probability of a household being poor by 3.5 per cent (Sundaram and Tendulkar, 2006).[13]

In Indonesia (1999), the incidence of poverty was found to decline monotonically with level of education. Mean schooling for the poor and non-poor was 6 and 7.4 years respectively. The incidence of poverty was 47.5 per cent for households whose workers had no schooling, and only 13 per cent in the case of households with workers having secondary education. For households with tertiary education, the incidence of poverty was only 2 per cent (Islam, I., 2006).

In Vietnam (1997–98), probit regression showed statistically significant effect of education of the head of household as well as of average years of schooling of adult members in the household on poverty (in separate models). A one-year increase in attending school by the head of household would result in reduction of the probability of the household being in poverty by one percentage point. Likewise, a one-year increase in the average years of schooling of adult members of the household would reduce the probability of the household being poor by 3 percentage points (Huong *et al.*, 2006).

Empirical evidence is also found to support the hypotheses of indirect effect of education on poverty discussed earlier and depicted in Figure 6.1. As for the impact of parent's education on the education of children (and thus the level of education of future generations), a study on Bangladesh (Rahman, 2006) finds statistically significant impact of the education of both the head of household as well as the wife of the head on enrolment at primary as well as secondary level enrolments (in separate regressions). In fact, the impact of wife's education is found to be stronger in the case of primary enrolment. These results point to strong intergenerational impact of education. The same study also finds that poverty of households has strong negative effect on enrolment at both primary and secondary levels. It also points out that poverty induced exclusion from education occurs more at the primary level and due to a variety of reasons (e.g. small amount compared to needs, late disbursement, etc.); stipends have only a limited effect on ameliorating the situation.

Going beyond country studies, Islam, R. (2006a) shows with cross-country regression analysis that education has a statistically significant effect on the incidence of poverty. Adult literacy rate is found to have a significant negative effect on poverty, and 42 per cent of the country level variation in the incidence of poverty is explained by this variable alone.[14]

Education and inequality

The literature on economic development has long recognized the effect of education on income inequality.[15] Although popular notion may regard education as a means of reducing inequality, theoretical studies point out that the relationship between education and inequality may be ambiguous. For example, the human capital model of income distribution that stems from the work of Becker, Mincer and Schultz implies that the distribution of earnings (and income) is determined by the level and distribution of schooling across the population. While the model predicts a positive relationship between educational inequality, as measured by the variance of schooling, and income inequality, the effect of increased average years of schooling on income inequality may be either positive or negative, depending on the evolution of rates of return to education. This is because of the operation of two different types of effects of education, the 'composition' effect and 'wage compression' effect (Knight and Sabot, 1983).

The composition effect refers to change in the size of the population with education. As the share of the educated population in a developing country is low at the early stages of development, more education would initially tend to increase income inequality because of the advantage that the educated would get in the labour market. However, as the supply of educated labour increases, the premium on education would decline, thus setting off the wage compression effect, which in turn would lower inequality. Thus the net effect of education at any point would depend on the relative strength of the composition and wage compression effects. Gregorio and Lee (2002) explains this further by using a formal expression to express variance in income as being dependent on variance in schooling, rate of return to schooling (r), the average years of schooling (S), and the covariance between rate of return and average years of schooling. If the rate of return and schooling level are independent, an increase in the level of schooling would increase inequality. However, if the covariance between rate of return and schooling is negative, as is often found to be the case, increase in schooling can reduce inequality. Inequality in the access to schooling also plays an important role in whether education would reduce or accentuate income inequality.

As for empirical evidence on the effect of education on inequality, early studies (reported in Gregorio and Lee, 2002) showed that higher level of schooling by and large reduces inequality, although inequality in educational attainment increases it. Using data on income distribution and education for 100 countries over the period of 1960 to 1990, Gregorio and Lee (2002) provide useful empirical evidence on how education and income relate to inequality. Their findings indicate that 'educational factors – higher attainment and more equal distribution of education – play some role in changing income distribution' (Gregorio and Lee, 2002, p. 413). They also argue that the small quantitative effects of educational expansion on income distribution are due in part to the impact of educational expansion on inequality of educational attainment in the population.

A meta-regression analysis (Abdullah *et al.*, 2011) covering 64 empirical studies that report a total of 868 estimates of the effects of education on income inequality finds that education affects the two tails of income distribution, reduces the income shares of the top earners and increases the share of the bottom earners, but has no effect on the share of the middle class. So, the impact of education on inequality as a whole may be ambiguous. Like Gregorio and Lee (2002), Abdullah *et al.* (2011) also finds that inequality in access to education leads to higher income inequality. Moreover, secondary education appears to be more important in reducing income inequality than primary education. These findings may have useful implications for policies aimed at improving income distribution. One obvious strategy has to be to undertake policies that can ensure equitable access to education, or even better, provide the poor with greater access to education. Furthermore, rather than focusing only on expansion of primary education (which may be useful from the point of view of universal primary education), attention needs to be devoted to higher levels of education and skills. As will be discussed in the next section, post-primary education can be important from the point of view of improving the employability of people in countries that are at a slightly higher level of economic development than low income countries.

Interesting evidence on the role of education on income inequality comes from the experience of Latin American countries, some of whom witnessed declines in inequality during the 2000s. A number of studies reviewed by Torre and Messina (2013) show that there has been a reduction in income inequality after 2003. According to this study, a dominant factor contributing to the reduction of income inequality at the household level is the reduction in labour related incomes. In trying to understand what lies behind the decline in labour earnings, they consider return to skills as an important factor. An examination of the evolution of the returns to different levels of education for a number of countries of the region leads them to conclude that they moved in tandem with the Gini for labour related income increasing till 2002–03 and falling thereafter. The conclusion that emerges is that an important explanation for the post-2003 decline in income inequality in Latin America is the reduction in the skill premium, measured indirectly through the returns to education.

Education and employment

Education, employment and mobility in the labour market

Better educated and trained people have a greater probability of being employed because education and training can raise qualifications and make labour force more productive. This should be reflected in (1) a higher rate of employment, measured, for example, by the ratio between employed and working age population, and (2) a lower rate of unemployment for those with higher levels of education. But such a positive relationship between education and employment may hold better in situations where the labour market as a whole seeks educated people and sectors that are larger and grow at higher rates seek more educated workers. This may not be the case in developing countries where labour markets are often found to be segmented and the educated find jobs only in certain segments of the economy.

For example, in a dual economy with a predominantly traditional segment that consists of agriculture and allied activities, educated workers are likely to find jobs only in the modern sector which is typically small, especially at the early stages of development. Such sectors may not require many educated workers, except perhaps in research, extension service, etc. Likewise, construction, traditional crafts and other informal sector activities also may not require formally educated and trained workers. As an economy grows, the modern sector is also likely to grow in size, thus raising demand for a more educated and skilled workforce. Hence, in developing countries, one may not find a clear positive relationship between education and employment in terms of the simple indicators mentioned above.

How, then, is the importance of education for the labour market of developing economies likely to be manifested? As mentioned above, with economic growth, a dual economy is likely to witness expansion of its modern sectors which in turn is expected to lead to increased demand for educated and skilled labour. In such a situation education and skill training would be important to facilitate mobility of workers from the traditional to the modern segments of the economy. Likewise, developing countries are expected to witness changes in the composition of labour force in terms of the status of employment, for example, from casual workers in agriculture to regular wage and salaried workers in manufacturing and other modern sectors. This may also imply a greater demand for more educated people. All these developments are likely to mean higher wages and earnings of workers with more education.

As for empirical evidence, it will be shown in Chapter 7 that while there is a negative relationship between average years of schooling and youth unemployment rate in developed countries, for developing countries the opposite is the case. For overall employment also, a positive relationship is found between education and employment in developed countries. A study on OECD countries (OECD, 2011) finds that 84 per cent of the population with tertiary education is employed, and it falls to 74 per cent for people with upper secondary and post-secondary non-tertiary education. For those without upper secondary education, the figure goes down to just above 56 per cent.

In OECD countries, an upper secondary education is typically considered the minimum needed to be competitive in the labour market. The average unemployment rate among those who have completed this level of education is close to 5 percentage points lower than among those who do not have (OECD, 2011).

Coming to developing countries, it will be seen in Chapter 7. that in contrast with developed countries, the relationship between unemployment amongst the youth and average years of schooling is positive. This apparently perverse result may not appear very surprising if one remembers the observations made above about the nature of the labour market in such countries, especially the segmented nature of the labour market and the demand for educated labour being limited mainly to the modern sectors of an economy. In such a situation, an expansion of education, especially at the secondary and tertiary levels may not correspond directly with the demand for the products. This becomes clear from country level data on unemployment by levels of education. For purposes of illustration, such data for Bangladesh, India and Malawi are presented in Figures 6.2, 6.3 and 6.4.

For Bangladesh, if one ignores the inexplicable dip in the rate of unemployment for degree holders, one can see a positive relationship between the rate of unemployment and level of education: those with higher education suffer from higher rate of unemployment! The relationship is similar in the case of India and Malawi, with of course some variation in details. In India, the rate of unemployment is particularly high for diploma/certificate holders. But more significantly, those with secondary and tertiary education suffer from higher unemployment

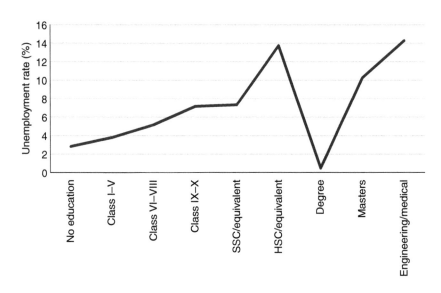

Figure 6.2 Bangladesh: unemployment rate by level of education (source: constructed by using data from BBS (2011)).

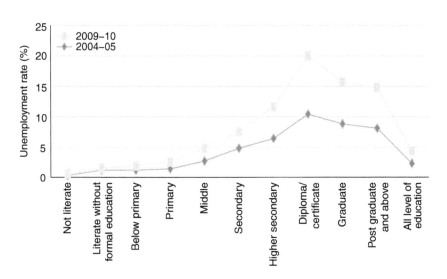

Figure 6.3 India: unemployment rate by level of education (source: constructed by using data from the National Sample Survey data reported in Government of India (2013)).

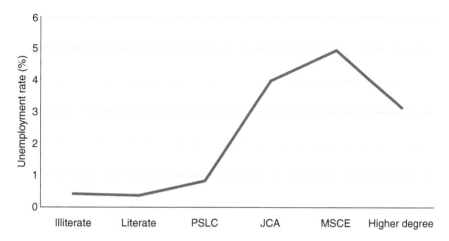

Figure 6.4 Malawi: unemployment rate by level of education (source: prepared by using data from Castel *et al.* (2010)).

rates than those who are illiterate or have only primary education.[16] In Malawi also, those with degree and secondary education face higher unemployment rates than the illiterate and primary education holders. Do these data imply that education is not of much use in employment? Why then is there so much demand for higher education? In order to understand this, it may be useful to look at some more data relating to employment and education.

Table 6.3 presents data on the distribution of various sectors' employment by level of education as well as the share of the sectors in total employment for Bangladesh. It is clear from this data that employment in the major sectors of the economy like agriculture, trade, manufacturing and construction is dominated by workers who are either illiterate or have less than primary education. On the other hand, sectors where the proportion of employment with secondary and higher levels of education is high (say at least 20 per cent), e.g. electricity and gas, information and communication, professional and scientific work, administration including public administration, education, real estate, financial services, etc. account for very small proportions of total employment. In the circumstances, it is possible to hypothesize that those with secondary or higher levels of education would look for work outside sectors like agriculture, transport, construction, etc. and keep waiting until they find a job that matches their aspiration. And that, in turn, may, at least partly, explain the observed relationship between education and unemployment. Education – especially secondary and higher level – is most likely being used as a mechanism for getting jobs in the modern sectors of the economy.[17]

That education may provide a means of another type of mobility is indicated by data on the distribution of employment by status and level of education for Bangladesh that are presented in Table 6.4. It may be noted from that data that

Table 6.3 Bangladesh: distribution of employed persons (15 years and over) by sector and level of education, 2010

Industry	Total	No education	Class I–V	Class VI–VIII	Class IX–X	SSC	HSC	Degree and higher	Share in total employment (%)[a]
Agriculture, forestry and fishing	100	46.5	23.3	13.0	9.0	5.0	2.1	1.1	47.56
Manufacturing	100	35.4	26.0	17.1	9.0	6.5	3.1	2.9	12.47
Electricity, gas, etc.	100	8.2	11.6	32.4	13.2	12.1	10.3	12.2	0.18
Water supply, sewerage, etc.	100	38.2	15.0	27.1	2.4	3.4	0	14.0	0.05
Construction	100	46.3	28.7	13.4	5.7	2.7	1.6	1.4	4.84
Wholesale and retail trade	100	36.1	22.9	15.0	9.9	8.3	4.1	3.7	13.97
Transportation and storage	100	53.9	24.3	10.9	5.0	3.2	1.6	1.0	7.36
Hotel and food	100	35.9	31.2	13.6	10.1	5.3	1.9	2.0	1.54
Information, and communication	100	10.2	10.1	38.5	5.6	10.6	7.7	17.5	0.10
Financial services	100	4.0	7.2	13.7	9.2	9.9	16.7	39.3	0.67
Real estate	100	26.4	20.5	11.2	14.0	14.1	3.0	10.8	0.06
Professional, scientific and technical	100	13.4	11.4	9.7	8.5	17.4	8.3	31.3	0.21
Administration and support services	100	6.2	5.1	16.7	11.3	15.3	15.9	29.5	0.90
Public administration	100	5.4	3.6	27.0	11.7	21.6	15.1	15.8	1.0
Education	100	6.0	2.6	10.0	5.1	12.6	17.8	45.9	2.38
Health and social work	100	17.5	11.0	13.7	10.4	13.3	13.7	20.3	0.80
Other services	100	26.2	26.8	19.7	11.7	6.5	3.3	5.8	4.36
Total	100	40.8	23.0	14.1	8.7	6.0	3.4	4.0	100

Source: Bangladesh Bureau of Statistics (2011).

Note
a The figures in this column do not add up to 100 because some minor sectors like mining and quarrying, recycling, entertainment and recreation, household employment, etc. have not been included in the table.

Table 6.4 Bangladesh: distribution of employed persons by status in employment and education, 2010

Status in employment	Total	No education	Class I–V	Class VI–VIII	Class IX–X	SSC	HSC	Bachelor degree	Master	Technical and vocational
Regular paid employee	14.6	5.1	10.1	21.9	17.1	27.4	40.6	63.0	70.7	48.7
Employer	0.2	0.2	0.2	0.1	0.3	0.3	0.6	0.7	0.9	0
Self-employed (agr)	22.8	28.6	21.3	17.4	19.8	19.0	15.9	10.0	6.1	7.5
Self-employed (non-agr)	18.0	17.7	19.5	16.7	15.9	19.3	17.9	15.8	23.6	24.2
Unpaid family worker	21.8	16.9	23.9	27.7	34.9	25.8	18.6	9.3	0	16.3
Irregular paid worker	2.7	1.9	3.3	3.6	3.5	3.4	3.8	2.4	0	3.3
Day labourer (agr)	10.7	17.0	10.6	5.6	3.7	2.5	1.7	0	0	0
Day labourer (non-agr)	8.9	11.7	11.0	6.9	4.9	2.7	1.7	0	0	0

Source: authors' compilation from BBS (2011).

for those who have no education or less than primary level, the major categories of employment are self-employment and day labourer in both agriculture and non-agriculture. On the other hand, even for those with just secondary education, regular paid employee accounts for the highest share followed by unpaid family work. For this level of education, the share of day labourer and other irregular paid worker is very low (and falls drastically compared to those with no or primary education). If one looks at those with post-secondary level education, the share of regular paid employee shows a big jump (nearly two-thirds or more for those with degree and higher level education). Thus it seems that education provides one with entry to salaried jobs, and one perhaps is willing to accept a period of unemployment in order to get one. Moreover, the fact that the rate of return to education is quite significant, and in some cases is found to be higher for higher levels of education, implies that it must be economically worthwhile to accept a period of unemployment.

Data on relationship between education and employment status in Malawi (Table 6.5) shows a broadly similar pattern as observed for Bangladesh. More than three-quarters of the illiterate workers are engaged in agriculture. The share engaged in agriculture declines monotonously with the level of education, but remains over 50 per cent even for those with junior certificate. However, this figure drops sharply for those with school certificate (i.e. secondary education). Over 58 per cent with that level of education are engaged in wage employment. For those with higher degress, the proportion in wage employment is over 77 per cent. The role of education in enabling people to move away from agriculture to other sectors and espeically to wage employment is clear.

Apart from mobility in terms of the sector and status in employment, education also brings direct income benefit which is already apparent from the rate of return estimates. The income premium due to education can be seen by direct comparison of incomes associated with different levels of education. Data on Malawi and Tanzania (Tables 6.6 and 6.7 respectively) should serve to illustrate the point. In Malawi, for example, education at each level yields an income premium ranging from 44 per cent between literates without primary level certificate and those with primary certificate to a staggering 200 per cent difference

Table 6.5 Malawi: distribution of employed persons by status in employment and level of education, 2004–05

Level of education	Farmer	Self-employed	Casual	Wage employment	Total
Illiterate	77.8	8.9	7.5	5.3	100
Literate	70.0	14.0	6.9	8.8	100
PSLC	65.3	16.3	4.8	12.8	100
JCE	51.0	15.2	3.7	26.1	100
MSCE	18.1	16.1	2.3	58.5	100
Higher Degree	10.0	7.8	1.6	77.4	100
Total	68.8	12.4	6.5	11.43	100

Source: adapted from Castel *et al.* (2010).

Table 6.6 Tanzania: mean monthly income (in Tshs) of paid employees and self-employed by educational attainment, 2006

Education	Mean monthly income of paid employees	Difference between the previous level of education (%)	Mean monthly income of the self-employed	Difference between the previous level of education (%)
Never attended school	40,134	n.a.	48,920	n.a.
Primary not completed	45,777	14.1	48,394	–1.1
Primary completed	67,462	47.4	82,060	69.6
Secondary and above	207,433	207.5	129,494	57.8
Total	98,454	n.a.	75,693	n.a.

Source: authors' compilation from URT (2006).

Table 6.7 Malawi: median hourly income (in Malawi Kwacha) by educational attainment, 2004–05

Level of education	Median hourly income	Difference between the previous level of education
Illiterate	7.2	n.a.
Literate (no degree)	10.9	51.4
PSLC	15.7	44.0
JCE	22.7	44.6
MSCE	38.5	69.6
Higher degree	115.4	199.7
Total	15	n.a.

Source: Adapted from Castel *et al.* (2010).

between secondary certificate and higher degrees. Similar differences can be seen in the case of paid employment in Tanzania. Data on Tanzania shows that the education premium can be earned in self-employment also, although the difference is much lower than in paid employment.

Evolution of education and skill requirement with economic growth

Two types of changes take place in the structure of economies that experience growth. First, changes occur in the sector composition of the economy through shifts in the relative contribution to GDP and employment of various sectors like agriculture, manufacturing, construction, trade, transport and services. Second, changes also take place within sectors. For example, the composition of manufacturing changes as the share of simple labour intensive industries declines and that of more capital and skill intensive industries increases. Likewise, the composition of the service sector may also change towards more modern sectors like banking, insurance, communication, and personal and social services, etc. During the early stages of economic development, it is the first type of structural change that is likely to predominate while in the subsequent stages, structural changes may be more within sectors.

In line with the structural changes outlined above, education and skill requirements of an economy are also likely to vary depending on its stage of development. For most jobs at the early stages of economic development (when traditional sectors like agriculture and simple manufacturing predominate), primary and secondary education may be adequate. For example, farmers with such education may be able to adopt new technologies and farming methods. Likewise, for production workers in simple manufacturing like textiles and garment making, food processing, etc., primary or secondary education may be adequate for them to be able to undergo necessary skill training.

As for skills, in economies at early stages of development, most jobs involve routine manual work that require more cognitive skills and less of thinking and creativity. But as an economy grows into higher levels of development, the porporation of jobs that require some thinking and higher level skills starts rising. As a result, the need for workers with post secondary educaiton and vocational and technical skills grows.

An illustration of how the nature of jobs and skills requirement of an economy changes is provided by the figures presented in Tables 6.8 and 6.9. In the US economy, during the last 30 years of the twentieth century, the proportion of blue-collar workers declined from over a third to a quarter. On the other hand, the proportion of technicians, professionals and managers increased substantially from less than a quarter in 1969 to a third in 1999. Jobs relating to sales and services also increased. This obviously had implications for skill requirements. The demand for cognitive skills and routine manual work skills declined while that for expert thinking and complex communication increased. When demand for education and skill requirement undergoes such changes, the education and skill training system of a country has to undergo reforms to be able to cater to the changing demand. How some countries that attained economic growth in recent decades addressed this challenge is illustrated by the experiences of countries like Republic of Korea and Taiwan (China) during the 1970s and 1980s and that of Malaysia since the 1980s.

The Republic of Korea once had a typical labour surplus economy, and the government intervened selectively to promote industrialization. During the early phase of export-oriented industrialization, it benefited from the availability of

Table 6.8 Changing mix of jobs in the US economy, 1969–99

Type of jobs	Percentage of adult employment	
	1969	*1999*
Blue-collar workers	38	25
Administrative and support workers	18	14
Sales related occupations	8	12
Technicians, professionals, managers and administrators	22	33
Service workers	12	14

Source: authors' compilation from Levy and Murnane (2004).

Table 6.9 Changing skills demand in the US economy, 1969–99

Type of skills	Percentage change during 1969–99
Routine cognitive	−7.5
Routine manual	−2.9
Expert thinking	+8.4
Complex communication	+13.5

Source: authors' compilation from Jerald (2009).

workers that had some basic education (as the country had already achieved universal primary education in 1960 (Tzannatos and Johnes, 1997). However, once the surplus was exhausted (by about mid-1970s), the Government embarked on a strategy of structural change towards heavy and chemical industries involving high technology. That created demand for higher level of education and skills.

As in industrialization, the government was also playing an important role in education and training. During the 1960s, it expanded vocational education substantially. However, the formal vocational schools were not in a position to meet the changing demand for skilled human resources that emerged in the wake of structural change in industries. The government responded to the situation by undertaking measures to strengthen technical and vocational education at the secondary level by expanding the number of public vocational training institutes and legally mandating in-plant vocational training in most private enterprises. By enacting a law for vocational training in 1976, large companies in certain industries were required to provide in-plant training for a certain proportion of their employees. Those companies were obliged to pay a training levy if they did not provide in-plant training.[18]

In line with the human resource needs of heavy and chemical industries, the government reorganized five-year junior technical colleges (comprising three years of secondary and two years of post-secondary) into two-year junior vocational colleges directed towards the preparation of technicians and engineers who would be able to perform specific technical tasks in the heavy and chemical industrial fields.

In the 1980s, the government of Korea expanded opportunities for higher education in order to meet social demand. But there was a decline in enrolment in vocational secondary schools and in in-plant training. That resulted in a shortage of skilled workers in industries. Faced with that and in order to meet the changing demand, the Government introduced various measures to strengthen the vocational education and training system. The target was to increase the enrolment of vocational senior secondary schools and increase the the enrolment ratio of general versus vocational senior secondary schools from 68:32 to 50:50 by 1995.

Based on the performance of the reforms mentioned above, further reforms in the vocational education and training system were undertaken during the 1990s. In addition, private companies began to emphasize skill upgrading for their workers while placing less emphasis on the initial training for workers prior to employment. What is clear from the various reforms introduced by the government of Korea and efforts by the private sector is that there was awareness about the changing skill requirements and steps were being taken to respond to the changes.

Taiwan (China) provides another good example of how the education and skill training system was modified to respond to the changing demand for education and skills as the country went through various stages of development. When industrialization started, the country benefited from an initial high literacy rate. As the composition of the industrial sector started changing during the 1960s, the government's emphasis shifted from compulsory primary education to compulsory secondary education.[19] Total expenditure on education increased from 2.1 per cent of GNP (11 per cent of the budget) in 1955 to 4.6 per cent of GNP (20 per cent of the budget) in 1970. Expenditure per student increased sixfold between 1960 and 1975.

When the economy was about to face a scarcity of skilled workers, emphasis was given to vocational training as opposed to academic education at the secondary level. As the share of labour in the non-agricultural sector started increasing, vocational training increased sixfold between 1966 and 1974. Only 40 per cent of Taiwan's high school students were in the vocational track in 1963; by 1972, the figure had risen to 52 per cent and, by 1980, to almost 70 per cent. It is thus clear that, as in the Republic of Korea, there was awareness in Taiwan about the changing nature of demand for human capital and the government responded flexibly by shifting the emphasis of the structure of education to keep it in line with the changing needs of the economy (Ranis, 1995, p. 524).

Malaysia is another country that attained rapid economic growth and underwent significant structural changes since the early 1980s. How those changes got reflected in the structure of employment and occupations are captured by data presented in Tables 6.10 and 6.11. A few aspects of changes on the sector composition of employment are clear from Table 6.10. First, there has been a sharp decline in the share of agriculture. Second, and as is common with countries experiencing economic growth, the share of manufacturing increased initially and then declined. Third, the share of finance, real estate and various services increased substantially.

Some idea of how the shift in the structure of employment got reflected in the occupational structure can be obtained from data presented in Table 6.11. As expected, the share of agriculture declined sharply from over a third to a little

Table 6.10 Malaysia: sector composition of employment, 1982–2010

Sector	1982	1990	2000	2010
Agriculture and fishery	31.17	26.0	16.74	13.25
Manufacturing	15.54	19.94	23.45	16.89
Construction	7.20	n.a.	n.a.	9.16
Trade	16.40	n.a.	n.a.	16.24
Transport	4.25	n.a.	n.a.	4.77
Finance and real estate	3.85	n.a.	n.a.	7.29
Community, social and personal services	19.95	19.88	21.69	39.26
Total	100	100	100	100

Source: Department of Statistics, Government of Malaysia (2013).

Notes
Columns may not add up to 100 because some small sectors, e.g. mining, have been excluded from the table.
The sector classification has been changed somewhat in 2000. Hence the figures for comunity, personal and social services for 2010 may not be strictly comparable to those of earlier years under the same category.

Table 6.11 Malaysia: percentage share of employment by major occupational groups, 1980–2010

Occupational groups	1980	1990	Occupational groups	2000	2010
Administration/ management	1.7	2.4	Senior officials and managers	6.9	7.5
Professionals and technicians	6.7	8.8	Professionals	5.8	6.3
			Technicians/associate professionals	12.0	14.7
Clerical workers	8.2	9.8	Clerical workers	9.6	10.1
Service and sales workers	9.7	11.5	Service and sales workers	13.0	16.8
			Craft and related trade workers	9.1	11.7
Production workers and technicians	28.5	27.6	Plant and machine operators and assemblers	16.1	11.7
Agriculture and fishery	35.7	28.3	Agriculture and fishery	15.0	11.3

Source: Department of Statistics, Government of Malaysia (2013).

over 11 per cent. Likewise, the share of production workers also declined after an initial period of economic growth (i.e. since the 1990s). Occupations that registered substantial increase in their share include administrators and managers, professionals and technicians, service and sales workers and skilled workers (the last indicated by the increase in the share 'craft and related trade workers'). There has thus been a clear change in the structure of occupations, first, from agriculture to production workers (presumably in manufacturing), and then to more knowledge and skill oriented occupations.

How did policy makers in Malaysia respond to the changes in education and skill requirements that came along with the changes in the structure of employment and occupation described above? As in the Republic of Korea, the Government of Malaysia undertook steps to expand post-secondary education including vocational education and training. The result was a shift in the composition of the labour force from one of predominance of primary educated to that of secondary and tertiary educated (Table 6.12). In 2011 nearly one in four members of the labour force had tertiary education compared to just over 6 per cent in

Table 6.12 Malaysia: distribution of labour force by educational attainment, 1982–2011

Level of education	1982	1990	2000	2010
No formal education	15.44	9.60	5.57	3.17
Primary	41.92	33.79	24.91	16.86
Secondary	36.52	24.91	55.05	55.46
Tertiary	6.11	16.86	14.47	24.51

Source: Department of Statistics, Government of Malaysia (2013).

1982 and less than one in ten in 1990. The proportion with secondary education increased to 55 per cent in 2000 and has remained at that level since then.

It needs to be noted, however, that an increase in the proportion of labour force with secondary and tertiary education does not tell the whole story because the key question is what type of qualifications within those categories are needed in the economy and whether the education system of the country is capable of meeting that requirement. If fragmentary evidence is taken as an indicator, there is a mismatch between the supply of and demand for graduates in Malaysia. One study (Fleming and Soborg, 2012, p. 14), quoting data from the Ministry of Higher Education, reports that 50 per cent of the graduates in 2006 and 2007 had difficulty finding employment, and 28 per cent remained unemployed after one year of graduating, while another 27 per cent went for further studies and re-training or were still waiting for jobs. The country thus faced the typical situation of employers having difficulty finding the right skills while graduates remained unemployed. That, in turn, created difficulties in the country's transformation process from a middle income to higher income status and from a producer of basic industrial products to one producing high technology products.

The report of the National Economic Advisory Council titled *New Economic Model for Malaysia* (NEAC, 2010) recognized the problem mentioned above as the 'middle income trap', and underscored the need for a shift in the approach to education from 'rote learning' to 'creative and critical thinking' because an advanced economy needs more of the latter kind of skills. The report also pointed out the importance of skill upgrading through continuous education and training and suggested partnership between industry and government in attaining that goal. It may be recalled in this context that the Republic of Korea also adopted a policy of private sector participation in skill training when the economy moved from labour intensive manufacturing to heavy and chemical industries.

The need for emphasis on different levels (and types) of education in different economies is also illustrated by the projections of gap between demand and supply of human resource with various levels of education in China and India (Table 6.13). Projections for the year 2020 made by McKinsey Global Institute

Table 6.13 Projected demand and supply of manpower with different levels of education, China and India, 2020 (million)

Level of education	Demand	Supply	Gap (%)
China			
Tertiary	140	117	−16
Secondary	509	514	+1
Primary	172	192	+10
India			
Tertiary	68	74	+8
Secondary	133	120	−10
Primary	319	346	+7

Source: authors' compilation from McKinsey Global Institute (2012).

(2012) and presented in Table 6.13 point out interesting differences between the two countries that might otherwise seem to be at similar level of development. While China is projected to experience a shortage of human resource with tertiary education, India is projected to experience an excess of human resource with that level of education but a shortage of secondary level qualification. What is, however, common between the two countries is that they will have excess supply of primary educated human resource. It thus seems to be clear that both countries need to move beyond producing human resource with just basic education because they need higher level of education and skills. With respect to post-primary education, India appears to need an expansion of secondary education more than its tertiary education. This may reflect two phenomena: while demand for human resource with secondary education may be growing at high rates, there may already have been a rapid expansion of tertiary education compared to what the economy can absorb. In China, the opposite may have happened, and the country now needs to move more towards expansion of tertiary education.

Concluding observations

The data and analysis presented in this chapter should enable one to draw a few conclusions regarding the relationship between the requirement of human resource with different levels of education and skills at different levels of development. First, at the early stage of economic development of a country, basic education may be adequate for many of the jobs that may open up in segments of the economy that register high growth (e.g. manufacturing, construction and services). However, as an economy attains higher levels of development and the composition of the sectors attaining higher growth changes, the requirements of education and skills are also likely to change. On the side of general education, there would be a growing need for people with post-primary and post-secondary education. On the side of skills, requirements evolve from basic cognitive skills to the ability to think and create. A country's education and skill development system must undertake reforms to gear itself to meeting such changing requirements. Experience also shows that there may often be a tendency to simply expand higher education or vocational education without due regard to the type of education and skills for which demand is expanding. The result often is unemployment of the educated. A careful exmaination of the factors responsible for such a situation may show that that is more due to the expansion of education and training that is not required rather than due to the inadequacy of education itself.

Notes

1 The term human capital may be conceptualized in a broad sense to include education, skills and health of workers that determine their overall ability. However, in the present context, education and skill of a worker will be used as a surrogate for human capital; and hence, these terms will be used interchangeably.

2 World Bank (1993) points out that education and skill development played an

important role in the high rate of economic growth achieved by the countries of East and South East Asia region during the 1970s and 1980s.

3 Kuznets (1966), for example, pointed out that for developed countries, only a portion of economic growth can be explained by the growth in the quantity of capital and labour, and that quality of the inputs is one major explanatory factor of the unexplained residual.

4 There is a large body of literature on the contribution of human capital to economic growth. An excellent survey is provided by Schultz (1991). For an exposition of how human capital can be incorporated in growth models, see Ray (1999).

5 Drèze and Sen (2013) enumerate a number of ways in which education plays a role in process of development and social progress that include ability to communicate better and be better informed, giving a voice, especially to women, tackling the health problem, providing greater access to economic opportunities and reducing inequality.

6 This is the famous Mincerian wage equation (due to Mincer, 1974) that postulates wage as a function of years of education, years of work experience and ability of an individual. At the micro level, private rate of return to education can be estimated by regressing an individual's income on the level of education and other characteristics.

7 For formal expositions of these two approaches and references to the relevant literature, see Stevens and Weale (2003).

8 For surveys, see Glewwe *et al.* (2007); Hanushek and Woessmann (2008); Hawkes and Ugur (2012); Stevens and Weale (2003), among others.

9 The role of education in improving cognitive skills is demonstrated in a number of other articles in the *Oxford Bulletin of Economics and Statistics*, vol. 58, no. 1, Special Issue on 'Human Capital in Economic Development'.

10 See Glewwe *et al.* (2007) for a more detailed list of possible econometric problems that may lead to biased estimation of parameters in regression analysis.

11 The OECD launched the PISA programme in 1997 as a means of monitoring the outcomes of the education systems in terms of student achievement within an internationally agreed common framework. Tests cover mathematics, science and reading for three different age groups: primary education (age 9/10), lower secondary education (age 13–15) and the final year of secondary education (generally grade 12 or 13). For details of the methodology and the data, see OECD (2010).

12 By showing that the number of per capita patent applications is positively related with PISA scores in Mathematics, Filho (2013) argues that the quality of education helps innovation and economic growth.

13 Another study (Tilak, 2006), based on cross-section regression with state level data on India, found a significant relationship between poverty ratio and the proportion of adults with secondary or higher level of education in different Indian states. Interestingly, that study found that mere literacy or primary education does not contribute to poverty reduction.

14 The regression mentioned here uses data from 38 developing countries. The figures for poverty incidence are for a year between 1991 and 2000 while the literacy figure is for 1995. It may be noted that the regression equation with poverty incidence as the dependent variable and adult literacy as the independent variable was estimated by using the OLS method and the issue of simultaneity between the variables was not addressed.

15 Notable in the early literature are Adelman and Morris (1973); Ahluwalia (1976); Chenery and Syraquin (1975).

16 A positive relationship between the rate of unemployment and level of education is found for Sri Lanka as well. See World Bank (2012).

17 It is also possible that educational attainment acts as a proxy for socio-economic background, where higher educational attainment is correlated with individuals from relatively well-off backgrounds. Given that social protection systems, such as unemployment benefits are not widely available in developing countries, one could argue

that individuals with higher educational attainment can 'afford' to be unemployed, while those with poorer educational background cannot.

18 This mandate initially applied to firms with more than 500 employees, and the number was gradually reduced to 150 and 100 in 1991 and 1995 respectively. For further details, see KRIVET (n.d.).

19 The data presented in this and the next paragraph are from Ranis (1995).

Bibliography

Abdullah, A.J., Doucouliagos, H. and Mannin, E. (2011) *Education and Income Inequality: A Meta-Regression Analysis*, Deakin University, Melbourne.

Ahluwalia, M.S. (1976) 'Inequality, Poverty and Development', *Journal of Development Economics*, vol. 6, pp. 307–342.

Adelman, I. and Morris, C.T. (1973) *Economic Growth and Social Equity in Developing Countries*, Stanford University Press, Stanford.

Barro, R. (1991) 'Economic Growth in a Cross-Section of Countries', *Quarterly Journal of Economics*, vol. 106, no. 2, pp. 407–444.

BBS (Bangladesh Bureau of Statistics) (2011) *Report of the Labour Force Survey 2010*, Government of Bangladesh, BBS, Dhaka.

Behrman, J.R. (1990) *Human Resource Led Development? Review of Issues and Evidence*, ILO-ARTEP, New Delhi.

Blaug, M. (1976) 'Human Capital Theory: A Slightly Jaundiced View', *Journal of Economic Literature*, vol. 14, no. 3, pp. 827–855.

Castel, V., Phiri, M. and Stampini, M. (2010) *Education and Employment in Malawi*, Working Paper No. 10, African Development Bank, Tunis.

Chadha, G.K. (2003) *What is Dominating the Indian Labour Market? Peacock's Feathers or Feet?* Presidential Address, 45th Annual Conference of the Indian Society of Labour Economics, 15–17 December 2003.

Chenery, H.B. and Syraquin, M. (1975) *Patterns of Development, 1950–1970*, Oxford University Press, London.

Cohen, D. and Soto, M. (2007) 'Growth and Human Capital: Good Data, Good Results', *Journal of Economic Growth*, vol. 12, no. 1, pp. 51–76.

Demeke, M., Guta, F. and Ferede, T. (2006) 'Ethiopia: Growth, Employment, Poverty and Policies', in Islam, R. (ed.): *Fighting Poverty: The Development-Employment Link*, Lynn Rienner, Boulder and London.

Drèze, J. and Sen, A. (2013) *An Uncertain Glory: India and its Contradictions*, Princeton University Press, Princeton and Oxford.

Filho, N.A.M. (2013) 'Education and Human Capital', in Cazes, S. and Verick, S. (eds) *Perspectives on Labour Economics for Development*, ILO, Geneva.

Flemming, D. and Soborg, H. (2012) *Malaysian Skills Development and the Middle Income Trap*, Department of Society and Globalisation, Roskilde University, Denmark.

Gemmell, N. (1996) 'Evaluating the Impact of Human Capital Stocks and Accumulation on Economic Growth: Some New Evidence', *Oxford Bulletin of Economics and Statistics*, vol. 58, no. 1, pp. 9–28.

Glewwe, P., Maiga, E. and Zheng, H. (2007) *The Contribution of Education to Economic Growth in Sub-Saharan Africa: A Review of Evidence*, Mimeo, Department of Applied Economics, University of Minnesota.

Government of India, Planning Commission (2013) *India Twelfth Five-Year Plan (2012–17), Social Sectors, Vol. III*, Delhi.

Government of Malaysia, Department of Statistics (2013) *Labour Force Survey Time Series Data, 1982–2011*, Putrajaya, Malaysia.

Gregorio, J.D. and Lee, J-W. (2002) 'Education and Income Inequality: New Evidence from Cross-Country Data', *Review of Income and Wealth*, Series 48, no. 3, pp. 395–416.

Hanushek, E.A. and Woessmann, L. (2008) 'The Role of Cognitive Skills in Economic Development', *Journal of Economic Literature*, vol. 46, no. 3, pp. 607–668.

Hawkes, D. and Ugur, M. (2012) *Evidence on the Relationship between Education, Skills and Economic Growth in Low-Income Countries: A Systematic Review*, EPPI Centre, Social Science Research Unit, Institute of Education, University of London, London.

Huong, P.L., Tuan, B.Q. and Minh, D.H. (2006) 'Employment-Poverty Linkages and Policies for Pro-Poor Growth', in Islam, R. (ed.) *Fighting Poverty: The Development-Employment Link*, Lynn Rienner, Boulder and London.

Islam, I. (2006) 'Indonesia: Poverty, Employment and Wages', in Islam, R. (ed.) *Fighting Poverty: The Development-Employment Link*, Lynn Rienner, Boulder and London.

Islam, R. (2006a) 'The Nexus of Economic Growth, Employment and Poverty Reduction: An Empirical Analysis', in Islam, R. (ed.) *Fighting Poverty: The Development-Employment Link*, Lynn Rienner, Boulder and London.

Islam, R. (ed.) (2006b) *Fighting Poverty: The Development-Employment Link*, Lynn Rienner, Boulder and London.

Islam, R. (2010) 'The Role of Human Resource in Sustaining Economic Growth in South Asia', in Alam, M. and Barrientos, A. (eds) *Demographics, Employment and Old Age Security: Emerging Trends and Challenges in South Asia*, Macmillan India, New Delhi.

Jemio, L.C. and Choque, M. (2006) 'Bolivia: Employment-Poverty Linkages and Policies', in Islam, R. (ed.) *Fighting Poverty: The Development-Employment Link*, Lynn Rienner, Boulder and London.

Jerald, C.D. (2009) *Defining a 21st Century Education*, Centre for Public Education, available at: www.centerforpubliceducation.org/Main-Manu/Policies/21st-Century/Defining-a-21st-Century-Education-Full-report-PDF.pdf (accessed 10 August 2013).

Knight, J.B. and Sabot, R.H. (1983) 'Educational Expansion and the Kuznets Effect', *American Economic Review*, vol. 73, pp. 1132–1136.

KRIVET (Korea Research Institute for Vocational Education and Training) (n.d.) *Reform and Innovation of Technical and Vocational Education in the Republic of Korea*, Seoul.

Krueger, A. and Lindahl, M. (2001) 'Education for Growth: Why and for Whom?', *Journal of Economic Literature*, vol. 39, no. 4, pp. 1101–1136.

Kuznets, S. (1966) *Modern Economic Growth: Rate, Structure and Spread*, Yale University Press, New Haven, CT.

Levine, R. and Renelt, D. (1992) 'A Sensitivity Analysis of Cross-Country Growth Regressions', *American Economic Review*, vol. 82, no. 4, pp. 942–963.

Levy, F. and Murnane, R.J. (2004) *The New Division of Labour: How Computers are Creating the Next Job Market*, Russell Sage Foundation, Princeton, New Jersey.

Mankiw, G., Romer, P. and Weil, D. (1992) 'A Contribution to the Empirics of Economic Growth', *Quarterly Journal of Economic Growth*, vol. 107, no. 2, pp. 407–437.

McKinsey Global Institute (2012) *The World at Work: Jobs, Pay and Skills for 3.5 Billion People*, available at: www.mckinsey.com/insights/employment_and_growth/the_world_at_work (accessed 9 August 2013).

Mincer, J. (1974) *Schooling, Earnings and Experience*, Columbia University Press, New York.

NEAC (National Economic Advisory Council) (2010) *New Economic Model for Malaysia, Part I, Strategic Policy Directions*, NEAC, Putrajaya.

OECD (Organisation for Economic Co-operation and Development) (2010) 'The High Cost of Low Educational Performance: The Long-run Economic Impact of Improving PISA Outcomes', OECD Programme for International Student Assessment, Paris. Available at: www.oecd.org/pisa/44417824.pdf (accessed 28 July 2013).

OECD (Organisation for Economic Co-operation and Development) (2011) 'How Does Education Affect Employment Rates?', in *Education at a Glance 2011: Highlights*, OECD Publishing, Paris. Available at: http://dx.doi.org/10.1787/eag_highlights-2011–16-en (accessed 5 August 2013).

Palmer, R., Wedgwood, R. and Hayman, R. (2007) *Educating out of Poverty? A Synthesis Report on Ghana, India, Kenya, Rwanda, Tanzani and South Africa*, Centre for African Studies, University of Edinburgh, Edinburgh, and DFID, London.

Pritchett, L. (2001) 'Where has All the Education Gone?', *World Bank Economic Review*, vol. 15, no. 3, pp. 367–391.

Psacharopoulos, G. (1985) 'Returns to Education: A Further International Update and Implication', *Journal of Human Resources*, vol. 20, no. 4, pp. 583–604.

Psacharopoulos, G. (1994) 'Returns to Education: A Global Update', *World Development*, vol. 22, pp. 1325–1343.

Psacharopoulos, G. and Patrinos, H.A. (2004) 'Returns to Education: A Further Update', *Education Economics*, vol. 12, no. 2, pp. 111–134.

Ray, D. (1999) *Development Economics*, Oxford University Press, Delhi, Oxford, New York.

Rahman, R.I. (2006) *Access to Education and Employment: Implications for Poverty*, PRCPB Working Paper No. 14, Bangladesh Institute of Development Studies, Dhaka and Institute for Development Policy and Management, Manchester University, Manchester.

Rahman, R.I. and Islam, N. (2006) 'Bangladesh: Linkages among Economic Growth, Employment and Poverty', in Islam, R. (ed.) *Fighting Poverty: The Development-Employment Link*, Lynn Rienner, Boulder and London.

Ranis, G. (1995) 'Another Look at the East Asian Miracle', *The World Bank Economic Review*, vol. 9, no. 3, pp. 509–534.

Sala-i-Martin, X., Doppelhofer, G. and Miller, R. (2004) Determinants of Long-Term Growth: A Baysian Averaging of Classical Estimates (BACE) Approach', *American Economic Review*, vol. 94, no. 4, pp. 813–835.

Schultz, T.P. (1991) 'Education Investment and Returns', in Chenery, H. and Srinivasan, T.N. (eds) *Handbook of Development Economics*, North-Holland, Amsterdam.

Stevens, P. and Weale, M. (2003) *Education and Economic Growth*, National Institute of Economic and Social Research, London.

Sundaram, K. and Tendulkar, S.D. (2006) 'India: Employment-Poverty Linkages and Policy Options', in Islam, R. (ed.) *Fighting Poverty: The Development-Employment Link*, Lynn Rienner, Boulder and London.

Tilak, J. (2006) *Post-Elementary Education, Poverty and Development in India*, Working Paper Series No. 6, Centre for African Studies, University of Edinburgh, Edinburgh.

Torre, A. and Messina J. (2013) *The Trend Reversal in Income Inequality and Returns to Education: How Bad is This Good News for Latin America?*, available at: www.voxeu.org/article/trend-reversal-income-inequality-and-returns-education-how-bad-good-news-latin-america (accessed 24 March 2013).

Tzannatos, Z. and Johnes, G. (1997) 'Training and Skills Development in East Asian Newly Industrialised Countries: A Comparison and Lessons for Developing Countries', *Journal of Vocational Education and Training*, vol. 49, no. 3, pp. 431–453.

URT (United Republic of Tanzania) (2006) *Report of the Integrated Labour Force Survey 2006*, Dar Es Salaam.

World Bank (1993) *The East Asian Miracle*, Oxford University Press, London.

World Bank (2012) *World Development Report 2013: Jobs*, World Bank, Washington, D.C.

7 Youth employment

Introduction

It has already been argued in Chapter 2 of the present volume that productive employment has to be a major element of inclusive economic growth. It has also been pointed out that economic growth in many parts of the developing world has been associated with low and declining employment intensity. And that provided a strong justification for strategies and policies for making economic growth more employment intensive. Why, then, does one need to devote special attention to the issue of youth employment?[1]

First, it is well known that unemployment rates are much higher among the youth compared to overall and adult unemployment rates – and this is true of developing countries as well.

Second, young men and women may face special difficulties in transiting from the world of learning to the world of work. This may not be a development issue as such, in the sense that similar problems may be faced in countries irrespective of the level of development. However, in situations where levels of economic growth are either low or unstable and opportunities for productive employment remain inadequate even with high and stable growth, it is important to understand such specific difficulties that may burden youth with additional disadvantages.

Third, while there are costs associated with unemployment itself, costs associated with youth unemployment may have implications for an economy in terms of missing the potential demographic dividend. This is an important issue in that development literature includes this as a factor that could contribute to economic growth in developing countries.

Fourth, the delay in entering the labour market and unemployment during the early phase of one's life and career is likely to have a 'scarring effect' on longer-term employment and earnings prospects of the youth. This would represent a cost not just for an individual but also for the economy and society as a whole in terms of lost productivity, earnings, tax revenue and other contributions to the economy.

Hence, a strategy for making economic growth more inclusive needs to include an understanding of why youth unemployment is so high and explore what special measures are needed to address the problem in addition to those that are required to promote the growth of productive employment as a whole. The present chapter purports to undertake this task. It is organized as follows.

The next section presents some data to demonstrate that youth unemployment is much higher than overall and adult unemployment. The data presented would also show that the situation worsened during and in the wake of the global economic crisis of 2008–09. The discussion in this chapter deals with the costs associated with youth unemployment, as well as their potential scarring effects. The chapter also provides an overview of various factors that may be responsible for youth unemployment. Finally, the chapter reviews strategies, programmes and policies undertaken in response to the challenge of youth unemployment with a view to examining what has worked better.

Youth unemployment rate: levels and trends

Even when an economy functions normally, the youth face disadvantages in the labour market and tend to be more vulnerable to unemployment than adults. Unemployment amongst the youth is normally found to be two to three times higher than that for adults. The situation tends to become worse during periods of economic downturns, not least because young people may be the first ones to be laid off when labour markets face a decline in demand. Apart from retrenchment, an important way in which labour markets adjust to lower demand is through reduced hiring of new workers. And that is why when the youth face the adverse effects of an economic downturn, the transition from education to the world of work becomes much more difficult in such a situation.

An ILO report (ILO, 2010, p. 4) states:

> At the peak of the crisis period, the global youth unemployment rate saw its largest annual increase ever. The youth unemployment rate rose from 11.9 to 13.0 per cent between 2007 and 2009. Between 2008 and 2009, the rate increased by 1 percentage point, marking the largest annual change over the 20 years of available global estimates and reversing the pre-crisis trend of declining youth unemployment rates since 2002.

(See Figure 7.1.) Globally, the youth unemployment rate was 12.1 per cent in 2008, compared to 5.8 per cent for total unemployment rate and 4.3 per cent for adult unemployment rate (see Figure 7.2). Thus, the ratio of youth-to-adult unemployment rate was 2.7 in 2009, implying that the youth were almost three times more likely to be unemployed than adults (see Table 7.1).

For OECD countries, the ratio of youth-to-adult unemployment rate increased from 2.4 in 1998 to 2.8 in 2008, thus pointing to a worsening of the situation. Between the fourth quarter of 2008 and the corresponding period of 2009, the youth unemployment rate for this group of countries registered a rise of 5.9 percentage points compared to 2.5 percentage points rise for total unemployment (Scarpetta *et al.*, 2010).

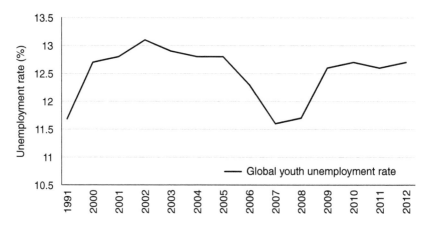

Figure 7.1 Global youth unemployment rates, 1991–2012 (source: prepared by the authors using data from ILO (2012c)).

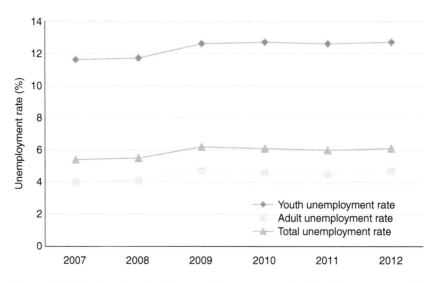

Figure 7.2 Global youth and adult unemployment rates, 2007–12 (source: prepared by the authors using data from ILO (2012c)).

As for developing countries, ILO data (ILO, 2010: Table A5, p. 63) indicate some variation between regions. The rise in youth unemployment rate in 2009 appears to be the sharpest for Latin America, with Sub-Saharan Africa at the other extreme showing no increase in the rate. Other regions, i.e. East Asia, South East Asia and South Asia, experienced small increases in youth unemployment rates. However, it may be noted in this context that as in the case of adults, the impact of the global economic downturn on youth employment in

Table 7.1 Youth unemployment rate in different regions, 2009

Region	Youth unemployment rate (%)	Ratio of youth to adult unemployment
World	13.0	2.7
Developed Economies and European Union	17.7	2.5
Central and South Eastern Europe (non-EU) and CIS	20.8	2.5
East Asia	8.9	2.6
South-East Asia and the Pacific	14.7	5.0
South Asia	10.3	3.1
Latin America and the Caribbean	16.1	2.7
Middle-East	23.4	3.8
North Africa	23.7	3.7
Sub-Saharan Africa	11.9	1.9

Source: authors' compilation from ILO (2010).

developing countries may have been felt more in the form of underemployment, precarious employment or employment in the informal economy. Indeed, ILO (2010) mentions that the impact has been felt more in shorter hours, reduced wages, increase in casual labour and in an increasingly crowded informal economy.

Costs of youth unemployment

Scarring effects on individuals and cost to families

The most obvious and immediate cost of unemployment to the individual is the foregone earnings. But the cost to the individual goes beyond the loss of earnings during the period of unemployment. There can be a long-run 'scarring effect' of the inability to transit smoothly into the labour market. Scarring means that the mere experience of unemployment increases the risk of future unemployment and can have an adverse effect on future earnings. This can happen through (1) the human capital channel, e.g. through a deterioration of skills and foregone work experience, and (2) the 'signalling effects': periods of unemployment conveying a signal of low quality and productivity to potential employers. The longer the unemployment spell lasts, the more individual productivity may be affected. Likewise, the lower the level of initial qualification, the longer the scarring effects are likely to last (Scarpetta *et al.*, 2010).

There are studies[2] pointing out that joblessness at an early stage of life can negatively affect the youth's long-run earnings prospects and job opportunities. Those who suffer unemployment in the early part of their life are more likely to suffer subsequent spells of unemployment. Students graduating during recession start work with lower paying employers and only slowly manage to make transition to better paying firms. Such negative wage effects may persist for more than a decade. For example, a study on the UK showed that an extra three months of unemployment before age 23 led to an extra two months out of work between ages 28 and 33. Several studies also show the adverse effects of lost work experience on future wages. Unemployment immediately upon graduation from college is associated with substantial future earnings losses (Scarpetta *et al.*, 2010).

Furthermore, high youth unemployment also leads to higher incidence of unhappiness, mental health problems and higher incidence of crimes of various kinds. Bell and Blanchflower (2011) find evidence that spells of unemployment while young often create permanent scars through its harmful effects on a number of outcomes – happiness, job satisfaction, wages and health – many years later.

Unemployment of the youth from lower income and disadvantaged families is likely to have an adverse effect on the family's resources, and hence on the overall welfare of such families. Youth unemployment is also reported to contribute towards increasing income inequality (Morsy, 2012).

Cost to the economy

Costs of youth unemployment are not limited to individuals and families. High and persistent youth unemployment can impose significant costs to the economy which, in turn, can arise from at least two different sides. The first is cost to public finance that would include: (1) cost of welfare benefit payments to the unemployed; (2) the loss of tax revenues engendered by the underutilization of human resources; (3) lower contribution to national insurance payments.

The second broad element of cost to the economy would take the form of lower than potential output represented by the difference between the current and potential output had the youth labour force been fully employed. Cost to the economy may also arise from lower productivity and efficiency of the youth when they get employed after a period of unemployment.

Estimating the cost of youth unemployment

The process of estimating the cost of youth unemployment can be divided into four stages: (1) identification and outline of the possible elements of costs;[3] (2) attaching cost estimates to these elements; (3) estimating the number of people experiencing the various elements of cost; (4) estimating the total costs by using the cost elements and cost per person.

Estimates of the cost of youth unemployment are available for developed countries like Canada, USA, UK and other EU countries. For example, Schwerdtfeger (2013) uses estimates of long-term 'wage penalties' (a term used to refer to the scarring effect mentioned above) suffered by those who experience a spell of youth unemployment to gauge the potential aggregate earnings losses in a group of European countries, Canada and the USA. The estimated impact varies from a high of 12 per cent of GDP in Ireland to 1.3 per cent for Canada and the

USA. For countries like Greece and Spain, the estimates are lower than for Ireland but are quite significant. Likewise, estimates for 26 EU countries (Eurofound, 2012) indicate that the cost increased from 1 per cent of GDP in 2008 to 1.21 per cent of GDP in 2011. The increase clearly reflects the impact of the increase in youth unemployment in the wake of the global economic crisis of 2008–09.

According to one estimate for UK, the net present value of the cost to the Treasury, even looking only a decade ahead, is approximately GBP28 billion (ACEVO Commission on Youth Unemployment, quoted in Matsumoto *et al.*, 2012).

But the situation does not have to be as described above. Instead of counting the costs of youth unemployment, with appropriate policies and effective action, it should be possible to benefit from the youth population and their participation in the labour market. Many countries, especially in the developing world, have the potential to reap the demographic dividend from an increase in the proportion of working age population. Labour being an important factor of production, effective utilization of this factor can make a significant contribution to economic growth, especially if the quality can be enhanced through appropriate investment in human capital. For example, World Bank (2007) refers to a study attributing more than 40 per cent of the higher growth in East Asia over Latin America during 1965–90 to the faster growth of its working age population and better policies for trade and human capital development. There are country level studies (for example, James, 2008, on India) providing evidence of growth in working age population having a significance influence on GDP growth.[4]

The demographic dividend mentioned above could also be converted into a 'youth dividend' with appropriate targeting of policies and action to integrate the youth into the labour market more effectively than has been the case. But in order to be able to do so, it would be necessary to have a good understanding of the factors that are responsible for the high level and persistence of youth unemployment.

Causes of youth unemployment

The fact that youth unemployment rates are usually much higher than adult unemployment rates indicates that there must be some specific reasons for youth unemployment. Of course, some factors, e.g. low growth of an economy and low employment intensity of growth, are common to both adult and youth unemployment. But the youth face special difficulties in making entry into labour markets and in staying there when labour markets adjust to sharp downturns in economy. From a policy point of view, it is essential to understand the factors that are common to youth and adult unemployment as well as those that are specific to the former.

The debate on the causes of youth unemployment revolves around two broad strands of analysis. One line adopts a structural and supply side view and argues that the problem arises out of a lack of appropriate education and skills of workers on the one hand and rigidities in the labour market on the other.[5] The other line argues that youth unemployment is due mainly to the pace and pattern of growth that results in inadequate employment growth. The first of these approaches has become popular amongst policy makers at the country level as well as at the level of international organizations, not least because it is easy to derive policy and action needed to respond to the education and skill deficit and mismatch.

As for the relationship between education and skills on the one hand and youth unemployment on the other, evidence from developed countries seems to be quite clear: As educational attainment increases, the incidence of unemployment decreases. This comes out of a number of studies by the OECD reported in ILO (2012c). For example, the employment rate for young persons aged 15–29 who left school with an upper secondary education is significantly higher than the rate for young persons who left school with no diploma. However, in low and middle income countries, there appears to be a reverse relationship. Countries with longer average years of schooling tend to have higher youth unemployment rates.[6] One could of course point out that education by itself may not guarantee access to jobs because of possible mismatch between the type of education and skills obtained by the young persons and the requirements of the labour market.[7]

Another factor that is often cited as responsible for high youth unemployment relates to rigidities in the labour market in the form of high minimum wages and high severance pay. This view argues that regulations relating to the labour market discourage employers from hiring young persons as the cost of employing them becomes too high. For example, one study (Yasser, 2011, quoted in Matsumoto *et al.*, 2012) attributes the high rate of youth unemployment in the Middle East and North Africa to the overly rigid labour market regulations. However, studies by the ILO (IILS, 2012) find that the impact of employment protection legislation on employment is rather weak. The relationship between labour market regulations and employment is found to be non-linear, with both too lax and excessive regulations leading to poor employment outcomes. Another study (Matsumoto *et al.*, 2012, p. 10) shows that both among high income and low middle income countries, 'youth unemployment rates are only minimally and insignificantly associated with the average level of minimum wages'. The same study points out that the relationship between youth unemployment and labour market regulations is complex and diverse across countries, especially in low and middle income countries, and it is not possible to judge the implications of such regulations for youth employment.

Based on regression analysis with pooled cross section and time series data covering both high income and low and middle income countries, the above mentioned study comes to a number of interesting conclusions. First, youth unemployment is negatively associated with the share of labour force with tertiary education at the 10 per cent significance level. In low and middle income countries, there is no statistically significant relationship between secondary school enrolment and youth unemployment rate. Hence, increasing skills via higher education may not be the most effective policy tool to combat youth unemployment. On the demand side, youth unemployment is negatively associated with investment at the 1 per cent significance level (for both groups of countries). Investment, in turn, is a negative function of the cost of credit (real rate of interest), the share of debt in GDP and the current account balance. That youth unemployment is closely related to the overall economic and employment situation becomes clear from another piece of evidence: a strong positive correlation between youth unemployment rate and overall unemployment rate. With regression analysis based on cross-section data on G20 countries, ILO (2012b) finds that in 2010 adult unemployment rate explains 58 per cent of the variation in youth unemployment rate. That study also found a similar relationship for the same group of countries for the period 1990–2010. The evidence mentioned above relating to the influence of overall employment situation and of investment and GDP growth indicates the importance of aggregate demand as a factor influencing youth unemployment.

If low aggregate demand leading to low output and employment growth is a factor that is responsible for overall and adult unemployment as well as for youth unemployment, what is different for the youth? First, the youth often face special difficulties in entering the labour markets. Studies on school-to-work transition[8] show that while long periods of transition are quite common, for some transition never ends in success. While long periods of job search are common even in times of normal economic activities, the situation becomes worse during periods of economic downturns. Quite often, the youth end up in jobs which they do not find satisfactory either in terms of wages/salaries or in terms of the nature of work. Second, the youth themselves may 'shop around' and change jobs before settling down in a job. Thus frictional unemployment may be higher for the youth. Third, the youth may be more vulnerable to economic fluctuations, and they may be the first ones to be fired when a recession starts. Employers may find it less costly to fire the youth compared to the adult both in terms of the severance pay involved and loss of skill.

To conclude this brief overview of evidence relating to the causes of youth unemployment and labour market barriers faced by the youth, it may be mentioned that while factors operating from both supply and demand side play an important role, there are factors that may not fall neatly into either of these categories. On the demand side, the important factors are slow and volatile economic growth, low (and in some cases, declining) employment intensity of growth, and reluctance in hiring the youth. On the supply side, the relevant issues include mismatch between educational qualifications and the requirements of the labour market, mismatch between training provided and skills required on the job, and inadequacy of training on the job. Matching of the demand for and supply of workers is an area of weakness, especially in developing countries. In the absence of appropriate career guidance, counselling and information about labour markets, the youth face difficulty in judging the prospects of career in different fields and in making the right choice regarding the field of study.

Youth unemployment and national development strategies

Given the seriousness of the youth unemployment problem and its implications, it is natural for the issue to receive attention at the political and policy making levels. The attention and priority given to the issue is evident in the policy pronouncements (in the form of national plans, development strategies and other policy documents) in various countries. Of course, there is a good deal of variation in the manner in which the issue is treated, i.e. whether priority is expressed in terms of concrete action, measurable targets and monitoring and evaluation of progress. Various assessments and reports by the ILO provide valuable information and insight in these respects.

A review by the ILO of policy frameworks of 138 countries (ILO, 2012b) shows that since 2005, there has been an increasing commitment at the country level to place youth employment in national policy agendas. As for Poverty Reduction Strategies that became major vehicles of articulating development strategies and qualifying for external assistance, while the issue was nearly absent in the first round, nearly half of the second generation strategies contain youth employment as a strategy. Similar conclusions were reached by several other ILO surveys undertaken since 2010. Most countries are reporting inclusion of youth unemployment in their policy priorities. Nearly 30 per cent of the 138 countries mentioned above have an explicit youth employment policy or strategy, while many others have articulated youth employment provisions in their youth development policies. But the way youth employment is prioritized varies from country to country. While some countries make it a cross-cutting theme in their policy framework, others treat the issue through specific sectors and measures.

National youth employment action plans represent another vehicle for expressing the commitment to address the challenge of youth unemployment. These plans aim to ensure coherence between youth employment measures included in various policies and to identify clear youth employment priorities and measurable outcomes using specific resources within a given time frame. By 2012, only 35 countries had formally adopted such action plans.

The ILO review mentioned above (ILO, 2012b) concludes that national policies and programmes on youth employment generally concentrate on supply side measures, with skill development receiving major attention. Interventions to increase the demand for young workers are less frequent. This bias reflects either a bias in viewing the youth unemployment problem as mainly a supply side issue or simply the adoption of measures that appear more visible and targeted. However, the brief review of the causes of youth unemployment presented in the earlier section brought out clearly that both demand and supply side factors are responsible for the phenomenon, and hence measures are needed to tackle both sides of the problem. Indeed, inadequate demand for young workers was a problem even before the global economic crisis when the global economy was experiencing high rate of overall economic growth. It has become even more serious in the wake of the Great Recession that came in the wake of the global economic crisis. Hence, a more balanced strategy would be essential if a significant dent were to be made into this formidable problem.

Employment policies to address the challenge of youth unemployment

The analysis of the causes of youth unemployment presented in a previous section made it clear that both demand and supply side factors are responsible for the problem. Stimulating demand and putting employment at the centre of macroeconomic policies are essential for creating employment in general and for the youth in particular. Macroeconomic and sectoral policies can play an important role in influencing the pattern of growth which in turn is important for making growth job-rich. On the supply side, education and training that equips the youth with skills and work experience can contribute to improving their employability.

Experiences with employment policies adopted during previous crises provide useful lessons that could be utilized in formulating necessary policies and strategies to address the current challenge. Apart from macroeconomic and sectoral policies, active labour market policies as a whole can be very useful. Measures to mediate between labour supply and demand can mitigate inadequacies of the education and training system and the failure of the labour market. Assistance in job search and job matching can help the youth find jobs and the employers find the required work force. Training and retraining programmes can enhance the employability of disadvantaged youth, especially if they are combined with on-the-job learning opoprtunities. Support for self employment and entrepreneurship can be helpful in situations where the growth of wage employment lags behind the growth of the labour force. Such support can be more effective if it is combined with skill training and help in accessing credit.

During the global economic crisis of 2008–09 and in subsequent years, the above mentioned measures were adopted by various countries in varying degrees (Table 7.2). A number of countries introduced employment subsidies for hiring young people in the form of contributions to salary, waivers to social security contributions and tax breaks. Apart from general subsidies for hiring the youth which were introduced in many countries, subsidies took several other forms including: (1) bonuses for hiring apprentices and wage subsidy for hiring interns on regular contracts (France); (2) wage subsidy for SMEs; (3) financial support for engaging youth on internship; (4) subsidy/incentive payment for hiring long-term unemployed (UK); (5) tax credit for hiring long-term unemployed (USA). In addition to the measures mentioned above, there are examples of innovative measures undertaken in support of job creation. Examples include (i) the local mentoring project in Sweden and (ii) the Future Jobs Fund of the UK. Under the former, local entrepreneurs and managers in Sweden provide support to the young unemployed in their endeavour to create employment for themselves. In the UK, the part of the Future Jobs Fund is utilized to encourage local authorities and others to create 150,000 new jobs of benefit to the local community.

Table 7.2 Types of youth employment programmes and examples of countries adopting them

Type of programme	Countries
Employment subsidies	Chile, China, France, Greece, Ireland, Republic of Korea, New Zealand, Portugal, Romania, Slovenia, Switzerland, Turkey, UK, USA
Entrepreneurship promotion	Belgium, Belize, China, Greece, Italy, Kenya, Tanzania, Uganda
Public works programme and community services	Bangladesh, Bulgaria, Hungary, Kenya, Pakistan, Poland, Paraguay, Spain, USA

Source: authors' compilation from ILO (2011).

Note
Countries undertaking programmes of skill training and employment services are not mentioned in this table because most countries have such progrmmes.

Many countries sponsored skill development programmes to enhance the employability of disadvantaged youth. A number of countries allocated additional resources for public employment services with a view to strengthening job search assistance and other labour market services. Measures were also undertaken to promote youth entrepreneurship. There are good examples of innovative mechanisms of financing youth entrepreneurship (see Box 7.1). Public works programme and community support services were introduced in a number of countries.

Box 7.1 Innovations in Financing Youth Entrepreneurship

There are good examples of innovative mechanisms to finance youth entrepreneurs. One such example is youth-friendly micro finance in Kenya, Tanzania, Uganda and Zimbabwe. In Kenya and Zimbabwe, a project titled Youth Employment Support (YES) provides for skill training combined with micro finance. The latter is provided through building capacity of micro finance institutions, NGOs and youth-led saving and credit cooperatives (SACCOs) to offer financial services to young entrepreneurs who have followed the Start and Improve Your Business modules. The SACCOs promote democratic business institutions that allow youth members to make decisions on major issues like interest rates, repayment period and collaterals to make credit more accessible to young entrepreneurs. In these two countries, the project has been able to create 2,956 jobs (53.6 per cent being women) against the target of 2,000 jobs.

A similar funding mechanism has been tried with good results in two other countries (Tanzania and Uganda) under a project titled Youth Entrepreneurship Facility. Kenya's (largely government financed) programme titled *Kazi Kwa Vijana* (Youth for Work) has a national youth fund to finance youth business and entrepreneurship. It involves engagement with micro finance and other financial institutions to provide credit at repayment rates that the youth can afford. The management and implementation structure of the fund is also led by the youth.

Zimbabwe has an innovative private youth fund provided by a multi-national business entitled 'Old Mutual's US$10 million Kuerra-Ukondla Youth Empowerment Fund'. It is meant to provide funding for youth entrepreneurship development in agriculture, manufacturing and services.

Although the full impacts of the projects mentioned above are not yet known, preliminary results indicate that skill training combined with improved access youth friendly credit can be a catalyst for creating employment for the unemployed youth.

Source: Prepared by the authors using information from ILO (2012d).

In the absence of in-depth evaluations of the effectiveness of various programmes in support of youth, it is not possible to say much about how successful they have been in achieving their goals and which of them have been more successful. However, an ILO report (ILO, 2011) does mention a number programmes as 'examples of successful programmes' (Table 7.3), although nothing is mentioned about the criteria of success used in identifying them as such.[9] However, the above-mentioned ILO note does provide a list of the main features of youth employment programmes that have been more effective. They include:

- Formulation and implementation at early stages of joblessness;
- Design that responds to labour market requirements;
- Targeting and tailoring to individual needs and labour market disadvantages;
- A comprehensive approach providing various services in a package;
- Link to work experiences and involvement of the private sector;
- The involvement of social partners, i.e. employers and workers themselves.

Table 7.3 Selected examples of successful youth employment programmes

Type of programme	Examples of successful programmes
Training	PLANFOR (Brazil); Jovenes Programmes (several countries of Latin America); Employability Improvement Programme (Canada)
Employment services	New Deal for Young People (UK); Active Labour Market Programme (Finland)
Public works and community services	American Conservation and Youth Service Corps (USA); Temporary Employment Programme (Bulgaria)
Employment subsidies	Employment Plan (Belgium); Wage Subsidy Programme (Czech Republic); Works Programme (Poland)
Entrepreneurship promotion	Self-employment Programme (Bulgaria); Youth Entrepreneurship Training amd Microenterprsie Programmes (Peru)

Source: authors' compilation from ILO (2011).

Concluding observations

The world is facing a serious employment challenge which is even more daunting for the youth. While the problem existed even during periods of high growth of the global economy, the Great Recession exacerbated the situaiton. It is true that the developed countries were more affected by the recession and its adverse effect on employment. But the developing countries were not spared, although the timing and the extent of the impact varied depending on the structure of their economies and linkage with the global economy. The labour markets also adjusted through a variety of mechanisms, with quantity adjustment (i.e. increases in unemployment) being only one. Other mechanisms of adjustment include wage rates, hours of work, type of contract employed and composition of employment in terms of sector, status and the degree of formality.[10]

For the youth, the situation was worse. While youth unemployment was much higher than adult unemployment even during normal times, they were worse hit by the recession. And many faced the danger of a 'scarring effect' with long-term impact on their career and earnings. An analysis of the causes of youth unemployment indicates that a variety of factors operating from both the demand and supply sides are in force. Yet strategies and policies adopted at the national level are often found to be biased towards supply side interventions.

Measures of fiscal stimulus were adopted by many countries in response to the shock inflicted by the recession. The size, composition and timing of the packages varied a good deal, and so did their effectiveness. While some contained measures that had good potential to support emplyment alongside economic growth, in other cases, there was no specific focus on employment – the assumption being that revival of growth in output will lead to a recovery of the labour market. There were also cases where measures focused on labour market did not produce the desired result due to inadequacies in the design and implementation of the measures (Islam, R., 2011).

When the global economy started to recover around the middle of 2009, recovery in the labour market did not start simultaneously. As is well-known, labour markets start their recovery with a lag, and there was no exception this time. However, the lag in the start of the recovery in developing countries appeared to be shorter than in other crises.

But the policy stance changed gear soon after the start of economic recovery. Faced with increases in budget deficit and public debt and pressures for cutting deficit and debt, most developed countries adopted a strategy of fiscal consolidation. As a result, growth faltered, and many countries, especially in the Eurozone, faced double-dip recession. The impact on the employment and labour market situation was also felt quickly, and there was a reversal of the nascent recovery. The impact on youth unemployment has been particularly severe.

The employment policies pursued in response to the global economic crisis include (1) macroeconomic policies; (2) policies focused on specific sectors; (3) policies to augment demand for labour; and (4) active labour market policies. A comparison between the percentage of countries that adopted various measures shows some interesting differences and similarities between developed and developing countries. Within fiscal policies, developing countries appear to have relied more on expenditure increase than tax cuts. In monetary policy, a higher percentage of the developed countries relied on cuts in interest rate and quantitative easing. Within sectoral policies similar proportions of both developed and developing countries provided support to manufacturing, construction and export sectors. More developing countries supported agriculture.

As for measures to augment demand for labour, employment subsidy was employed more by developed countries while direct job creation measures were adopted by both groups in similar proportions.

In the area of active labour market policies (ALMPs), more developed countries used public employment service and training both for the unemployed and the employed. Similar proportions (but rather low) in both groups adopted youth training measures. As for subsidy for youth employment, it is mostly the developed countries that adopted this measure. Promoting youth entrpreneurship was used by both group of countries in similar proportions.

It thus appears that higher proportions of developed countries adopted measures requiring budgetary allocations with the exception of direct job creation measures. This is indicative of the constraint of fiscal space faced by developing countries. Promotion of youth entrepreneurship appears to have been used widely for general employment as well as for the youth. And it is in this area that some innovations have also been made, especially in providing access to finance. Moreover, the probability of success with such programmes appears to increase when they are delivered in the form of a package consisting of training, access to finance and other services.

Measures of direct job creation, especially through public works programme, also have been employed in several countries with a degree of success. In fact, such programmes, by acting as an instrument of social protection (in the absence of standard forms of social protection), may also play the role of automatic stabilizers in periods of recession. However, their adoption and success depends on a variety of factors including fiscal space and the institutional capacity and preparedness to design and implement them. Given the limited fiscal space in developing countries, programmes often have to depend on the availability of external resources.

The overview of employment policies provided in the present chapter indicates the alternatives that are available for addressing the general employment challenge as well as the challenge of employment for the youth. One feature that is striking is the extent of reliance on supply side measures (e.g. training, entrepreneurship development) in many countries even though their limitations are clear, especially in developing countries and in the context of slow economic growth and overall demand for labour. Clearly, greater attention needs to be given to augment demand for labour both when economic growth is normal and when there is a downturn. A few points may be worth making in this context.

First, under normal circumstances, demand for labour – at least a large part of it – should be growth-induced. For that to happen, it is essential to have a high rate of growth on a sustained basis, and growth must also be employment friendly. Macroeconomic and sectoral policies can play a vital role in achieving both the above goals. Quite often, macroeconomic stability is regarded as the goal rather than an instrument for achieving the broader goals of economic growth and employment.[11] This needs to change, and the tools of macroeconomic policies would need to be applied with due attention to these broader goals of development.

Second, in applying macroeconomic policies, care has to be taken to ensure that interventions do not distort the structure of incentives and provide wrong signals to entrepreneurs and investors. For example, if the price of capital is artificially lowered and the relative price of capital and labour favours the use of capital rather than labour,[12] the situation would not be conducive to an employment friendly pattern of growth. As mentioned at the outset (and has been corroborated by empirical evidence), it is not only inadequate economic growth but also the pattern of growth that has been responsible for the disappointing employment performance in many developing countries. That, in turn, has been due, at least partly, to the incentive structure that has prevailed. In formulating policies, care has to be taken to avoid that kind of situation.

Then comes the issue of fiscal space for measures like subsidies to preserve exisitng jobs and create new ones, and allocation for direct job creation programmes. Quite often, the absence of fiscal space is looked at in a static context without considering the possibility of creating necessary space for some programme. In reality, careful costing and planning may show that a sizeable programme can be accommodated within a country's own budget – as has been the case with India's Mahatma Gandhi National Rural Employment Guarantee Programme. There may also be situations where the costs of porgrammes may appear beyond the fiscal capacity of a country, yet the revenue generating potential of the country may offer the possibility of creating the necessary space in the budget.[13] What is important is to have the needed political will backed up by administrative machinery for implementing the necessary measures.

If fiscal space is really a constraint, or if a country has to go for fiscal consolidation due to genuine reasons, it should be possible to find fiscally neutral measures for job creation. One example of such a measure (provided by Islam and Chowdhury, 2012) is to make it mandatory for public sector organizations to to hire long-term unemployed youth for a certain period and spend, for this purpose, an equivalent of the unemployment and job search benefit that would have been spent on them. This means that the government, instead of providing unemployment benefits, would become the employer of last resort. Of course, this kind of measure may be applicable mainly to developed countries and those developing countries that have unemployment benefits in place. But there are many developing countries, especially LDCs, where there is no unemployment benefit from where funds can be diverted for use in job creation. In such situations, one would have to look for sectors from where resources could be diverted for this purpose. In identifying sectors for possible reallocation of expenditures, one would have to identify those which have low fiscal multipliers from where resources could be diverted to sectors characterized by high multipliers. One study (IILS, 2012) shows that fiscally neutral change in the composition of expenditures and revenues can lead to the creation of a substantial number of jobs. The direction of change in the composition of expenditure would be different for developing and developed countries. For the former, greater emphasis has to be on public investment and social protection to reduce poverty and inequality. Such measures can augment aggregate demand and lead to higher growth of output and emloyment. For developed countries, the focus should be on ensuring that the unemployed, especially the youth, receive the required support to find jobs.

As for supply side measures, several points are worth noting:[14]

- Strong apprenticeship systems (as exemplified by several countries of Western Europe, e.g. Austria, Denmark, Germany and Switzerland) play an imporant role in keeping youth unemployment low. They can facilitate and smoothen school-to-work transition.
- Anticipation of skill needs and changes therein and adapting training to the requirement is a major challenge in fast changing economic environments. Training providers need to address this challenge in order to narrow the gap between what is required by the labour market and what is produced by the training system.
- Continuous training and upgrading of the skills of the employed and retraining of the unemployed are important areas where all stakeholders – governments, other training providers, employers and workers – need to work together. Effective systems to suit individual countries and sectors need to be put in place.
- ALMPs may not be very useful when an economy is in recession or when output growth is low. However, they can play an important role, especially in mitigating youth unemployment when economic growth becomes healthy and unemployment is caused more by skill mismatch and difficulty in matching demand and supply than by lack of demand.
- Support for entrepreneurship development can be a useful tool for addressing the employment challenge, especially of youth unemployment. But the possibility of success in this area has been found to be greater when the services are offered in a package containing training, access to credit and assistance in linking with markets.

Notes

1 ILO defines 'youth' as those belonging to the age group 15–24 years. This definition is intended to cover the normal period of entry into labour markets. But entry may get delayed due to a variety of reasons, and hence this demographic definition may be restrictive. It is not surprising that there are countries where this standard definition is not used for purposes of data collection or policy.

2 These studies are mostly on developed countries. For example, Bell and Blanchflower (2011) provides quantitative evidence on the UK and USA. For full references, see ILO (2012c) and Matsumoto *et al.* (2012).

3 It may be noted that all elements of costs may not be relevant to all countries. For example, the cost to the treasury in terms of benefit payments to the unemployed would be relevant only for countries where there is unemployment benefit for the unemployed. Likewise, the cost in terms of lower contributions to national insurance payments would apply to countries having such a system. On the other hand, certain cost elements, e.g. lost output and lower tax revenues because of lower than potential output/income, is likely to be applicable to all countries.

4 In addition to providing evidence on India, James (2008) cites a number of studies, cross-country as well as country level, that provide similar evidence.

5 Another supply side factor that is cited is the large size of youth cohort. See, for example, O'Higgins (2001).

6 These countries include Bolivia, Chile, Fiji, Sri Lanka and Swaziland. See Matsumoto *et al.* (2012).

7 World Bank (2012) considers preference for public sector jobs and the limited absorptive capacity of that sector to be the main cause of the problem in a number of countries of the Middle East and North Africa.

8 The ILO has carried out such studies in a number of countries. For a synthesis of those studies, see Matsumoto and Elder (2010).

9 See, also, Caliendo *et al.* (2011) for an empirical analysis of the effectiveness of various elements of active labour market policies in the context of some countries of Europe. For general discussions on active labour market policies, see Auer *et al.* (2005) and Betcherman *et al.* (2001).

10 See Islam, R. (2011) for a more detailed analysis.

11 It is not uncommon to see central banks in developing countries, either on their own or being prompted by IMF, applying restrictive monetary policy to contain inflation irrespective of the factors responsible for it. Likewise, finance ministries are usually under strict vigilance to keep budgetary deficits to predetermined levels like 5 per cent of GDP, as a result of which expenditures are cut with insufficient regard to their impact on growth and employment. For further discussion, see Chapter 3.

12 For examples of such instances, see Islam, R. (2011, 2012).

13 This has been demonstrated in an exercise on Bangladesh (Islam *et al.*, 2011) where it is found that if the country's revenue potential were to be tapped, the necessary fiscal space could be created for a package of programmes containing a national employment guarantee scheme and other labour market programmes for preserving employment in the face of economic downturns. For a good discussion on creating fiscal and policy space in developing countries, see Islam (2009, 2012).

14 See, also, ILO (2012b).

Bibliography

Auer, P., Efendioglu, U. and Leschke, J. (2005) *Active Labour Market Policies around the World*, ILO, Geneva.

Bell, D.N.F. and Blanchflower, D.G. (2011) 'Young People and the Great Recession', *Oxford Review of Economic Policy*, vol. 27, no. 2, pp. 241–267.

Betcherman, G., Dar, A., Luinstra, A. and Ogawa, M. (2001) 'Active Labour Market Policies: Lessons for East Asia', in Betcherman, G. and Islam, R. (eds) *East Asian Labor Markets and the Economic Crisis: Impacts Responses and Lesson*, World Bank and ILO, Washington, D.C. and Geneva.

Caliendo, M., Künn S. and Schmidt, R. (2011) *Fighting Youth Unemployment: The*

Effects of Active Labour Market Policies, IZA Discussion Paper Series No. 6222, Bonn.

Eurofound (2012) *NEETs – Young People Not in Employment, Education and Training: Characteristics, Costs and Policy Responses in Europe*, Publications Office of the European Union, Luxembourg.

IILS (International Institute for Labour Studies) (2012) *World of Work Report 2012: Better Jobs for a Better Economy*, ILO, Geneva.

ILO (International Labour Organization) (2010) *Global Employment Trends for Youth*, Geneva.

ILO (International Labour Organization) (2011) *Policy Options to Support Young Workers during Economic Recovery: Policy Brief*, Geneva.

ILO (International Labour Organization) (2012a) *Global Employment Trends 2012*, Geneva.

ILO (International Labour Organization) (2012b) *The Youth Employment Crisis: Time for Action*, Report V, International Labour Conference 101st Session 2012, Geneva.

ILO (International Labour Organization) (2012c) *Global Employment Trends for Youth 2012*, Geneva.

ILO (International Labour Organization) (2012d) *Africa's Response to the Youth Employment Crisis Regional Report: Synthesis of Key Issues and Outcomes from Eleven National Events on Youth Employment in the African Region March–May 2012*, Geneva.

ILO (International Labour Organization) and World Bank (2012) *Inventory of Policy Responses to the Financial and Economic Crisis: Joint Synthesis Report*, Geneva and Washington, D.C.

Islam, I. (2009) *Creating Policy Space for Developing Economies to Cope with the Global Economic Crisis: A Proposed Framework*, Employment Policy Department, ILO, Geneva.

Islam, I. (2012) *Revisiting the Economics of Fiscal Austerity: Rhetoric vs Reality*, Presentation made at the 66th Decent Work Forum, ILO, Geneva, 22 May 2012.

Islam, I. and Chowdhury, A. (2010) *Fiscal Consolidation, Growth and Employment: What do We Know?*, available at: www.voxeu.org/index.php?q=node/5312 (accessed 21 June 2010).

Islam, I. and Chowdhury, A. (2012) *Fiscal Austerity and the Youth Employment Crisis*, available at: www.voxeu.org/debates/commentaries/fiscal-austerity-and-youth-employment-crisis (accessed 31 October 2010).

Islam, I. and Verick, S. (2010) *The Great Recession of 2008–09: Causes, Consequences and Policy Responses*, IZA Discussion Paper Series No. 4934, Institute for the Study of Labour, Bonn, May 2010.

Islam, I. and Verick, S. (eds) (2011) *From the Great Recession to Labour Market Recovery: Issues, Evidence and Policy Options*, ILO and Palgrave Macmillan, Geneva and London.

Islam, R. (2011) 'The Employment Challenge in Developing Countries during Economic Downturn and Recovery', in Islam, I. and Verick, S. (eds) *From the Great Recession to Labour Market Recovery: Issues, Evidence and Policy Options*, ILO and Palgrave Macmillan, Geneva and London.

Islam, R. (2012) 'Addressing the Jobs Challenge', in ODI Development Progress, available at: www.developmentprogress.org/blog/2012/11/08/addressing-jobs-challenge.

Islam, R., Mujeri, M.K. and Ali, Z. (2011) *Fiscal and Policy Space for Crisis Response with a Focus on Employment and Labour Market: A Study of Bangladesh*, Paper prepared for the ILO, Geneva.

James, K.S. (2008) 'Glorifying Malthus: Current Debate on "Demographic Dividend" in India', *Economic and Political Weekly*, Mumbai, 21 June.

Martin, G. (2009) 'A Portrait of the Youth Labour Market in 13 Countries, 1980–2007', *Monthly Labour Review*, July, pp. 3–21.

Matsumoto, M. and Elder, S. (2010) *Characterizing the School-to-Work Transition of Young Men and Women: Evidence from the ILO School-to-Work Transition Surveys*, Employment Working Paper No. 51, ILO, Geneva.

Matsumoto, M., Hengge, M. and Islam, I. (2012) *Tackling the Youth Employment Crisis: A Macroeconomic Perspective*, Employment Working Paper No. 124, ILO, Geneva.

Morsy, H. (2012) 'Scarred Generation', *Finance and Development*, vol. 49, no. 1, March, pp. 15–17.

O'Higgins, N. (2001) *Youth Unemployment and Employment Policy*, ILO, Geneva.

Rosas, G. and Rossignotti, G. (2005) 'Starting the New Millennium Right: Decent Employment for Young People', *International Labour Review*, vol. 144, no. 2, pp. 139–160.

Scarpetta, S., Sonnet, A. and Manfredi, T. (2010) *Rising Youth Unemployment during the Crisis: How to Prevent Negative Long-Term Consequences on a Generation?* OECD Social, Employment and Migration Papers, No. 106, OECD, Paris, April.

Schwerdtfeger, M. (2013) *Assessing the Long Term Cost of Youth Unemployment*, Special Report, TD Economics, 29 January 2013.

World Bank (2007) *World Development Report 2007*, World Bank, Washington, D.C.

World Bank (2012) *World Development Report 2013: Jobs*, World Bank, Washington, D.C.

Yasser, A. (2011) 'Closing the Jobs Gap', *Finance and Development*, vol. 48, no. 2, pp. 73–79.

8 Labour market flexibility, informality and employment[1]

Introduction

One influential view in the development literature is that specific labour regulations – such as high minimum wages and employment protection legislation – depress the demand for labour. The price, it is claimed, is borne by workers, especially low skilled and young workers, who are then 'priced out' of the labour market. Such workers often have to endure long spells of unemployment or move into the 'informal economy' and join an interminable queue to obtain formal sector jobs that are in scarce supply. Thus, attenuating or removing onerous labour market regulations reduces the incidence of informality, empowers young and marginalized workers to gain a foothold in the formal labour market and contributes to the goal of inclusive development. How valid is this thesis both in analytical and empirical terms? The chapter revisits this important topic and seeks to extract relevant policy lessons for developing countries.

The chapter highlights the various analytical complications that can vitiate the validity of the naïve version of the labour market flexibility thesis. This sets the preamble for tracing the global nature of the debate on labour market flexibility. It points out how it has changed from a naïve version in which labour market flexibility is universally desirable to a more nuanced version in which so-called 'plateau' effects are highlighted. This thesis maintains that too much flexibility is as bad for employment as too little flexibility. Within these limits, there is a 'plateau' in which labour market regulations are essentially benign with respect to their impact on employment while engendering redistributive benefits. Despite this, the chapter notes that the G20 has made a renewed commitment to contentious structural and labour market reforms as a way of boosting growth and employment for both developed and developing countries.

The analytical review of the regulations–employment nexus allows one to assess the pertinent empirical evidence. This empirical review draws on a new dataset on labour market regulations to provide an overview of regional variations in various forms of labour market regulations and the extent to which they relate to regional variations in broad labour market indicators.[2] It will then briefly review the extent to which the G20 version of the structural and labour market reform agenda is upheld by model-based policy simulations on which policy makers seem to be placing considerable faith. This critical discussion will be followed by a brief overview of some econometric studies as they seek to offer new insights into the labour market flexibility debate. The chapter will argue that, while econometric investigations are useful, another way of examining the impact of labour regulations on employment and informality, both for adults and youth, is to assess the perceptions of the private sector on the importance attached to labour market regulations as a constraint on the expansion of business operations. The evidence suggests that, across all regions of the world, firms identify multiple constraints on business operations, labour market regulations being one of them, but by no means the most important one. The quality of governance, access to finance, use of a reliable transport network and reliable supply of electricity are usually more important constraints from a business perspective than labour regulations. Hence, if labour regulations are either substantially attenuated or removed, one cannot expect a major expansion of the private sector unless other remaining and more significant constraints are also tackled. What one needs are appropriately designed labour market institutions that can strike the right balance between protecting the rights of workers and promoting growth and employment.[3]

The case against labour market regulations: what the proponents say

Those who are concerned about the negative employment consequences of labour market regulations subscribe – implicitly or explicitly – to the paradigm of labour market flexibility. The latter may be regarded as a synonym for the textbook case of a competitive or neoclassical labour market. Workers are free to move in response to shifting relative wage and employment opportunities, while firms are free to adjust the workforce in response to shifting profit opportunities. In such a framework, collective bargaining driven by trade unions, strongly enforced hiring and firing rules, restrictions on casual and flexible modes of employment, severance pay, unemployment benefits, minimum wages and other regulations are regarded as undesirable institutional arrangements as they constrain the free choice of workers and firms. More importantly, arrangements meant to protect the interests of workers paradoxically hurt employment opportunities by raising the cost of labour above what the market will bear.

What the proponents of labour market flexibility ignore: the limitations of the competitive model and their implications[4]

The text-book model of a perfectly competitive market for labour services that informs the worldview of the proponents of labour market flexibility either ignores or pays insufficient attention to a number of analytical complications and their implications. This stems from some strong assumptions that are built into the basic model. Thus:

1   The model is static, being valid for a full employment, but zero-growth, economy with no demographic and structural changes. Hence, labour demand and labour supply can be held constant.
2   The model assumes the absence of any market power exercised by employers.
3   The model ignores efficiency wage considerations.
4   The model ignores the vulnerability of workers to labour market risks.
5   There is perfect compliance when regulations are enacted and implemented.
6   No 'learning' takes place among key stakeholders when the 'rules of the game' change.

Relaxation of some or all of these assumptions will mitigate the strong predictive power of the basic model. To start with, the assumptions of a zero-growth economy and lack of demographic and structural changes are clearly not valid for a typical developing economy. The (downward sloping) labour demand curve is derived in the conventional model from the production function. Growth in this framework can be depicted as a shift in the production function due to, say, increases in the investment rate, or increases in factor productivity. This will also cause a rightward shift in the labour demand curve.

In a typical developing economy, the (upward) sloping labour supply curve will also shift in response to rising labour force growth and urbanization. Under these circumstances, it is important to make a distinction between a movement along a given labour demand curve interacting with a static labour supply curve and shifts of both demand and supply. A perfectly enforced minimum wage and other non-wage labour standards that are above the 'market-clearing' level will cause involuntary unemployment and/or increase the incidence of informal unemployment. This can be conceptualized as an upward movement along a given labour demand curve interacting with a given labour supply curve. In a rapidly growing economy undergoing demographic and structural transformation, labour demand and supply will experience progressive shifts thus offsetting the regressive impact of minimum wage and other exogenously imposed labour standards. This dynamic framework offers a better representation of the evolution of the labour market in a typical developing economy than the conventional model.

It is also well known that monopsonistic employers will set wages below the marginal productivity of labour while employment will be below the competitive norm. In these circumstances, a fully enforced minimum wage and other exogenously imposed labour standards can increase wages and employment. One study of Indonesian rural labour markets has claimed that observed wages for the sample that was studied were below the estimated marginal labour productivity of workers – evidence that is consistent with monopsonistic practices.[5]

The basic model assumes that atomistic, profit-maximizing employers set wages that correspond to exogenously determined productivity. Yet it has been known for some time that productivity can be endogenously determined by wages.[6] This is the basis of the efficiency wage hypothesis. Profit-maximizing employers might consider the market-determined wages to be too low and raise them systematically above these market-determined norms in order to motivate workers to perform to higher standards and thus recoup the cost of higher wages through higher productivity. One should not expect any enforced change in the behaviour of employers if minimum wages and other non-wage minima are set at or below the efficiency wage. In this case, involuntary unemployment and search unemployment will be the result of the conduct of profit-maximizing employers rather than government intervention.

There is an implicit normative message in the basic model of a perfectly competitive labour market that 'any job is better than no job' – a message that has powerful adherents.[7] Such a view discounts the value of fortifying job security, because the conventional model ignores the vulnerability of workers to labour market risks. In the absence of formal risk-mitigation schemes, workers could be induced to readily accept low productivity jobs at low wages. This could propel a developing economy into 'low productivity, low pay' equilibrium. In this equilibrium, 'bad jobs' drive out 'good jobs'. Insecure workers behave rationally in this framework. In the absence of any job security and legal protection – such as laws against unfair dismissal, the absense of unemployment insurance – workers' pay a premium (in the form of low wages and the ready acceptance of any job) to employers in order to reduce the risk of being unemployed. Under such circumstances, the imposition of higher labour standards and various risk-mitigation schemes – such as unemployment insurance – could be both efficient (leading an economy towards 'high productivity, high wage equilibrium') and equitable (enabling vulnerable workers to deal with labour market risks).

A core assumption of the basic analytical framework that undergirds the thesis of labour market flexibility is that minimum wages and other regulations can be perfectly enforced. Hence, the compliance regime is infallible in its execution. Yet, non-compliance is widespread. As soon as one introduces the empirically plausible assumption of non-compliance, the strong results that one can derive from the basic model will no longer hold.

Critics concede that minimum wages and other regulations apply primarily to the formal sector but not the informal sector. In that case, one can show that the impact on overall employment of an economy becomes ambiguous: it depends on the magnitude of the minimum wage increase and the 'substitution effect' reflected in the changing composition of employment between the formal and informal sector.[8]

The issue of non-compliance and its implications have received renewed attention in the analytical literature on minimum wages. One insightful study considers the consequences of inserting imperfect compliance in models of imperfect competition and juxtaposes it with the assumption of imperfect commitment on the part of policy makers. It demonstrates that the wage–employment trade-off becomes more complex.[9]

Consider an economy where there is surplus labour and/or productivity is low. Consider too a political process that yields a government that has egalitarian preferences and thus uses an increase in the minimum wage as a signal to make a credible commitment to enforce the new wage regime. It can be shown that equilibrium wages and employment will go up in these particular circumstances, a result that relies on the assumption of imperfect compliance and the credible commitment of a distribution-sensitive government rather than on the assumption of imperfect competition.

The assumption of perfect compliance and infallible enforcement by policy makers entails the corollary that no 'learning' takes place among key stakeholders as the 'rules of the game' change; they inevitably do when there are major changes in the institutional and regulatory environment. Even the most populist government does not resolutely pursue regulations if the consequences are such that they adversely affect the welfare of large sections of the community. If, as argued, perfectly enforced statutory minima lead to significant unemployment while rewarding formal sector workers, then a distribution-sensitive government will have to manage the trade-off between improving the living standards of formal sector workers and looking after the interests of the unemployed and the informally employed. The tensions that are unleashed in managing this trade-off might well be significant enough to ensure that they attenuate a resolute political commitment to labour market regulations. There are many subtle ways that a government might 'signal' that they are not rigidly committed to statutory minima. One way might be to leave the onerous minimum wage legislation intact on paper, but allow the real value of minimum wages to fall.[10]

Firms in the formal sector can also become adept at circumventing labour regulations, without necessarily breaching legal limits. Alternatively, firms can seek to recoup the higher cost of complying with regulations by extracting a higher supply of effort from existing workers or by investing in human and physical capital that can boost productivity.[11] In other words, company level responses are likely to be much richer than just lay-offs and a reduced demand for labour services. Workers too can adapt to changing circumstances by aiming for more realistic wage settlements, if the alternative of pushing for a strict adherence to onerous labour regulations raises the risk of pushing business to bankruptcies. In sum, when one allows for 'learning' among key stakeholders to take place as they develop coping mechanisms to deal with large-scale changes in the institutional and regulatory environment, the wage–employment trade-offs might, over the course of time, become muted.

Labour market flexibility: the nature of the global discourse

Given that various analytical complications temper the core model of labour market flexibility as a key source of job creation, one would have thought that a nuanced view of the role that labour market reforms can play in the development process would be the norm rather than the exception. Yet the nature of the global discourse on labour market flexibility is in a state of flux. On the one hand, there is a movement in favour of a carefully enunciated version of the role that labour market reforms can play in engendering employment. On the other hand, there is resurgence, especially since 2010, among the G20 and other influential international actors, in favour of the view that policy reforms that make labour markets more flexible play a very important part in the job creation process. The rest of the discussion traces the changing nature of the global discourse on labour market flexibility.

In a seminal 1993 paper, Richard Freeman, one of the world's foremost labour economists, pointed out that preconceived notions about 'labour market rigidities' in developing countries often clash with the available evidence. For example, the iconic Harris–Todaro model posited an urban labour market in developing countries in which wages were institutionally determined and held above the market-clearing level. This served as a powerful signal for migrants from rural areas to join the queue of the unemployed in search of lucrative urban sector jobs. Yet, the notion of downward rigidity of wages – a salient feature of a regulated labour market – can hardly be reconciled with the widespread evidence of real wage variability across a wide range of developing countries with diverse labour market institutions and policies that Freeman observed in his 1993 paper. If there is de facto flexibility in developing country labour markets, despite the seemingly onerous nature of formal regulations, should one blame such regulations for impairing economic performance?

There was a time when neither the analytical literature nor the empirical discussions on the study of growth and development paid much attention to labour market institutions and policies. This appeared to change in the 1990s. A 1994 OECD Jobs study proclaimed that labour regulations were the primary determinant of wages and employment. It could explain the labour market woes of a sclerotic and highly regulated European labour market vis-à-vis a vibrant, job-creating and lightly regulated US labour market. Powerful international organizations (most notably the Bretton Woods institutions) that matter in setting the global development agenda became wary of endorsing regulations that seek to protect labour rights and impose higher labour standards in developing countries. Only the ILO, given its mandate, appeared to put up a defensive battle in favour of regulations that sought to protect and enhance labour standards, both in rich and poor nations.

The professional consensus on the adverse effects of labour market regulations appeared to change as an alliance of unions and civic activists in rich nations, most notably in the USA, began to focus attention on violations of labour rights and poor pay and working conditions in the subcontracted factories of many multinational companies in developing countries. 'Anti-sweatshop' activism came to the fore. It received considerable attention in the international media and a sympathetic response from the US administration. The 1995 World Bank report on the welfare of workers in an age of globalization evolved against such a background (World Bank, 1995). Unlike previous proclamations, the World Bank offered a nuanced account of labour market regulations and highlighted the desirability of an enterprise-driven and more democratic industrial relations system in developing countries.

As one goes through the first decade of the twenty-first century, what is the substance and tenor of the global debate on labour market institutions and policies and their impact on economic performance? Here, one detects some evidence of revisionism among influential international actors that have implications for the global development agenda.

As part of this revisionist view on the role that labour market reforms play in engendering employment, it would be useful to highlight the 'plateau' effects of employment protection legislation (EPLs) and minimum wages advanced by the World Bank's 2013 *World Development Report* on 'Jobs'. It notes:[12]

> New data and more rigorous methodologies have spurred a wave of empirical studies over the past two decades on the effects of labour regulations…
>
> Based on this wave of new research, the overall impact of EPL and minimum wages is smaller than the intensity of the debate would suggest. Most estimates of the impacts of employment levels tend to be insignificant…
>
> Many countries appear to set EPLs and minimum wages where impacts on employment or productivity are modest. Within that range or 'plateau', effects enhancing and undermining efficiency can be found side by side, and most of the impact is redistributive…
>
> However, when the edge of the plateau is reached … impacts are more negative…
>
> It does not follow that minimum regulation is the answer. If rules are too weak, or not enforced, the problems of poor information, unequal bargaining power, or inadequate risk management remain unaddressed. This cliff may be less visible than excessive labour market rigidity, but it is no less real.

Despite these caveats and qualifications, there appears to be a renewed commitment to labour market reforms as a source of job creation. This is spearheaded by the G20. Thus, the G20 Leaders Declaration at the Toronto Summit (June 2010) endorsed an ambitious agenda of 'structural reforms' cutting across both labour and product markets that would lift global output significantly, create 'tens millions more jobs', sustain poverty reduction and reduce global imbalances significantly.[13] Subsequent *Communiqués* in 2013 and 2014 of Finance Ministers and Central Bank Governors of the G20 sustain this commitment to structural reforms.[14]

The G20 Finance Ministers and Central Bankers rely heavily on the technical guidance offered by the IMF. It is perhaps not surprising that the IMF reflects this particular position of the G20. Thus, it is noted that '[i]n countries with high levels of youth unemployment and informality, labor market reforms can be critical in avoiding a lost generation'.[15]

The promises of significant employment and growth dividends of structural and labour market reforms is also influenced by the OECD's *Going for Growth* template in which wide-ranging policy initiatives that cut across product market regulations, labour market regulations, financial regulations, taxation, human capital and other areas unlock the growth potential of countries under review.

The OECD makes it clear that not all the proposed reforms apply to all countries with equal force at all times.[16]

The proposed labour market regulations under the OECD's *Going for Growth* template are worth highlighting. The suggested regulatory changes that are applicable to a range of countries include: (a) reform of (disability) benefit schemes; (b) reform of unemployment insurance schemes; (c) reforms to reduce labour restrictions on labour mobility; (d) reforms to reduce minimum cost of labour; (e) reforms to the wage bargaining system; (f) strengthening policies to promote female labour force participation; (g) improving incentives for formal labour force participation. Some of these initiatives, such as (c), (f) and (g) are desirable; others are more contentious and are likely to weaken labour market institutions. The OECD's position on the impact of these labour market policies on GDP are shown in Table 8.1.

Based on Table 8.1, one could argue that labour market reforms that reduce employment protection legislation, reduce the scope and coverage of collective bargaining, reduce unemployment benefits and their duration, increase the retirement age and restrict access to disability schemes are expected to have a positive impact on GDP in the long run. Increased spending on active labour market policies has a positive long run impact on labour demand. What about the short run? The OECD maintains that 'fears that reforms may depress economic activity in the short run are overblown'.[17] But this proclamation overlooks the caveats that are associated with the OECD's internal research. An OECD Economics Department Working Paper includes the following qualifications in its summary of findings (italics added):

> This analysis indicates that the benefits from reforms *typically take time to materialize* ... there is also tentative evidence that some *labour market reforms (e.g. unemployment benefits and job protection) pay off in good times than in bad times, and can even entail short-term losses in severely depressed economies.*[18]

Table 8.1 Selected labour market policies and expected impact on GDP

Selected labour market policies	Impact on GDP (–/+), with – denoting negative impact and + denoting positive impact
Employment protection	–
Intermediate (industry-wide) collective bargaining	–
Collective bargaining	–
Unemployment benefits and their duration	–
Early retirement and easy access to disability schemes	–
Spending on active labour market policies	+

Source: adapted from OECD (2014: 9).

IMF studies on labour market policies in advanced economies also note some of these concerns.[19]

Furthermore, the OECD study does not discuss the issue of quality of employment, since the impact of reforms is measured in terms of two aggregates: GDP growth and the employment rate. It is, of course, possible for the employment rate to increase, but the quality of new jobs created to decline.

There are also adverse distributional consequences associated with labour market and related reforms. In the case of the UK, one study commissioned by the *Financial Times* concluded that the current welfare benefit reforms will hit the poorer northern region five times harder than the richer south.[20] An IFS study draws attention to 'a £20 billion cut to the social security budget by 2015–16 [that will affect] the vast majority of ... working-age households and this inevitably tends to hit lower income households hardest'. The study then 'estimates the implications of these kinds of factors for the path of income poverty now and in future'. The projections are quite stark. A sharp rise in child poverty (based on a relative income standard) of six percentage points is anticipated between now and 2020. This will apparently negate all the reductions in child poverty attained during the 2000s.[21]

In sum, structural and labour market reforms might hold a good deal of promise in the long run, but their short-run and distributional consequences cannot be discounted. It is not, of course, possible to make the transition to the long run without negotiating the short run; neither does it make much sense to focus only on ex-ante aggregate benefits without considering the distribution of such benefits. A balanced policy discourse on structural reforms should focus on both their promises and pitfalls.

Labour market reforms and labour market outcomes: the mixed nature of the available evidence

The discussion in this section commences with an overview of regional variations in the incidence of labour market regulations. This overview draws on global data created by the IMF on labour market institutions covering a wide set of countries for the 1990–2005 period.[22]

Figures 8.1 to 8.3 highlight regional variations in key aspects of labour market regulations – minimum wages (relative to mean/median wages), severance pay (maximum amount measured in months of pay) and unemployment benefits coverage. As can be seen in Figure 8.1, for the 1990–2005 period, the global coverage in terms of unemployment benefits is quite low: 21 per cent only, with the coverage rate for the regions of the world where the low and middle income countries are concentrated ranging from basically zero (Asia and Africa) to 18 per cent (East Asia and Pacific). The highest coverage rate is in Western Europe (72 per cent) followed by North America (48 per cent), that is, in the developed parts of the world.

What makes the developing regions of the world conspicuous in relation to their developed counterpart is the incidence of severance pay. Here, the low and

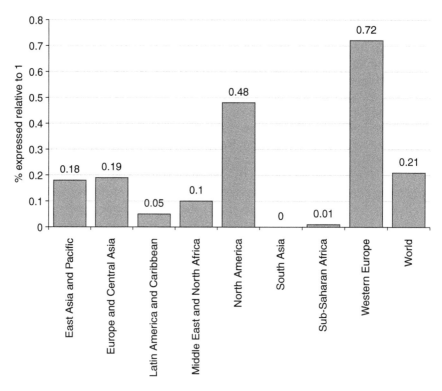

Figure 8.1 Unemployment benefits coverage (per cent) by region (average 1990–2005)
(source: authors' compilation based on Aleksynska and Schindler (2011)).

middle income countries – concentrated in Africa (including Middle East and North Africa), Asia and Latin America – have a higher incidence of severance pay than the more developed regions of the world entailing Europe and North America (see Figure 8.2).

For example, severance pay is more than three times higher than Western Europe in South Asia and more than five times higher than Western Europe in Latin America and the Caribbean. This can, at least partly, be explained by the fact that in richer countries of the world unemployment benefits provide a major source of dealing with risk of unemployment and redundancies. Less weight is placed on severance pay as a means of dealing with the risk of unemployment and redundancies. In the case of low and middle income countries, the opposite holds true, that is, unemployment benefits coverage even for formal sector workers is rather limited, so that the burden of dealing with the risk of unemployment among formal sector workers is placed on severance pay and hence on enterprises. In essence, unemployment benefits schemes and severance pay become substitutes rather than complements. This has important policy implications that will be highlighted at an appropriate juncture.

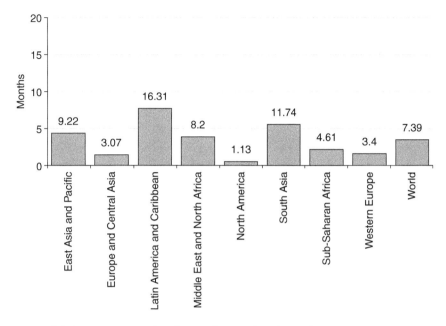

Figure 8.2 Severance pay (maximum, in months) by region (average 1990–2005) (source: authors' compilation based on Aleksynska and Schindler (2011)).

Consider now the case of minimum wages which are expressed here in relative terms, that is, relative to average wages, across different regions of the world. It is the highest in South Asia (58 per cent of average wages) and the lowest in Sub-Saharan Africa (18 per cent of average wages). Elsewhere, in other parts of the developing world, minimum wages as a proportion of average wages, is around 30 per cent of average wages – which is a little below the benchmarks (around 40 per cent of average wages) prevailing in North America and Western Europe. Hence, two regions – South Asia and Sub-Saharan Africa – really stand out as having either low or high minimum wages relative to global standards. (See Figure 8.3.)

What matters is the relationship between broad-based employment indicators and measured indices of labour market regulations reviewed here. Two illustrations are offered: one highlights regional variations in severance pay and their corresponding variations in employment rates (Figure 8.4); the other reflects regional variations in minimum wages and their corresponding variations in employment rates (Figure 8.5).[23] In both cases, there are no obvious patterns. Compare, for example, East Asia and the Pacific which has the highest employment rate (averaged over 1990–2005) in the world, but severance pay in the region is higher than Middle East and North Africa which has the lowest employment rate in the world. The ratio of minimum wages to average wages are almost identical (around 30 per cent) in the two regions, but they correspond to sharp differences in employment rates.

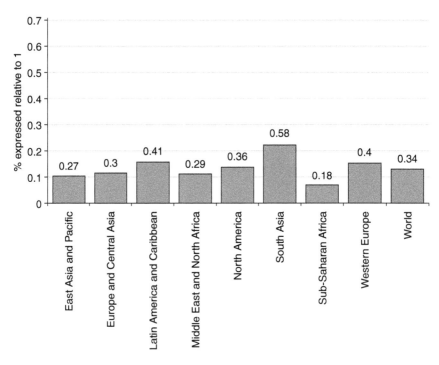

Figure 8.3 Ratio of minimum wage to mean wage by region (per cent) (average 1990–2005) (source: authors' compilation based on Aleksynska and Schindler (2011)).

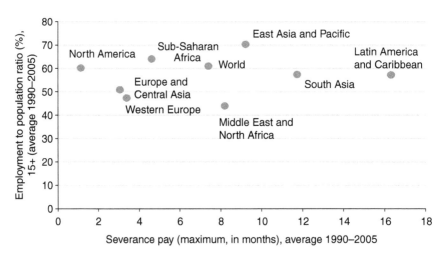

Figure 8.4 Severance pay and employment to population ratio (1990–2005) (source: authors' compilation based on Aleksynska and Schindler (2011)).

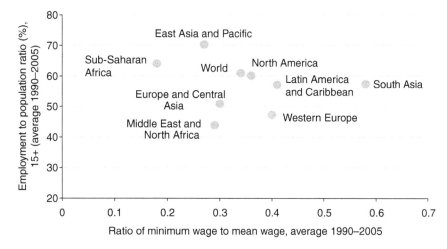

Figure 8.5 Minimum wage and employment to population ratio (1995–2005) (source: authors' compilation based on Aleksynska and Schindler (2011)).

Having set the broad global and regional context, it would be useful to consider the evidence from the perspective of the G20 that has spearheaded the new move to endorse labour market reforms as an important means of promoting global growth and employment in the post-crisis era. As noted, consistent proclamations have been made by the G20 policy makers (encompassing the political leaders, the finance ministers and central bankers) that the most effective and reliable long-run means of promoting global economic recovery lies in structural reforms, of which labour market reforms represent a core component. This is part of a policy package in which short-run support to aggregate demand is provided by monetary policy in the advanced economies, while fiscal consolidation seeks to rein in unsustainable public finances in the rich countries in the wake of the sovereign debt crisis in the Eurozone.

A particular paper – authored by the IMF, in conjunction with the OECD and the World Bank – has played a key role in shaping a 2014 G20 proclamation on this issue (IMF, OECD and World Bank, 2014). The notion that, largely as a result of structural reforms, global GDP growth can be 0.5 percentage points higher than the norm over the next years, has been literally extracted by the G20 Finance Ministers and Central Bankers from this paper. Yet labour market reforms seem to play a relatively modest role in the simulation exercises that have been provided in this paper (but understandably have not been reported in any depth by the global media). Consider Table 8.2 which shows in the case of four middle income G20 countries – Brazil, India, Indonesia and South Africa –the expected impact on factor productivity and the unemployment rate of selected labour market reforms based on the maximum amount possible over the implementation period (between 2014 and 2018) of reductions in employment

Table 8.2 Simulated impact of labour market reforms on productivity and unemployment in selected G20 middle income countries

Country	Simulated impact (2014 to 2018) on productivity if there is a 20% reduction in EPLs from their original levels (increase in per cent)	Simulated impact (2014 to 2018) on unemployment rate (reduction in percentage points) of a 10% increase in ALPMs)
Brazil	0.12	–
India	0.13	0.21
Indonesia	0.15	0.21
South Africa	0.12	0.21

Source: adapted from IMF, OECD, World Bank (2014), Table 2.

protection legislation (EPL) and increase in expenditures on active labour market policies (ALMPs) to improve the intermediation functions of labour market institutions.

As can be seen, model-based simulations suggest that the labour market reforms – including more positive measures, such as enhanced expenditure on ALMPs – are expected to have a modest impact (well below 1 per cent over five years) on productivity and unemployment rates on large and populous developing countries that form part of both the G20 and the famous BRICs. As the paper recognizes, most of the increased impact on productivity – and hence growth – comes from increased competition in product markets, rather than labour markets, brought about by reduced entry barriers to various industries, especially service industries.

So far, the focus has been on a critical evaluation of a G20-led initiative to advocate structural and labour reforms as a core plank of a new strategy to promote global growth and employment. The discussion now briefly reflects on three recent empirical studies that seek to shed new light on the impact of labour market reforms on labour market outcomes, growth and inequality.

The first (Bernal-Verdugo *et al.*, 2012a) uses panel data for 97 developed and developing countries from 1985 to 2008. The indicators for labour market regulations are based on the Fraser Institute's Economic Freedom of the World (EFW) database and the aim is to assess their impact on aggregate unemployment, youth unemployment and long-term unemployment. EFW in turn draws on the World Bank's 'Doing Business' reports that, as will be noted later, have attracted some controversy. There are six areas on which one could measure labour market flexibility (such as minimum wages, hiring and firing, etc), but the authors prefer a 'composite indicator of labour market flexibility'. The authors conclude:

> after controlling for other macroeconomic and demographic variables … increases in the flexibility of labour market regulations and institutions have a statistically significant negative impact both on the level and the change of unemployment outcomes. Among the different labour market flexibility

indicators analysed, hiring and firing regulations and hiring costs are found to have the strongest impact.

(Bernal-Verdugo *et al.*, 2012a, p. 12)

This conclusion holds both for OECD and non-OECD countries.

One can raise various caveats about these strong conclusions pertaining to the measurement of both the dependent (unemployment) and independent variables (labour market regulations). To start with, the authors restricted themselves to one database (Fraser Institute's EFW) which in turn relies on the controversial World Bank's 'employing workers index'. The standard practice in the 'Doing Business' series used to be a ranking of countries, with countries having less regulations on hiring and firing workers being rated higher than countries that had more regulations. As a result of sustained criticism from various quarters, the World Bank no longer uses 'employing workers index' in its cross-country rankings and thus carefully avoids making any explicit judgments on whether more or less labour regulations are desirable. The 'employing workers index' is now reported in an appendix in the World Bank's influential *Doing Business Reports*. This important change in the World Bank's position with respect to the 'employing workers index' is unfortunately not reflected in the aforementioned study. Furthermore, the authors – who are associated with the IMF – could have used the IMF database on labour market regulations which has been reported at a previous juncture in this chapter.

There is also the issue of measuring the dependent variable – unemployment in this case. As is well known, while this is a reasonable indicator of labour market outcomes in developed countries with a high incidence of formal labour markets, it is widely considered to be an inappropriate indicator of labour market outcomes in developing countries. The authors also concede that they have not taken into account the 'quality of employment' as well as the 'possible negative short-term effects' of enhanced labour market flexibility.[24]

This paper and related publications (such as Crivelli *et al.*, 2012) are not mere academic studies. They influence the IMF's country level policy advisory role on labour market reforms and its impact on employment outcomes. For example, the IMF released a template on 'analyzing and projecting labour market indicators' which, it claims, will over time be routinely incorporated in the Fund's bilateral surveillance of member states through its Article IV consultations (IMF, 2012). Here, one finds that one of the aforementioned studies (Crivelli *et al.*, 2012) is approvingly cited as a source to justify how specific policies, including labour market reforms, can increase employment elasticity and hence increase the employment creating potential of an economy. Thus, it states: 'Crivelli *et al.* (2012) find that structural policies aimed at increasing labor and product market flexibility and reducing government size have a significant and positive impact on employment elasticities' (IMF, 2012, p. 6).

The next study (Nataraj *et al.*, 2012) reviewed here deals exclusively with a meta-analysis of the impact of labour market regulations on employment in low income countries (LICs). This is a valuable addition to the empirical literature as it is probably the first systematic attempt to collate the evidence from a low income country perspective. The authors of the study readily concede that they could only identify a small number of studies – 17 in all – which use comparable econometric methods to identify the impact of labour market regulations on employment. Nevertheless, their conclusion is that 'labor regulations decrease formal employment but increase informal employment; the impact on overall employment is ambiguous' (Nataraj *et al.*, 2012, p. 3). They also use four studies (and 76 estimates based on those studies) to conduct a meta-regression analysis. This leads the authors to suggest that 'a 10 per cent increase in the minimum wage would reduce formal employment by 0.8 per cent' (Nataraj *et al.*, 2012, p. 3).

While these results are in line with the orthodox hypothesis on the labour market regulations–employment nexus, the authors clearly recognize that it would be hazardous to generalize the findings because of the paucity of the studies (four for the meta-regression analysis). In any case, given that the focus of the evaluation is on isolating the impact of labour market regulations on employment, no attempt is made to discuss other policy and structural variables that inevitably influence employment outcomes and how significant they are in quantitative terms in relation to indicators of labour market flexibility.

The final study (Campos and Nugent, 2013) reviewed here is distinctive because of its ambitious attempt to construct a new index of the rigidity of employment protection legislation (LAMRIG) for an unbalanced sample of more than 140 countries from 1960 onwards. The construction of LAMRIG draws heavily on ILO's NATLEX database and other sources. Higher values of LAMRIG are associated with higher labour market rigidity. The estimates show that, for the full sample, the average value of LAMRIG is 1.47 with a minimum value of zero and a maximum value of 3.50.

The study seeks to identify the factors that lead to changes in LAMRIG rather than just focusing on cross-country variations in levels of LAMRIG. The authors suggest that, apart from legal and institutional factors, economic crises often lead to reductions in employment protection legislation (that is, a decrease in the value of LAMRIG); episodes of trade liberalization end up increasing the value of LAMRIG, while episodes of financial liberalization often have the opposite effect. In general, countries with lower levels of per capita GDP have lower levels of LAMRIG. The study also briefly reports on results that suggest that increases in LAMRIG tend to be associated with increases in inequality (as measured by the Gini ratio), but do not have a statistically significant impact on per capita GDP growth when other factors (such as human capital and share of investment in GDP) are included in the regression analyses. No attempt is made in this study to examine how either levels of LAMRIG or changes in it affect employment outcomes. However, given that there is a typically positive relationship between growth and employment, the absence of any statistically significant impact on growth implies that the impact of changes in LAMRIG are likely to be benign with respect to employment outcomes.

An important aspect of the findings of this study is that employment protection legislation – as measured by LAMRIG – changes 'very slowly' in many cases

(Campos and Nugent, 2013, p. 14). The estimates that are provided for the full sample (988 observations for a period of more than 40 years) suggest that the average value of the change in LAMRIG amounts to a mere 0.32. This means a moderate increase in the average value of LAMRIG from 1.47 to 1.79 and hence a moderate increase in employment protection legislation for the full sample of countries over a long period. In annualized terms, this means an average increase of 0.007 per cent over 44 years. These hardly detectable changes in the average value of LAMRIG suggest that, in many cases, employment protection legislation behaves essentially like a fixed parameter rendering it ill-suited to explain major changes in labour market outcomes over a long period of time.

The econometric studies that purport to show the employment consequences of labour market regulations studies ignore the perceptions of employers on the role of labour market regulations in influencing business operations. If they are indeed as important as some of the econometric investigations claim, they should be reflected in the views that employers hold with respect to labour market flexibility. Yet, the world's largest survey of the perceptions of employers suggests a different picture. As Table 8.3, derived from the World Bank's *Enterprise Survey* shows, more than 80 per cent of employers in more than 100,000 firms in over 100 low and middle countries do not regard labour market regulations as a major impediment to their business operations. To such employers, the quality of governance (as reflected in crime and corruption), lack of a reliable transport network, lack of reliable supply of electricity, lack of access to finance and lack of a skilled workforce are much more pressing issues. Hence, if the purpose is to improve the business environment to promote private sector-led growth in developing countries, the survey results reported here suggest that labour market reforms are unlikely to play a major role. Improving the quality of governance, investing in infrastructure, promoting

Table 8.3 Major constraints to business operations as perceived by more than 135,000 firms in more than 100 countries (2009–14)

Variable name	Value[a] (%)
Corruption	36.8
Crime, theft and disorder	26.5
Access to finance	30.8
Electricity	36.3
Transportation	22.3
Tax administration	21.9
Business licensing and permits	14.8
Customs and trade regulations	18.4
Labour regulations	12.3
Inadequately educated workforce	27.4

Source: adapted from World Bank *Enterprise Survey*.

Note
a Simple average, all countries, 2009–14.

financial inclusion, investing in the education and training system are likely to be much more hospitable in enabling private sector-led growth.

Labour market flexibility and employment: which way now?

The mixed nature of the evidence on the labour market flexibility–employment nexus does not entitle one to adopt a nihilistic stance. The choice is not between 'no regulations' and 'maximum regulations', but between ill-designed and well-designed regulations that strive to strike the right balance between protecting workers against labour market risks and providing them with ample employment opportunities.

One way to conceptualize an appropriate policy framework is to draw on the salient principles that are embedded in the famous 'Tinbergen rule'.[25] Thus, for every policy goal there should be at least one appropriate policy instrument. This means invoking the Tinbergen rule which, when applied to labour market policies, suggests a scheme that is illustrated in Table 8.4.

There are several possible instruments for attaining specific policy goals. This means that one can use a combination of policy instruments to attain a specific set of policy goals. Thus, for example, the objective of reducing labour market risks can either be pursued through a single instrument, say, severance pay, or through a combination of multiple instruments that form part of an integrated labour market risk mitigation system. Similarly, in attaining the goal of reducing the incidence of in-work poverty or the 'working poor', one can exclusively use mandatory minimum wages or regard them as a menu of choices that policy makers have in improving the living standards of low-paid workers.

The diverse nature of the relationship between goals and instruments enables one to appreciate the current discourse on labour market regulations. It is not a

Table 8.4 Correspondence between goals and instruments in selected labour market regulations

Targets/goals	Instruments
Reduce labour market risks entailing spells of unemployment and underemployment	• Severance pay • Unemployment benefits or unemployment insurance • Mandatory individual savings account that self-finances periods of unemployment/underemployment
Reduce incidence of 'working poor'	• Mandatory minimum wage • Minimum wages as benchmark for 'living wages' that are incorporated in collective bargaining mechanisms • Productivity-enhancing measures, both the firm and aggregate level, that can support the payment of higher real wages

case of unilaterally reducing all forms of labour market regulations to extract employment dividends. This is analytically, empirically and ethically an indefensible position. After all, as the evidence shows, the majority of employers (more than 80 per cent) across the world do not think labour regulations are a major constraint on business operations. The aim is to find the right mix of regulations. This is where policy makers in developing countries need to engage more deeply with the philosophical premise and spirit of the Tinbergen rule. As discussed in a previous section, severance pay seems to be far more generous in developing countries than in developed countries. This is presumably because it has emerged as a sole, or primary, instrument for dealing with labour market risks faced by formal sector workers. Similarly, mandatory minimum wages have emerged as a sole, or primary, instrument for dealing with the incidence of in-work poverty. This one-to-one mapping between goals and instruments means that an undue burden is placed on particular policy instruments in attaining broad policy goals. Future policy discourse should, therefore, shift attention away from a singular approach to a pluralist approach that emphasizes complementary use of a range of measures for coping with labour market risks and the incidence of in-working poverty as suggested in Table 8.4.

Concluding observations

This chapter reviewed the contentious debate on labour market reforms in engendering desirable employment outcomes in developing countries. The orthodox variant of this debate regards all labour market regulations as a cost imposed on employers that induce them to reduce the demand for labour, especially for low-skilled workers. The result is either an increase in unemployment or a decrease in formal sector employment. Admittedly, there are a number of studies that empirically support this view, but one has to be much more circumspect in weighing the evidence. This is perhaps not surprising given the analytical complications that afflict the naïve version of the theory of labour market flexibility and the employment dividends that are supposed to flow from it. In essence, employment in developing countries – both in terms of quantity and quality – is the outcome of a complex interplay of various forces and factors, with labour market regulations being one such factor. Furthermore, labour market reforms need to strike the right balance between protecting workers from labour market risks and preserving broad-based employment opportunities. If reforms end up increasing inequality and imposing adverse short-run adjustment costs, then they militate against the goal of inclusive development.

Perhaps mindful of these concerns and the mixed nature of the evidence, the nature of the global discourse has become more nuanced, with the influential *World Development Report* of 2013 endorsing the notion of a 'plateau' effect of labour market regulations: too much regulation is paradoxically bad for workers, but so is too little regulation. Within these limits, there is a 'plateau' in which the impact of labour market regulations on employment is benign while yielding redistributive benefits.

The chapter noted that this nuanced view is confronted by a G20-led initiative to make a renewed commitment to structural and labour market reforms as an effective way of promoting global growth and employment in the post-crisis era. The chapter has warned that the renewed emphasis on structural and labour market reforms as the way forward for the global community rests on model-based policy simulations that show rather modest positive outcomes.

The chapter also argued that econometric studies that purport to show the negative employment consequences of labour market regulations become inevitably entangled in methodological debates pertaining to sample size, specification of dependent and independent variables and so forth. Furthermore, given that such studies are preoccupied with isolating the impact of labour market regulations on employment, they downplay by default the importance of a whole range of factors that shape employment outcomes. More importantly, such studies ignore the perceptions of employers on the role of labour market regulations in influencing business operations. If they are indeed as important as some of the econometrics claim, they should be reflected in the views that employers hold with respect to labour market flexibility. Yet, the world's largest survey of the perceptions of employers suggests a different picture. More than 80 per cent of employers in more than 100,000 firms in over 100 low and middle countries do not regard labour market regulations as a major impediment to their business operations. To such employers, the quality of governance, lack of a reliable transport network, lack of reliable supply of electricity, lack of access to finance and lack of a skilled workforce are much more pressing issues. In any case, the chapter noted, based on a new measure of employment protection legislation, that labour market regulations change very slowly for many countries. The evidence suggests an annual average change in this new index of labour market regulations of approximately 0.007 per cent over a period of more 40 years for more than 140 countries. It is unlikely that such a barely discernable change in a particular variable can bring about major changes in labour market outcomes across the world.

Finally, the chapter argued in favour of a pluralist approach to labour market regulations. This means invoking the spirit and philosophical premise of the 'Tinbergen rule'. One should avoid a one-to-one mapping between policy goals and policy instruments. Thus, one should aim for an appropriate mix of policy instruments in attaining the broad goals of mitigating labour market risks and in dealing with chronic in-work poverty. Such an approach is well suited to the notion of striking the right balance between protecting workers against adverse circumstances and preserving broad-based employment opportunities. Only then can labour market reforms play their rightful role in promoting inclusive development.

Notes

1 This chapter draws on Dhanani *et al.* (2009), chapter 6.
2 Aleksynka and Schindler (2011).
3 Berg and Kucera (2008).
4 See the collection of essays in McCann *et al.* (2014) that articulate a careful account

of the problems of labour market flexibility and how one can move forward with a pragmatic and alternative agenda.

5 Ezeala-Harrison (2005).
6 See Yellen (1984) and Akerlof and Yellen (1986, Introduction).
7 Harrison and Scorse (2005, p. 1) include Jagdish Bhagwati, one of the luminaries of the economics profession, and Nicholas Kristoff, influential *New York Times* op-ed writer, among the ranks of those who are wary of imposing higher labour standards in developing countries because of the 'any job is better than no job' mind-set.
8 Fields (2004).
9 Basu *et al.* (2007).
10 See Freeman (1993) who was among the first to assemble evidence to show that real minimum wages fell in the 1980s across a wide range of developing countries with diverse regulatory arrangements.
11 See Fraja (2003).
12 World Bank (2012, pp. 262–263).
13 The G20 Toronto Summit, available at: www.g20.utoronto.ca/2010/g20_declaration_en.pdf.
14 The G20 Communiqué of Finance Ministers and Central Bank Governors (18–19 April 2013) notes that: 'We will continue to implement ambitious structural reforms to increase our growth potential and create jobs'. See the Communiqué at: www.g20.org/events_financial_track/20130418/780961081.html.
15 Lagarde (2014).
16 OECD (2010, p. 3). An update is offered in OECD (2014) which sets out, in a single volume, the OECD position on 'growth policies and macroeconomic stability'. See Table 8.1 in this chapter which represents the OECD's interpretation of the impact of labour market reforms on GDP and, via this channel, employment.
17 OECD (2012).
18 Bouis *et al.* (2012).
19 Blanchard *et al.* (2013).
20 *Financial Times*, 11 April, 2013, available at: http://ig.ft.com/austerity-audit. As the *Financial Times* concludes:

> Cuts to welfare payments will hit the local economies of northern towns and cities as much as five times as hard as the Conservative heartland southern counties, according to research commissioned by the Financial Times into the impact of austerity.

21 The focus of the study is on Northern Ireland, but results for the UK as a whole are also reported. See the report from the Institute for Fiscal Studies (IFS, 2013).
22 The ILO maintains NATLEX which is a very text-rich source of data on labour market regulations. There is a project underway that will generate quantifiable indicators based on NATLEX. The IMF data used here is stored in numerical form and is relatively easy to use for graphical and statistical purposes. There are also other sources that compile cross-country data on labour market regulations, most notably the World Bank's *Doing Business* series and the Fraser Institute. See discussion in the text.
23 Employment rates (expressed as a proportion of the population) are used instead of unemployment rates because the latter is widely recognized to be an inappropriate indicator of labour market performance in developing countries.
24 Aleksynska (2014) critically discusses this paper and related publications (Bernal-Verdugo *et al.*, 2012b and Crivelli *et al.*, 2012) in considerable depth and demonstrates various methodological flaws that raise questions on the empirical validity of the papers.
25 Tinbergen (1952).

Bibliography

Abbas, S.K. and Zaman, A. (2005) 'Efficiency Wage Hypothesis: The Case of Pakistan', *The Pakistan Development Review*, vol. 44, no. 4, pp. 1051–1066.

Akerlof, G.A. and Yellen, J.L. (1986) *Efficiency Wage Models of the Labour Market*, Cambridge University Press, Cambridge.

Aleksynka, M. (2014) *Deregulating Labour Markets: How Robust is the Analysis of Recent IMF Working Papers?* Conditions of Work and Employment Series, no. 47, ILO, Geneva.

Aleksynka, M. and Schindler, M. (2011) *Labor Market Regulations in Low Income, Middle and High Income Countries*, IMF Working Paper No. 547, Washington, D.C.

Basu, A.K., Chau, N.H. and Kanbur, R. (2007) *Turning a Blind Eye: Costly Enforcement, Credible Commitment and Minimum Wage Laws*, IZA Discussion Paper No. 2998, Institute for the Study of Labour (IZA), Bonn.

Berg, J. and Kucera, D. (eds) (2008) *In Defence of Labour Market Institutions*, ILO, Geneva.

Bernal-Verdugo, L., Furceri, D. and Guillaume, D. (2012a) *Crises, Labour Market Policy, and Growth? A Cross-Country Analysis*, IMF Working Paper 12/218, Washington, D.C.

Bernal-Verdugo, L., Furceri, D. and Guillaume, D. (2012b) *Labour Market Flexibility and Unemployment: New Empirical Evidence of Static and Dynamic Effects*, IMF Working Paper 12/64, Washington, D.C.

Blanchard, O., Florence, J. and Loungani, P. (2013) *Labour Market Policies and IMF Advice in Advanced Economies During the Great Recession*, March, IMF Staff Discussion Note SDN 13/02, Washington, D.C.

Bouis, R., Causa, O., Demmou, L., Duval, R. and Zdzienicka, A. (2012) *The Short-Term Effects of Structural Reforms: An Empirical Analysis*, OECD Economics Department Working Papers No. 949, 26 March, Paris.

Campos, J. and Nugent, J.B. (2013) *The Dynamics of the Regulation of Labor in Developing and Developed Countries since 1960*, mimeo, May, Brunel University and IZA, University of Southern California and IZA.

Crivelli, E., Furceri, D. and Toujas-Bernaté, J. (2012) *Crises, Labor Market Policy, and Unemployment*, IMF Working Paper 12/65, Washington, D.C.

Dhanani, S., Islam, I. and Chowdhury, A. (2009) *The Indonesian Labour Market: Changes and Challenges*, Routledge, London and New York.

Ezelea-Harrison, F. (2005) 'Two-Tier Wage Systems in Agriculture: Evidence from Indonesian Microdata', *South Western Economic Review*, available at: www.ser.tcu.edu/2005/SER2005%20Ezeala-Harrison%201–12.pdf (accessed 27 October 2014).

Fields, G.S. (2004) 'Dualism in the Labour Market: A Perspective on the Lewis Model after Half a Century', *The Manchester School*, vol. 72, no. 6, pp. 724–735.

Fraja, D.G. (2003) 'Minimum Wage Legislation, Productivity and Employment', *Economica*, vol. 66, no. 264, pp. 473–488.

Freeman, R. (1993) 'Labour Market Institutions and Policies: Help or Hindrance to Economic Development?' *Annual Proceedings of the World Bank Conference on Economic Development*, pp. 117–156, World Bank, Washington, D.C.

Freeman, R. (2009) *Labor Regulations, Unions, and Social Protection in Developing Countries: Market Distortions or Efficient Institutions?* National Bureau of Economic Research Working Paper No. 14789, Cambridge, MA.

Harrison, A. and Scorse, J. (2005) 'Improving the Conditions of Workers? Minimum

Wage Legislation and Anti-Sweatshop Activism', *California Management Review*, Vol. 48, No. 2, pp. 144–160.

IFS (Institute for Fiscal Studies) (2013) *Child and Working-Age Poverty in Northern Ireland from 2010 to 2020*, IFS Report R78, Executive Summary, available at www.ifs.org.uk/comms/r78.pdf (accessed 27 October 2014).

IMF (International Monetary Fund) (2012) *A Template for Analyzing and Projecting Labor Market Indicators*, May, Middle East and Central Asia Department, Washington, D.C.

IMF/OECD/World Bank (2014) 'Macroeconomic and Reform Priorities', note prepared for meetings of G-20 Finance Ministers and Central Bank Governors, 22–23 February.

Lagarde, C. (2014) 'The Road to Sustainable Global Growth: The Policy Agenda', Speech delivered at the School of Advanced International Studies, Johns Hopkins University, 2 April.

McCann, D., Lee, S., Belser, P., Fenwick, C., Howe, J. and Luebker, M. (eds) (2014) *Creative Labour Market Regulation: Indeterminacy and Protection in an Uncertain World*, ILO and Palgrave Macmillan, Geneva and Basingstoke.

Nataraj, S., Perez-Arce, F., Srinivasan, S. and Kumar, K.B. (2012) *What is the Impact of Labor Regulations on Employment in LICs? How Does it Vary by Gender?* July, RAND Labor and Population Working Paper Series No. 957, Santa Monica, CA.

OECD (Organisation for Economic Co-operation and Development) (1994) *The OECD Jobs Study: Facts, Analysis, Strategies*, Paris.

OECD (Organisation for Economic Co-operation and Development) (2010) *Pursuing Strong, Sustainable and Balanced Growth: the Role of Structural Reforms*, October, Paris.

OECD (Organisation for Economic Co-operation and Development) (2012) 'Going for Growth 2012: Structural Reforms can Make the Difference', Remarks by Secretary-General, 24 February, Paris.

OECD (Organisation for Economic Co-operation and Development) (2014) *Growth Policies and Macroeconomic Stability*, OECD Economic Policy Paper, February, Paris.

Tinbergen, J. (1952) *On the Theory of Economic Policy*, North Holland, Amsterdam.

World Bank (1995) *World Development Report 1995: Workers in an Integrating World*, Oxford University Press, New York.

World Bank (2012) *World Development Report 2013: Jobs*, World Bank, Washington, D.C.

World Bank (various dates) *Enterprise Survey*, available at: www.enterprisesurveys.org (accessed 27 October 2014).

Yellen, J.L. (1984) 'Efficiency Wage Models of Unemployment', *American Economic Review*, vol. 74, no. 2, pp. 200–205.

9 Labour market risks and social protection

Introduction

At low levels of economic development, problems of low income and deprivation are compounded by the vulnerability of individuals and communities to risks of various kinds, idiosyncratic as well as covariant. While such risks make poverty more acute, they create the danger of even the non-poor falling into at least transient phases of poverty. The Great Recession of 2008–09 and the previous economic crises in different regions and countries of the world demonstrated in a stark fashion that countries at all levels of development face such risks. In view of the limited coverage of formal means of social protection in developing countries, people in such countries generally rely on informal means like support from the network of friends and family, or other non-traditional mechanisms (e.g. micro-credit or informal insurance) for coping with vulnerabilities. However, experiences with severe and prolonged economic crises, e.g. the global economic crisis of 2008–09 and the Asian economic crisis of 1997–98 have demonstrated the inadequacy of such mechanisms. Furthermore, it would be rather difficult to buy private insurance against labour market risks entailing spells of unemployment and underemployment. Hence, there is a strong case for countries at all levels of development to develop a comprehensive system of social protection that can provide individuals and households with necessary support during contingencies.

It is noteworthy that although poverty reduction was the first of the Millennium Development Goals adopted in 2000, the issues of vulnerability and risks of transient poverty and the importance of social protection in fighting poverty were not recognized at that time. This shortcoming of the MDGs became apparent in the wake of the Great Recession of 2008–09, and the international community took an initiative to promote the idea of social protection for all, regardless of the level of development of a country. This agenda (in which the ILO plays an important role) is a long-term one whose aim is to gradually move towards a comprehensive social protection system in developing countries while maintaining and strengthening existing ones in developed countries. The global economic crisis of 2008–09 and developments in its wake have given a boost to this incipient agenda. The idea of 'social protection floor', which was endorsed by the UN system as a whole in April 2009, calls for initiative towards ensuring that all citizens in both rich and poor countries at least have access to a minimum bundle of services that would enable people to cope with labour market risks and provide access to affordable healthcare, child benefits and incomes for those who are too old to work.

Two further initiatives are worth noting in the context of a discussion on social protection. The first is a programme under the rubric of 'conditional cash transfers' (CCTs) that started in the Latin American region, gradually gained circulation in other developing regions of the world, and can be said to have marked the beginning of almost a 'silent revolution' in the area of social protection. The basic premise is that income transfers directed towards poor and vulnerable households can be made incentive-compatible if such transfers are conditioned on ensuring that prospective beneficiaries use the resources received to invest in children's education and health. The second is the use of employment generation programmes (e.g. the national rural employment guarantee programme in India) as a safety net measure through guaranteeing jobs and livelihoods for the poor.

It is thus clear that the agenda of addressing labour market risks through social protection has become much broader than that of conventional social security schemes. In the present chapter, this broader approach is adopted to analyse the contribution of social protection in making economic growth more inclusive. The chapter opens by addressing definitional issues relating to various types of risks and modalities of social protection including the notion of social protection floor. The chapter is then devoted to a brief discussion on the challenge of social protection faced by developing countries in view of the particular characteristics of their labour markets. The relationship between social protection and economic growth is analysed from analytical as well as empirical angles. In that section, particular attention is given to CCT programmes and their role in attaining inclusive development. The interrelationship between social protection and employment is examined. The concluding section is devoted to an examination of the questions of cost, financing and affordability of social protection from the point of view of developing countries.

Social protection: definitions and concepts

Social security, social protection and social safety net

The concepts and definitions relating to social protection have evolved over time and have moved from particular perspectives associated with the term of 'social security' to a broader notion of social protection. In the early thinking that dates back to the mid-twentieth century, the idea behind social security was to cover risks (or contingencies) arising out of old age, ill health, unemployment, etc. with the goal of providing protection against 'contingent poverty'. The commonly used (or suggested) modality for addressing such risks is that of insurance based on risk-pooling over large populations and funding over the period during which a person works. Contributory schemes like pensions, provident funds and unemployment insurance fall under this category. In such schemes, payments are made before the contingency occurs, and a notion of guaranteed payment in case of contingency is associated with the contribution made.

Given the limited scope of social security measures covering only contingent poverty and the importance of addressing structural (or chronic) poverty, the notion of social protection came into circulation, and brought under its umbrella non-contributory schemes that could be used to tackle the latter type of situation. These are generally known as social assistance schemes which in turn may be means-tested (i.e. providing benefits only to those falling below a certain level of income) or non-means-tested. Such schemes could also be categorical, i.e. to cover certain categories (e.g. children, women, disabled people) of population. These would normally be financed out of governments' budgets. One particular form of such tax-financed schemes are the so-called conditional cash transfers that require beneficiaries to participate in prescribed public programmes, e.g. of education and health. Employment generation programmes aimed at generating incomes for the poor are also amongst such tax financed schemes, although payment under such a programme would be subject to participation in the labour market.

The earliest institutional underpinning for social protection was perhaps provided by the ILO's Philadelphia Declaration of 1944 when the annual conference of the ILO recognized its obligation to promote programmes which would achieve 'the extension of social security measures to provide a basic income to all in need of such protection and comprehensive medical care'.[1] According to the ILO Recommendation No. 67 of 1944, income security schemes should relieve want and prevent destitution by restoring, up to a reasonable level, income which is lost by reason of inability to work (including old age) or to obtain remunerative work, or by reason of death of the breadwinner. Income security should be organized as far as possible on the basis of compulsory social insurance, and the provision of needs not covered by compulsory social insurance should be made by social assistance. In the same vein, Recommendation No. 69 (1944) suggests that medical care should be provided either through a social insurance medical care service with supplementary provision by way of social assistance or through public medical service

ILO Convention No. 102 (1952) identifies nine areas for social insurance: (1) medical care; (2) sickness benefits; (3) unemployment; (4) old age; (5) employment injury; (6) family circumstances (in terms of size); (7) maternity; (8) invalidity; (9) widowhood. This addresses 'contingent poverty' rather than chronic/structural poverty of the type faced by many developing countries. In order to address the latter, it would be necessary to supplement social insurance by social assistance that is usually funded through public budget.

Over time, the use of the term social security evolved within the ILO as well. For example, according to the ILO's *World Labour Report 2000*, social security included social insurance (i.e. contributory schemes), social assistance (i.e. tax-financed benefits provided only to those with low incomes) and universal benefits (i.e. tax-financed benefits provided without being tested for income or means). That report defined social protection to include not only public social security schemes but also private or non-statutory schemes with a similar objective, such as mutual benefit societies and occupational pension schemes. It covered all sorts of non-statutory schemes, formal or informal, provided that the contributions to the schemes are not wholly determined by market forces. The report mentioned above acknowledges that employment guarantee may be seen as a form of unemployment insurance because it can provide income security (ILO, 2000, p. 165). In that sense, part of active labour market policies also becomes part of social protection policy.

It thus appears that the terms social security and social protection are being used interchangeably by the ILO, although its 2014 global report emphasizes the use of the term social protection.[2] This is indicated also by the inclusion, in its report of 2010 (ILO, 2010), of measures for addressing general poverty in the list of situations against which protection is needed.

Another term that has gained circulation in the discussion on social protection is 'social safety net' (SSN), which refers to non-contributory transfer programmes seeking to provide support to the poor and the vulnerable in the face of poverty and shocks of various kinds. They may be designed to serve a variety of purposes that include (i) reduction of poverty and inequality, (ii) encouraging human capital investment in human capital among the poor, (iii) enabling the poor to better manage risks both idiosyncratic and covariant, and (iv) protecting the poor from the adverse effects of economic reforms and adjustment.

SSN programmes are usually targeted at the poor or specific groups in society, and are financed from public budget. But the providers of SSNs also include private organizations (e.g. NGOs, charities, companies) and individuals. A variety of means are used for SSNs, e.g. food, in-kind transfers, cash transfers.

One particular type of social safety net (or social assistance) programme that has become prominent amongst measures of social protection are the so-called conditional cash transfer (CCT) programmes under which cash is transferred to the poor on condition of their participation in some publicly provided social and human development programmes, especially in the field of education and health-care. Typical programmes consist of providing cash on condition of children's enrolment and regular attendance in school, immunization of children, visits by women to pre- and post-natal healthcare centres, etc. The main objectives of such programmes are twofold: (1) to provide income support to the poor and (2) to promote human capital development, and through that mechanism, to promote increases in future incomes of the poor.

Basic social protection floor

The notion of basic social protection floor gained currency in the wake of the Great Recession of 2008–09 when it was found that in the absence of social protection, large swathes of population in developing countries not only suffer from chronic poverty, but many who are not normally poor find it difficult to cope with sudden external shocks and face the danger of lapsing into poverty. In discussions on ways and means of responding to the crisis at international forums like the UN and G20 countries, this issue featured prominently and the importance of putting in place some kind of basic social protection floor was recognized. The underpinning for this is provided by Article 22 of the Universal Declaration of Human Rights (1948) which states: 'Everyone, as a member of society, has the right to social security'. Article 25 of the Declaration formulates this right in a more precise manner as 'the right to security in the event of unemployment, sickness, disability, widowhood, old age or other lack of livelihood in circumstances beyond his control'. The Social Protection Floor (SPF) Initiative of the UN defines the term as a 'global and coherent social policy concept that promotes nationally defined strategies that protect a minimum level of access to essential services and income security for all in the present economic and financial crisis and beyond' (ILO and WHO, 2009, p. 1; see also 'Social Protection Floor Initiative', available at www.socialsecurityextension.org). According to this initiative, the main elements of SPF are:

1   Essential services: i.e. geographical and financial access to essential services (such as water, sanitation, adequate nutrition, health and education, housing, and other services including life and asset saving information);
2   Essential social transfers: i.e. social transfers, in cash and in kind, paid to the poor and vulnerable to provide a minimum income and health security.

(ILO and WHO, 2009, p. 2)

The ILO defines what it calls 'The Basic Social Security Floor' (BSSF) as 'a basic and modest set of social security guarantees – implemented through social transfers in cash and in kind – for all citizens' (ILO, 2008, p. 2). This set of guarantees includes (i) access to basic/essential healthcare benefits, (ii) income security for children at least at the poverty level through various family/child benefits, (iii) targeted income support to the poor and the unemployed in the active age group, and (iv) income security for the old and the disabled – at least at the poverty level – through pensions for old age, disability and survivors. The BSSF thus consists essentially of a guaranteed set of basic social transfers in cash or in kind to all. It is formulated as a set of guarantees rather than benefits. This leaves the option open to individual countries to implement them through means tested conditional or unconditional transfers. While conceptually this can be part of a country's social security architecture, in reality they may take the form of social assistance rather than social security benefits. As for financing, it is assumed that the SPF would be financed through general taxation (whereas defined benefits in social security schemes are the result of rights acquired on the basis of contributions).

Why social protection?

Economic growth, crises and social protection

As already mentioned in the first section of this chapter, till about the end of the twentieth century, social protection was not very high on the agenda either in developed or in developing countries. There was even a tendency to invoke the debate between the 'growth first model' versus the 'European social model' and the perceived superiority of the former as a justification for relegating the importance of social protection. Indeed, in the developed world, countries that achieved high economic and employment growth appear to be the ones charac- terized by lower unemployment rates as well as lower levels of unemployment benefits. Amongst the OECD countries, for example, the USA is known to have been able to achieve higher economic growth (in terms of GDP growth) than, for example, the countries in Western Europe – at least during the two decades before the global economic crisis of 2008–09.[3] And the duration of unemploy- ment benefit as well as expenditure on unemployment compensation has been consistently lower in the USA compared to the latter.[4]

Countries in the developing world generally did not have any unemployment benefits, and social protection in them – covering mainly the formal sector workers – basically was in the form of severance benefits (of varying duration), pensions and provident funds, and programmes of social assistance. For workers outside the formal sector, there was virtually no social protection except for some programmes of social assistance and labour market programmes targeted at specific groups. Even in countries that had achieved high rates of economic growth on a sustained basis for some time, e.g. those in East and South East Asia, there was not much thinking about unemployment benefit until they were hit by a severe economic crisis in 1997–98. High rates of output growth that were generally associated with high rates of employment growth in higher pro- ductivity activities like manufacturing, construction and services, and some increases in real wages appeared to have made it possible for policy makers in those countries to postpone thinking about social protection for workers.

The experiences mentioned above perhaps gave rise to the question whether high rates of economic and employment growth could obviate the need for social protection or at least make its case somewhat weaker. Even apart from the norm- ative issue of the desirability of social protection, two points need to be con- sidered in this context. The first relates to economic growth itself: what has been the experience with respect to growth, both in terms of rates and stability. The second point relates to the outcome of economic growth in terms of employment growth. Let us look at both points briefly.

As for the level of economic growth, during 1980–2000, annual GDP growth has been lower than during 1960–80 for the world as a whole. The same is true separately for the developing as well as developed countries.[5] Of course, the global economy as a whole attained a period of prosperity after the brief reces- sion of 2001. But even during the period of prosperity in the global economy, the working class did not benefit from growth in the same proportion as the higher income groups. In fact, the share of labour in total production has been declining during the periods of high growth and prosperity.[6] One can therefore imagine that workers may face additional pressure when either the global economy or the economy of a country is hit by some shock. From the point of view of equity, justice or efforts to reduce poverty, this outcome is neither desirable nor justifiable.

In addition, the volatility of both GDP and per capita GDP growth has increased.[7] While high rates of economic growth have not been a general achievement, lack of stability in growth has added to the insecurity that people (especially the poor ones) suffer from. How, in the absence of social protection, the levels of living of low income people are affected by economic instability can be illustrated with reference to the experience of the Asian economic crisis of 1997–98, as well as the global economic crisis and the Great Recession of 2008–09.

Before the financial and economic crisis hit the countries of East and South East Asia in 1997–98, most of them had the benefit of sustained rates of high economic growth for two decades or more. And yet, except for the Republic of Korea, no other country had any unemployment insurance. In Korea also, the coverage of the scheme was limited (only to firms with more than 30 employees). The other countries had mandatory severance payments, the magnitude of which varied from three months of salary in the Philippines to four and six months respectively for Indonesia and Thailand (Lee, 1998). In some countries, the workers could withdraw from their provident funds.[8] But on the whole, the degree of coverage under social protection measures was rather low, ranging from 12 per cent of total employment in Indonesia to 48 per cent in Malaysia (Lee, 1998).

It may be recalled that one immediate impact of the East Asian economic crisis was sharp recession in the affected countries (although the degree of the impact varied), GDP growth rates in 1998 ranging from –0.6 per cent in the Philippines to –13.2 per cent in Indonesia (Islam, 2003). The labour markets adjusted in various ways with both quantity and price adjustments taking place. While unemployment rates increased sharply in all the affected countries (i.e. Indonesia, Korea, Malaysia, Philippines and Thailand), real wages declined in all of them, the most severe being in Indonesia (Betcherman and Islam, 2001).

As a result, all the countries suffered a setback in their fight against poverty; and the impressive achievements they had made in reducing poverty were reversed. In Indonesia, the incidence of absolute poverty increased sharply from 17.7 per cent in 1996 to 24.2 per cent in 1998. It was only in 2000 that the incidence of poverty in Indonesia went back to the pre-crisis level. Likewise, poverty increased temporarily in Malaysia, Philippines and Thailand (Islam, 2003). It is thus clear that in the absence of effective social protection systems, the countries were unable to cope with the adverse effects of the economic crisis on the social aspects.

Of course, the countries affected by the economic crisis did introduce a variety of measures to cope with the adverse social effects of the crisis. But the measures varied in their details. Korea, for example, expanded their unemployment benefit scheme gradually to cover all workers except those hired on a daily basis. In addition, conditions for qualifying for the benefits were relaxed and the benefit levels were increased. In addition, wage subsidies and public works programme were introduced. Thailand focused on employment creation schemes, and also attempted to address possible effects of the crisis on education and health services. The other countries also introduced public works programmes and other measures to promote employment and incomes for the poor; but the effectiveness of the programmes varied.[9] The data on poverty mentioned above indicate that except Korea (where unemployment benefits were introduced before the economic crisis and were expanded during the crisis), the other countries were not able to prevent a substantial worsening of the living conditions of the lower income groups.

As for the Great Recession of 2008–09, it is by now well-known that the economic crisis not only started in the USA, but the impact of the resulting recession on the labour market was sharper in that country compared to some of the countries of Western Europe (except countries like Greece and Spain). Unemployment in the USA increased from 4.4 per cent in May 2007 to 10 per cent in October 2009, and remained well over 9 per cent throughout 2010 and much of 2011.[10] As mentioned earlier in this section, the USA is also the country where the duration of unemployment benefit was shorter and the proportion of expenditure on unemployment compensation in GDP was smaller compared to the countries of Western Europe. Therefore, it is not surprising that the USA had to take measures to extend the duration of unemployment benefits[11] as well as to increase benefits under other programmes of social assistance (e.g. the food stamps programme, health insurance for those who lost their jobs). In comparison, the countries of Western Europe (with some exceptions, of course) already had in place solid programmes of social protection that provided basic support to those losing their jobs. Of course, they have undertaken measures to strengthen their active labour market programmes, and some have also extended their unemployment benefits.[12] The conclusion that tends to follow from the above experience is that although the USA has been able to achieve higher GDP growth rate during periods of economic boom, the 'European social model' with its emphasis on social protection appears to have provided better support to workers during periods of instability and economic downturn.

The impact of recession in developed countries got transmitted quickly to other parts of the global economy and labour markets started adjusting through a variety of measures including retrenchments, lowering of wages, etc. (Islam *et al.*, 2011). Moreover, the experience of the Asian economic crisis and its aftermath indicates that when economic recovery starts, labour markets do not start readjusting immediately. There is usually a lag between economic recovery and recovery in the labour market which can vary depending on the situation (Islam, 2003; Reinhart and Rogoff, 2009). In the absence of social protection, workers (and their families) in such situations face the danger of reverting back into poverty, as was seen during the crises mentioned above.

To sum up, the market-based economies of the present day world give rise to uncertainties of different kinds; and given the interdependence between various economies, the adverse effects of such risks and uncertainties get transmitted to countries outside the origin. While there are benefits of globalization, there is also the risk of the negative effects of economic shocks spreading beyond national boundaries. It is the general people, especially those dependent on their own labour, who ultimately suffer from such uncertainties. Measures are needed to provide them with protection and ability to cope with such an environment.

Coming to the second point, i.e. the outcome of economic growth in terms of employment, it needs to be noted that employment intensity of economic growth is critical for translating the benefits of growth into poverty reduction on a sustained basis. Empirical evidence and analysis already presented in Chapter 2 of the present volume showed that there is no invariant relationship between economic growth and poverty reduction. The pattern of growth is critical from the point of view of its effectiveness in reducing poverty. Productive employment and labour market variables (e.g. real wages) play a key role in that regard.[13]

The contrasting experience of the countries of East and South East Asia, on the one hand, and of South Asia, on the other, lends support to the observations made above. Countries like the Republic of Korea, Malaysia, Thailand and Indonesia (the latter, till the time it was hit by economic crisis in 1998) not only achieved high rates of economic growth, their growth was more employment intensive in nature than in South Asian countries. And the rates of poverty reduction achieved by the former were also more impressive than the latter (Islam, 2006, 2013; Khan, 2007).

In fact, employment intensity of economic growth in many developing countries has been low and declining in recent years. Growth of employment in the formal sector has been rather low, and much of the employment growth takes place in the informal segments of the economy. In this kind of a situation, the prospects of high rates of employment intensive growth of the kind achieved by the East and South East Asian countries during the past few decades do not appear to be bright.[14] Unless there is willingness on the part of policy makers to rethink and reorient development strategies, economic growth may not become significantly more employment intensive than at present. Hence, it would be important to develop a strategy for social protection alongside the growth strategy.

Structural poverty and social protection

The phenomena of economic crises and ups and downs in incomes caused by them are temporary in nature. Structural and chronic poverty is a problem faced by many in low income developing countries. Although it is expected that economic growth would help them get out of poverty, and poverty has indeed declined in many countries, it is well known that the process and rate of decline in poverty reduction vary a great deal between countries, and growth often bypasses many poor people. It is essential to find ways and means to bring them out of poverty, and social protection is important in that context. Data presented in Table 9.1 illustrates this point with examples from a few developing countries.

The countries for which data are presented in Table 9.1 not only had different rates of growth of per capita GDP and poverty reduction per annum, but more importantly, the elasticity of poverty reduction with respect to economic growth has been very different in these countries. While per capita GDP growth required for one percentage point of poverty reduction was the highest for India (followed by Chile), it was the lowest for Brazil (followed by Indonesia and Mexico). The contrast between Brazil and India does not remain limited to this. It is well known that since the late 1990s, Brazil has successfully implemented an effective conditional cash transfer programme that has contributed substantially to poverty reduction in the country. On the other hand, economic growth in India has not resulted in much growth of productive employment in the formal sector. Neither has there been an effective social transfer programme like that of Brazil. Although India has been implementing a national employment guarantee programme since 2006, its contribution to poverty reduction has not been as substantial as that of Brazil's CCT programmes (more on this will be said later in the present chapter). Mexico also has been implementing CCT programmes, and the rate of per capita GDP growth required for a unit decrease in poverty in the country has also been low. These examples show the importance of adopting social protection programmes without waiting for economic growth to take care of the problem of poverty.

Figures 9.1 and 9.2 also show that countries can pursue social protection policies without waiting to reach a high level of per capita income and reap benefits accordingly. The examples of Asian countries presented in Figure 9.1 show that similar levels of per capita GDP can be associated with different levels of expenditure on social protection as percentage of GDP. For example, GDP per capita in Sri Lanka and Vietnam are similar to those of Indonesia and the Philippines, but their social protection expenditures in relation to per capita GDP are

Table 9.1 Per capita GDP growth and poverty reduction in selected countries, 1990/93 to 2009/2010

Country	Annual change (%) in per capita GDP	Change (% point) in poverty (US$2 a day)	Change (%) in GDP per % point decrease in poverty
Brazil	1.4	−0.6	1.7
Chile	3.7	−0.6	6.2
China	9.5	−3.0	3.1
India	5.7	−0.8	7.0
Indonesia	3.4	−1.9	1.8
Mexico	1.0	−0.6	1.7
South Africa	1.5	−0.6	2.5
Vietnam	6.3	−2.8	2.2

Source: adapted from Schweighofer (2013).

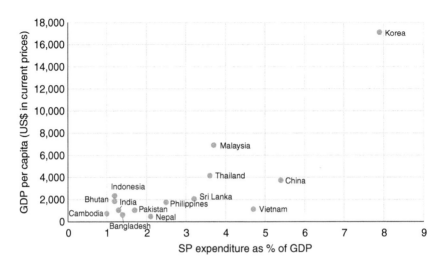

Figure 9.1 GDP per capita at current prices (US$) and social protection expenditure as percentage of GDP, 2009 (source: prepared by the authors using data from ADB (2013)).

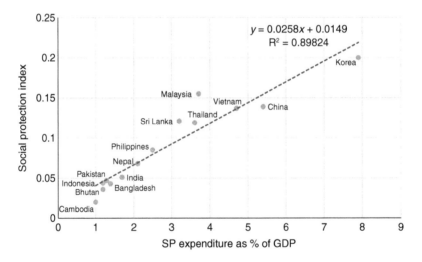

Figure 9.2 Social protection index and SP expenditure as percentage of GDP in selected countries of Asia, 2009 (source: prepared by the authors using data from ADB (2013)).

much higher. And Figure 9.2 shows that they have attained results from their social protection policies as they score higher in terms of the social protection index. The conclusion that follows from the evidence presented above is that attaching priority to social protection is not necessarily a function of the level of per capita income of a country, and countries can reap the benefits of allocating resources for social protection.

The challenge posed by a large informal sector

In the context of developing countries, an important aspect of the structure of labour markets is the duality that characterizes them – a small formal sector co-existing with a large informal sector. This has important implications for the coverage and type of social protection. For example, higher employment growth in the formal sector can facilitate a greater coverage of workers through various social insurance schemes. If, on the contrary, a high proportion of the labour force is engaged in the informal economy, alternative mechanisms for providing social protection are required. The high proportion of the employed labour force in self-employment and in informal employment does pose an additional challenge for developing countries in this respect. For those who are self-employed, it is not so easy to arrange for insurance against ill health and inability to work due to unforeseen contingencies and make provision for incomes during old age.[15] The same applies to those who are in informal employment, because it is difficult to use formal mechanisms of social protection, especially those based on insurance, in such cases. Conventional mechanisms of social protection, e.g. unemployment allowance and pensions, may not be applicable to the vast number of people in these categories. But rather than overlooking and ignoring the need for social protection for them, it is essential to identify alternative measures and, if necessary, innovative mechanisms for providing social protection.

In situations where social protection system is weak or inadequate, the poor usually depend on traditional support systems based on family and community. For example, during the Asian economic crisis of 1997–98, many workers who lost jobs in Indonesia and Thailand had to return to their rural households and rely on support from their families. At that time, there was a good deal of talk about so-called 'Asian values'. But what happened in reality was sharing of family's incomes, and the creation of a new class of poor. On the other hand, in the Republic of Korea, the social protection system was strengthened at that time by increasing the number of people covered by unemployment insurance. In addition, an attempt was made to prevent increase in the rate of unemployment by introducing public works programme. In Thailand as well, debates and discussion on the possibility of introducing unemployment insurance started at that time.

While conventional thinking is that social protection may not be economically feasible in developing countries, empirical exercises show that it should be possible to introduce at least some basic social protection measures, e.g. old age allowance and unemployment benefits, in such countries. One exercise (Lee, 1998) showed that in Indonesia and Thailand, the expenditure that will be needed to replace half of the regular incomes for unemployment for a period of six months can be feasibly shared between the government, employers and workers. A good example of what can be done to provide social protection for those engaged in the unorganized sector is demonstrated by the adoption, in

India in 2008, of the Unorganized Workers' Social Security Bill. Under this Act, provision was made to bring 340 million people (out of a total labour force of 458 million) under the cover of pension, basic health, life and disability insurance, as well as group accident insurance, within a period of five years. This shows that it is not unpractical or a luxury to think of providing social protection to those who are engaged in the informal economy. What is important is political will and the adoption of innovative approaches.

Social protection and inclusive development

Social protection and economic growth

The conventional perspective about the relationship between social protection and economic growth is that social transfers may discourage people from working and taxes may discourage entrepreneurs from investing, and thus the impact on growth may be negative. Such views, however, are at best based only on partial analysis of the factors and mechanisms that influence economic growth and of how various elements of social protection are affected by such factors. While some of the mechanisms may be negatively affected by social protection initiatives, thus creating a negative impact on growth, other factors may be boosted by social protection, thus creating a positive impact on growth. In order to have a more balanced view of the relationship, it would therefore be necessary to undertake an analysis of such factors and mechanisms.

While discussing the relationship between social protection and economic growth, it would be important to start from two broad aspects of the former, namely, how it is financed (i.e. whether through taxes and public budget or through contributions of participants) and what mechanisms are used to provide support to potential beneficiaries (i.e. whether through active measures like labour market policies or through passive measures like unemployment benefits, healthcare support, support for education, etc.).

As for factors that influence economic growth, the list would depend on the approach that is adopted. In the classical approach (following the traditions of Adam Smith and David Ricardo, for example), the major factor in economic growth is savings. And social protection may have an adverse effect on growth via the savings route because taxes for providing social assistance as well as redistribution resulting from benefits may discourage savings. However, the picture would be different if one adopts growth models (e.g. those of Solow and Keynes) where, in addition to savings and capital, factors like the supply of labour, skills, technological change, aggregate demand, etc. apply. In fact, there are situations where political instability may also have an adverse effect on growth. Once such a broad-based approach is adopted, the situation becomes different. Table 9.2 provides a stylized description of different aspects of social protection (i.e. the mode of financing and benefits provided), mechanisms through which they might affect growth, and the possible direction of their impact on growth. Before looking at the contents of this table, it needs to be noted that it provides only a basic structure for

Table 9.2 Mechanisms through which social protection may affect economic growth

Aspect	Mechanism of the impact	Boosting or depressing the mechanism	Direction of the impact on growth (positive or negative)
Financing			
Taxation and	Informality	B	+/−
social security	Labour supply	D	−
contributions	Labour demand	D	−
	Savings	D	−
	Income inequality	D	+
	Private investment	D	−
Expenditure			
ALMPs	Income inequality	D	+
	Income fluctuations	D	+
	Employment	B	+
	Investment	B	+
	Infrastructure	B	+
	Other public investment	D	−
	Social stability and cohesion	B	+
Health services	Human capital	B	+
	Income fluctuation	D	+
	Public investment	B	+
	Social stability	B	+
Transfers to the	Market-based insurance	B	+
unemployed	Job matching	B	+
	Income fluctuation	D	+
	Labour market flexibility	B	+
	Informality	B	+/−
	Labour supply	D	−
	Other public investment	D	−
	Social stability	B	+
Child benefit	Human capital	B	+
	Social stability	B	+
	Other public investment	D	-
Others (old age,	Income fluctuation	D	+
disability and	Consumption smoothing	B	+
survivors'	Labour supply	D	−
benefits)	Overall labour productivity	B	+
	Informality	B	+/−
	Other public investment	D	−
	Social stability	B	+

Source: adapted from Damerau (2011).

analysing the growth effect of social protection. Rather than looking at its various components in isolation, the various elements should be treated as possible factors whose workings and interactions are important.

Even looking at the various factors listed in Table 9.2 in isolation, one would note that while the growth effect of taxation and contributions needed for providing social protection may appear to be negative (via a depressing effect on labour supply and investment), there are many other factors that may create a positive growth effect. Hence, the net effect would be difficult to predict.

And the situation changes when possible interactions between various factors are taken into account. For example, benefits provided by social protection do not necessarily have a negative effect on labour supply, especially if they are combined with other active labour market policies (e.g. skill training and job search), in which case the impact on labour supply may be positive. The latter may have a growth enhancing effect through other channels as well, e.g. (1) creation of infrastructure through public works programmes, (2) reduction in fluctuations in income and smoothening of consumption and (3) improvement in social stability and cohesion. This kind of interaction may exist in other cases as well, turning the apparent negative effect into a positive one. For example, the positive impact of reduction in inequality on social cohesion and stability, and reduction of uncertainties in income may make it easier to implement needed reforms, and may thus encourage investment.

As for developing countries, it is important to recognize the difference in their situation which, in turn, may have differential implications for the growth effect of social protection. The relevant literature (e.g. Barrientos and Scott, 2008; Dercon, 2011) mentions several areas where measures of social protection may unleash a growth-generating impulse. First, social transfers and other social assistance can provide the poor with access to productive assets that are needed to participate in productive activities.[16] A related factor is credit constraint and the extent to which that is lifted through social protection. If social transfers and assistance can help facilitate access to credit and in building an asset base, the poor may have a chance get out of the poverty trap and participate productively in economic activities. To the extent that happens, social protection would have a positive impact on inclusive growth.

A second important issue is the extent to which social assistance provides the poor with greater ability to cope with shocks of various kinds and deal with uncertainties. In situations of uncertainty and their own ability to cope with shocks, poor households may limit the adoption of risky investments (for example, in higher yielding crops, newer products in cottage industries). By providing them with support for managing such risks, social protection may facilitate investments with higher yields.

Third, social transfers may also facilitate improved household resource allocation and dynamics. Examples are transfers aimed at supporting children's education and health which in turn may not only prevent child labour but also contribute to human resource development and higher returns to labour in future.

Fourth, well-designed social insurance can plug gaps in private insurance markets. By overcoming market failures, it can contribute to efficiency and enable households to use their resources more efficiently and encourage risk-taking and innovation (Ahmad *et al.*, 1991; Dercon, 2005).

Fifth, when transfers are used to create infrastructures through public works programmes, they enable the building of public goods and infrastructure in local communities which, in turn, can contribute to growth of output.

The above discussion indicates that there are strong reasons to expect a positive effect of social protection on economic growth. However, quantification of the magnitude and statistical significance of such effect may not be easy, especially in developing countries where the channels of causation are diverse, and many of them may operate over a period that is longer than can be captured by a simple relationship between expenditure on social protection and economic growth.

Studies that attempt to quantify the effect of social protection (measured by social expenditure) on economic growth in developed countries have produced results showing a positive, negative as well as inconclusive effect. One study that reviews 25 studies (mostly covering OECD countries) reports positive effect for ten of them, negative effect for six and inconclusive results for another nine (Damerau, 2011).

One study covering OECD countries (Arjona *et al.*, 2002) and reporting results based on regressions using pooled time series data from 21 countries for the period 1970–98 show: (1) statistically significant negative impact of social expenditures on GDP growth; (2) a similar result when expenditure on health is deducted from the total; (3) a similar result when the exercise is done for only expenditure on working age population. Results of regressions using data from 17 countries for 1984–97 show: (i) statistically significant positive impact of spending on active policies; (ii) statistically significant negative impact of spending on non-active policies.

As for developing countries, an ILO study (ILO, 2014) covering 136 developing countries and using data for the period 1990–2012 shows that expenditure on social protection has significant positive effect on GDP per capita. The results of the exercise (presented in Table 9.3) show that 1 per cent change in social protection expenditure per capita leads to a 0.353 per cent change in GDP per capita. Looking at the difference between categories of developing countries, it is noteworthy that the strength of the relationship increases as one moves from LDCs to lower middle income countries and upper middle income countries.

Can conditional cash transfers contribute to inclusive development?

The analysis and evidence presented above of the impact of social protection measures, and especially of social transfers, on economic growth covers conditional cash transfers (CCTs) as well. However, given the increasing use of the latter as an instrument for social safety in recent years, it may not be inappropriate to devote particular attention to it and examine its possible contribution to economic growth and making it more inclusive.

From three countries in 1997 (Brazil, Mexico and Bangladesh), CCTs were in operation in 28 countries around the world in 2008.[17] As for modality and approach, most of the programmes transfer cash on condition of child enrolment in schools and regular visits to healthcare centres. India's Mahatma Gandhi National Rural Employment Programme adopts a different approach of transferring cash as wage for unskilled work in infrastructure projects (see Table 9.4).

Table 9.3 Regression results of the impact of social expenditure on economic growth in developing countries, 1990–2012

	Log GDP per capita in constant 2005 US$				
	All developing	*Only LDCs*	*Only LMIs*	*Only EEs*
Log social protection expenditure per capita	0.353[a] (0.027)	0.245[a] (0.038)	0.353[a] (0.039)	0.477[a] (0.047)
Constant	5.741[a] (0.113)	5.482[a] (0.102)	5.678[a] (0.158)	5.568[a] (0.274)
R2	0.515	0.374	0.551	0.646
R2 (overall)	0.820	0.670	0.536	0.424
R2 (including fixed effects)	0.977	0.951	0.931	0.901
Observations	887	287	276	324
Number of countries	136	45	41	50

Source: ILO (2014).

Note

a denotes that the coefficient is statistically significant at less than 1 per cent level.

Table 9.4 Implementation of India's Mahatma Gandhi Rural National Employment Guarantee Programme, 2006–12

	2006–07	2007–08	2008–09	2009–10	2010–11	2011–12
Number of districts covered	200	300	All	All	All	All
Number of households covered (million)	21	34	45	53	55	50
Percentage women workers	40	43	48	48	48	48
Work-days per household	43	42	48	54	47	42
Budget (Rs billion)	113,000	120,000	300,000	391,000	401,000	400,000
Expenditure (Rs billion)	88,240	158,570	272,500	379,050	393,770	373,030
Share of unskilled labour in total expenditure (%)	66	68	67	67	65	66

Source: authors' compilation from GOI (2012).

The programmes vary in basic objectives, size and coverage. While some of them focus narrowly only one aspect, there are others that target the poor in general. For example, the female stipend programme in Bangladesh focuses only on gender difference in enrolment and covers only girl students. On the other hand, programmes like *Bolsa Familia* of Brazil cover the poor as a whole. The size and coverage of the porgrammes also vary a great deal, ranging from 40 per cent of the population in Ecuador to 20 per cent in Brazil and Mexico to just 1 per cent in Cambodia.[18]

Although some of the CCTs focus narrowly on only education or health, the basic objectives of the first generation programmes when they started in Latin America were twofold: to reduce poverty and inequality in the short term and to contribute to human development in the long run through the conditionality of school enrolment and accessing public health services. The programmes thus have built-in mechanisms for contributing to inclusive development. Coming to their actual impact, from our present perspective, it is important not only to look at their impact on economic growth but also to see if they can play a role in addressing labour market risks.

The basic rationale for CCTs is provided by the inadequacy of the poverty reducing effects of economic growth in many situations and the need to supplement market-driven outcomes with public policy aimed at accelerating the rate of poverty reduction. The rationale behind making transfers conditional on some required behaviour on the part of the beneficiaries is provided by two broad sets of arguments (Fiszbein and Shady, 2009). The first set is premised on the hypothesis that private investment in human capital, especially in education, is too low for a variety of reasons. One reason could be a wrong perception about possible returns to investment (or expenditures) in education and health as a result of which private investment is lower than is warranted by the actual or estimated rates of returns. In addition, parents may discount the future more heavily than they should (a phenomenon dubbed as 'incomplete altruism'), and even discriminate against girls. Furthermore, the 'privately optimal' investment in education and health may be lower than the 'socially optimal' if there are externalities associated with expenditures on education and health.[19]

The second set of arguments is provided by the political economy of anti-poverty measures, and a belief that such measures would be politically more attractive to voters when they are conditioned on what is considered as 'good behaviour' rather than given out as dole.

Whatever the rationales, CCTs have established a good track record in terms of both the immediate objective of poverty reduction and the longer-term objective of human development, although questions regarding the latter are being raised.[20] Some of the studies also throw light on the impact on growth mediating mechanisms. Although it is not possible to come to firm conclusions on the basis of such studies, a few remarks may be made with some confidence.

First, there seems to be strong support for the view that social transfers facilitate increased investment in human development via increased school enrolment and utilization of health services.[21]

Second, social transfers lead to increases in savings among households which in turn may facilitate investment in more productive activities.

Third, an important question is whether transfers may boost asset levels sufficiently to provide the poor with access to credit and help them overcome the credit constraint.[22] The evidence on this is not very strong – at least for physical assets. There is, however, some evidence to show that transfers enable the poor to invest in productive activities with high returns.[23] Also important in this regard is to compare the performance of other anti-poverty programmes like micro-credit. Reviewing a number of micro-credit initiatives in a range of countries (Ghana, India, Philippines and Sri Lanka), Dercon (2011) concludes that they also do not have large effects on asset holding and poverty reduction. An additional problem with micro-credit is that it is not easy to reach the poorest of the poor through the programme, while social transfers can be quite effective.

Despite the positive track record of CCTs in general, a number of questions have come up, especially in the context of the goal of human development. First, although the basic assumption behind transfers as a mechanism for increasing enrolment is that demand is the major constraint and there is no supply bottleneck, in many countries, especially in low income developing countries, availability and quality of facilities may be an important issue. Indeed, studies (for example, Handa and Davis, 2006; IEG, 2011) have mentioned the importance of addressing the supply issue alongside transfers to families to overcome the demand constraint.

Another important issue from the point of view of long-run impact on human development is the quality of learning. From the point of view of creating an impact on long-term human development and upward mobility through formation of human capital, the quality of learning is important. Evaluations focusing on cognitive achievement of students do in fact point to mixed results on learning (Fiszbein and Shady, 2009; Handa and Davis, 2006; IEG, 2011).

Third, if programmes target only poor households with children for assistance, they may leave out many poor families whose demographic situation is different. Likewise, employment-based programmes can cover only those households having members who are capable of manual labour.

From the point of view of the impact on labour market, it would be important to examine whether social transfers are having a negative impact on labour supply. Evidence in this respect shows that transfers of the kind provided by standard CCTs focusing on children's education may result in reallocation of resources within households, e.g. reduction in labour supply by children (as school enrolment rises). However, that is often more than compensated by increases in labour supply by working age adults, so that no significant adverse effect on total labour supply is found (Barrientos and Scott, 2008; Barrientos and Villa, 2014).

Can CCTs be useful in addressing labour market risks, especially risks faced in situations of economic crisis? Although the programmes with focus on human development are not normally geared towards that objective, there have been situations where they have been helpful in providing a safety net at times of crisis. For example, Handa and Davis (2006) mention that the programmes in Mexico and Nicaragua have provided a safety net in the face of the Tequila crisis and coffee price crisis respectively. But the employment-based programmes are more suitable for responding to the adverse effects of economic crisis on labour markets. This has been demonstrated during various crises, e.g. the Asian economic crisis of 1997–98 (Betcherman and Islam, 2001), the economic crisis in Argentina in 2001 (Devereux and Solomon, 2006).[24]

On the whole, it appears that if measures of social protection, and especially social transfers, can be designed and implemented well, they can have positive impact on the ability of poor households to invest in their productive capacity and better participate in the growth process – thus making growth more inclusive.

Social protection and employment

The inter-linkage between social protection and employment can work in two directions. Like its impact on economic growth, social protection may have an impact on employment and the functioning of labour markets. On the other hand, active labour market programmes, especially if they include employment generation programmes, can be a useful component of social protection strategy of a country. This is particularly so if the latter takes the form of guaranteed employment, e.g. in the Mahatma Gandhi National Rural Employment Guarantee Programme (MGNREGP) of India. In this section, we first look at the possible impact of social protection on employment, and then use MGNREGP as an example of how employment guarantee programmes may act as a means of social protection.

Possible impact of social protection on employment and labour market functioning

Conventional wisdom points out that a generous social protection, by raising the cost of hiring labour, can have an adverse effect on economic and employment growth – thus leading to higher unemployment and putting further pressure on the social protection system. But this view is not necessarily supported by available evidence.

There is an ongoing and unresolved debate on this issue. On Europe, a widely cited article by Bean (1994) argues that the evidence available does not show that the existence of generous unemployment benefits was the cause of persistent unemployment. Nickel (1997) also shows that unemployment benefits do not have an adverse effect on unemployment rates. A study by Forteza and Rama (2002) covering 119 countries (i.e. both developed and developing) shows that minimum wages and mandated benefits do not hinder economic growth. They argue that curtailing social security benefits might not contribute much towards economic performance. ADB (2005, p. 66) points out that 'effective social protection provides economic benefits ... can lead to higher productivity'.

In market-based economies, periodic fluctuations in economic activities and frictional unemployment that results from such fluctuations are common. In such situations, an important aspect of the functioning of the labour market is the efficiency with which unemployed workers can reintegrate into the labour force. In order to facilitate the reintegration of the unemployed into the labour force, it may be useful to link social protection (especially, unemployment benefit) to training and job search.

Active labour market policies in Sweden and other European countries, and labour market reforms in Germany – the so-called Hartz IV reforms – provide examples of such interventions in the labour market. The latter, introduced in 2005 (approved in 2004) replaced the open-ended unemployment benefit by a fixed-duration one and restricts full unemployment pay to 12 months in general and 18 months for over 55 year olds and reoriented ALMPS. The recipients can now be assigned to employment schemes in the 'secondary labour markets' (in 'work opportunities') lasting six months. Persons in work opportunities retain the full amount of the unemployment benefit and receive a supplementary payment of between €1 and €2 per hour. Job acceptability requirements have also been tightened, so that the long-term unemployed receiving benefits cannot refuse job offers irrespective of pay and occupational characteristics.

Evidence shows that re-employment rates can be increased if conditions for job search are tightened via the imposition of sanctions in case of non-compliance with job search requirements. Monitoring of job search is thus important for reducing unemployment duration (Wurzel, 2006).

OECD (2006) notes that while generous unemployment benefits might have negative effects on the aggregate employment rate, they have no effect whatever when coupled with ALMPs. Hence, spending on ALMPs should be a corollary of generous unemployment benefits, as it constitutes a 'work test', avoiding the disincentive effects usually associated with generous benefits. The rate of open unemployment in countries with good ALMPs and high spending on them, e.g. Sweden, Denmark and Netherlands, is lower than in countries like France, Germany and Spain (Auer *et al.*, 2005).

The conclusion that follows from the evidence cited above is that measures of social protection do not necessarily cause unemployment to increase. On the contrary, they can, especially if combined with appropriate active labour market policies, facilitate labour market adjustment.

Social protection through employment generation programmes: the case of MGNREP in India[25]

In September 2005, the Indian Parliament passed the National Rural Employment Guarantee Act (NREGA) which represents a bold step in the realm of public policy for employment and social protection not only in the country but also for the developing world as a whole. While the primary goal of the Act is to generate employment for the poor in rural areas, it also provides for basic economic security for them. The Act guarantees at least 100 days of wage employment per household in infrastructure construction schemes. Although the remuneration is linked to the amount of work performed, the mechanism for calculating the wage ensures that the daily wage will not be less than the prevailing minimum wage in agriculture. Moreover, the Act provides for an unemployment allowance if work cannot be provided within 15 days of application. There are a number of other aspects of the Act that are worth noting which include: (1) allocation of at least one-third of the jobs to women; (2) providing work within five kilometres of one's place of residence, and a payment of transport allowance in case the job is located farther than that; (3) allowing local bodies (namely, the village *panchayets*) to execute at least half of the work; (4) introduction of job cards, written application, direct payment of wages to bank accounts, etc. as measures to ensure transparency in the execution of the programme.

In addition to the goal of providing employment and social protection, the Act also envisaged ensuring that the schemes selected under the programme would contribute to the development of infrastructure in rural areas and thus contribute to economic growth. With that aim, the Act provides a list of the type of schemes that could be undertaken for creating employment.

Apart from providing employment and social protection and contributing to rural development, the Act has some other positive features. For example, by creating employment in rural areas, the programme was expected to strengthen the overall demand for labour in the rural labour market. That, coupled with the application of minimum wages in the jobs created, was expected to improve the bargaining position of the workers and lead to an improvement in the overall situation of labour in the rural economy.

Of course, critics have pointed out possible negative aspects of the employment programme in India described above. One major concern was whether it could have an inflationary effect on the economy, if production, especially of food grains, did not increase alongside increases in employment (Ghose, 2011). Although the Act does specify that the schemes selected should be such that they contribute to rural/agricultural development, what happens in reality would depend on how the schemes are selected and implemented.

Unlike CCTs in Latin America, there has not been much of in-depth evaluation of MGNREGP; but a few observations may be made on the basis of official documents and other studies.[26]

- While the programme was initially launched in 200 districts of the country, within three years it was extended to the rural areas of all the districts.
- In six years, the number of households covered by the programme increased to two-and-a-half times.
- The share of women in the total number of participants was 48 per cent in 2012, thus exceeding the target of one-third.
- But the average number of days of employment per household peaked at 54 days, although the target was 100 days. Of course, it is possible that the demand for jobs does not require offering 100 days. In fact, there is substantial variation in the number of days of jobs provided in various states

of the country – with the number very low in developed states, thus indicating that this number perhaps reflects demand for jobs.

• In 19 states the average wage rate in schemes under the programme was higher than the prevailing wage rates in agriculture. This may have created a pressure on rural wages as a whole. Whether the rise in rural wages may have had an inflationary effect is difficult to say. However, if one looks at the type of schemes taken up under the programme it would appear that they should have created possibilities of a positive impact on growth in agriculture. Moreover, there is evidence to show that the magnitude of employment created was countercyclical with seasonal variation in the demand for labour in agriculture.

Based on the experience of India's MGNREGP, a few observations may be made, albeit tentatively, about the use of employment programmes as a mechanism for social protection. First, the Indian programme is indicative of the adoption of a rights-based approach to employment. And by enacting a law in this respect, the guarantee of jobs has been given a legal backing. These two elements distinguish this programme from similar programmes elsewhere in the world; and they are critical if such a programme has to effectively serve as a measure of social protection.

Second, although the programme's basic objective is to guarantee a minimum level of income for the poor and thus address structural poverty, the guarantee element enables it to address labour market risks and provides workers with a choice of falling back on it when faced with unemployment.

Third, the programme is financed from the country's own resources without depending on external resources as is often the case with such programmes in low income developing countries. Initially, the estimated cost of the programme was about 1 per cent of the country's GDP, and it was thought that the country should be able to afford to spend that amount for providing a safety net to the country's poor. A country's ability and willingness to commit such resources towards its social protection programmes is extremely important, an issue to which we turn now.

Concluding observations

While awareness about the need and importance of social protection has grown in recent years, a question that is increasingly being asked is that of the cost of the relevant programmes and of financing them. Can developing countries, especially those at the lower end of the income scale, really afford to finance social protection from their own resources? Earlier in the present chapter, references have already been made to studies showing that with contributions from the governments, employers and workers, it should not be difficult to finance an unemployment benefit plan in developing countries. Likewise, experience with CCTs has shown that developing countries can afford to finance them. But what about the cost and affordability of a more comprehensive social protection floor?

One exercise by the ILO (ILO, 2008) covering 12 countries (of which seven are LDC) estimates the cost of implementing a social protection floor that includes universal pension, basic healthcare, child benefit and employment scheme; it shows that in 2010, the cost as percentage of GDP would range from 3.7 per cent in India to 10.6 per cent in Burkina Faso (Table 9.5). Based on that exercise, the ILO takes the view that such a programme should be affordable.

Of course, the question of affordability would depend not only on the cost but also on the availability of resources in a country. Given the fiscal space of low income countries where revenue earnings as percentage of GDP are typically less than 20 per cent of GDP and the typical spending on safety net programmes is around 2 to 3 per cent of GDP, a programme costing 5 to 10 per cent of GDP may not be considered cheap. However, rather than taking a diffident approach, it may be more useful to look at the issue in a disaggregated and practical manner.

On the side of costs, the cost of the universal pension and the employment guarantee programmes would typically cost less than 1 per cent of GDP each. On the other hand, many developing countries anyway spend about 2 per cent of their GDP on safety net programmes. So, with some reorganization of programmes and resource allocation, it should be possible to implement these two programmes without much addition to the budget.

It is the child care and the health services that appear more expensive in the ILO estimates (ILO, 2008, Appendix Table A2.1). However, these amounts should not be looked as net additions to what is already spent by countries in these areas. Again, with a bit of effort towards strategic reorientation of programmes and resource allocation, it may not be unrealistic to spend 4 to 6 per cent of a country's budget on these two items.

Furthermore, fiscal space should (and need) not be looked at as a fixed parameter. A bit of investigation would show that in many low income developing

Table 9.5 Estimated cost (percentage of GDP) of implementing basic social protection floor in selected developing countries of Africa and Asia, 2010 and 2020

Countries	2010	2020
Burkina Faso	10.6	9.9
Cameroon	5.9	5.6
Ethiopia	8.9	9.2
Guinea	4.3	4.1
Kenya	8.2	8.4
Senegal	6.5	6.1
Tanzania	8.0	8.4
Bangladesh	6.0	5.6
India	3.7	3.3
Nepal	7.2	7.9
Pakistan	3.9	4.2
Vietnam	4.4	4.3

Source: adapted from ILO (2008).

countries, the actual revenue resources are well below what could potentially be raised.[27] Moreover, there could be other innovative means of finding resources for social protection programmes.[28]

Notes

1 See reference to it in ILO (2010). Details of various ILO Conventions relating to social security, including Convention No. 102 mentioned below can be found in ILO (2010).
2 ILO (2014).
3 For example, according to data presented in OECD *Employment Outlook 2006*, GDP growth in the USA during 1993–2003 was 3.2 per cent per annum compared to 2.3 per cent for the 15 EU countries and the OECD average of 2.7 per cent per annum. During 2004–07 also growth in the USA has been higher than that achieved by EU-15. Unemployment rate in the USA has been much lower (5.3 per cent on an average during 1993–2003) than in EU-15 (8.8 per cent during the same period).
4 In 2004, according to OECD (2006), the duration of unemployment benefit was 6 months in the USA compared to 30 and 12 months respectively in France and Germany and an average of 34 months in Nordic countries (Denmark, Finland, Norway and Sweden). Likewise, public expenditure as percentage of GDP was much lower in the USA (0.55 per cent in 2002) compared to 1.39 per cent and 2.1 per cent in France and Germany respectively (Auer *et al.*, 2005).
5 There are of course exceptions like China and India where annual rate of GDP growth increased sharply during the latter two decades.
6 Data on 16 industrialized countries provided by one IMF study (IMF, 2007) show that during 1980–2004, the share of labour in GDP declined from 58 to 55 per cent. This kind of trend is observable in developing countries as well (Jaydev, 2007). The ILO *Global Wage Report* of 2012–13 points out that the average wage share in 16 developed economies dropped from 75 per cent of national income in the mid-1970s to 65 per cent in the mid-2000s. In a group of 16 developing and emerging economies, it dropped from 62 per cent of GDP in the early 1990s to 58 per cent in the mid-2000s. See ILO (2012).
7 China and India are notable exceptions in this regard as well. The comparative data on GDP growth and variations in it referred to in this paragraph are from ILO (2004).
8 For more information on labour market institutions in the countries of East and South East Asia in the 1990s, see Betcherman and Islam (2001).
9 For a summary of the various measures undertaken, see Betcherman and Islam (2001).
10 These figures are from US Bureau of Labour Statistics website: www.bls.gov/time-series/LNS14000000 (accessed on 10 June 2014).
11 The Bill under which the economic stimulus package was approved by the US Congress provides for an extension of the unemployment benefit by 33 weeks. The amount of unemployment benefit has also been increased. See Robert Longley, 'Economic Stimulus Package for Workers Hurt by the Recession', available at: http://usgovinfo.about.com/od/moneymatters/a/ecstimworkers.htm?p=1 (accessed 27 October 2014).
12 See ILO (2009, Table 4) for concrete examples.
13 See Chapter 2, as well as the country studies in Islam (2006).
14 For a more detailed analysis of this aspect, see Islam, 2009.
15 This, of course, is not to say that it is impossible for the self-employed to organize social protection for themselves. For a description of some such efforts, see ILO (2014).

16 Contingent transfers may help prevent depletion of assets when the poor are experiencing shock of some kind.

17 Out of the 28, 17 were in the Latin American and Caribbean region, six in Asia, and three in Africa. The other two countries were Turkey and Yemen.

18 Fiszbein and Shady (2009).

19 It is not difficult to think of such externalities, e.g. community members following health measures transmitted to beneficiaries, increasing returns to education and skills in places of work.

20 There is a large body of literature on CCTs, and many focus on their impact. A detailed evaluation of a large number of programmes is provided by Fiszbein and Shady (2009). The Independent Evaluation Group of the World Bank has undertaken an evaluation (IEG, 2011) of the social safety nets (including CCTs) supported by the Bank. One may also see other studies like Barrientos and Scott (2008), Barrientos and Villa (2014), Dercon (2011), Handa and Davis (2006) and Rawlings (2004).

21 There are, of course, those who argue that cash transfers (even conditional ones) may be blunt instruments for achieving this goal. For some references, see Dercon (2011).

22 This is predicted by some models (as referred to in Dercon, 2011).

23 In Mexico, 12 per cent of the beneficiaries of PROGRESA invested some of their cash in productive activities like agriculture and micro-enterprises, and the rates of return were quite high (ranging between 30 and 50 per cent). In the case of Ethiopia's Productive Safety Net Programme, some increase in livestock among the beneficiaries was noted, although the rate of graduation out of poverty was slower than expected. See Dercon (2011).

24 Although India's rural employment guarantee scheme (MGNREGP) was not designed for purposes of crisis response, and allocation for the programme was not increased during the global economic crisis of 2008–09, it nevertheless provided those affected by the crisis a choice.

25 It needs to be mentioned in this context that the objectives pursued by programmes of employment generation through infrastructure construction need not be limited to providing social protection. By creating infrastructure, they can contribute to the development objective as well. They also have other advantages, e.g. saving on foreign exchange (due to reliance on locally available technology). For an analysis of labour-based approaches to infrastructure in such a broader framework, see Islam and Majeres (2001).

26 Data and information provided in the following paragraphs are mainly from the studies included in GOI (2012).

27 One study on Bangladesh (Islam *et al.* 2011) points out that the revenue-GDP ratio of the country was around 10 per cent of GDP (in 2010), although the revenue potential was estimated to be in the range of 14–15 per cent of GDP.

28 As pointed out by Moss (2011), in resource-rich countries, a part of the revenue earned from natural resources could be set aside for financing social protection.

Bibliography

ADB (Asian Development Bank) (2005) *Labour Markets in Asia: Promoting Full, Productive, and Decent Employment*, Asian Development Bank, Manila.

ADB (Asian Development Bank) (2013) *The Social Protection Index: Assessing Results for Asia and the Pacific*, Asian Development Bank, Manila.

Ahmad, E., Dreze, J., Hills, J. and Sen, A. (eds) (1991) *Social Security in Developing Countries*, Oxford University Press, Oxford.

Arjona, R., Ladaique, M. and Pearson, M. (2002) *Social Protection and Growth*, OECD Economic Studies No. 35, 2002/2, OECD, Paris.

Auer, P., Efendioglu, U. and Leschke, J. (2005) *Active Labour Market Policies around the World*, ILO, Geneva.

Barrientos, A. and Scott, J. (2008) *Social Transfers and Growth: A Review*, BWPI Working Paper Series 52, Brooks World Poverty Institute, University of Manchester, Manchester.

Barrientos, A. and Villa, J.M. (2014) *Economic and Political Inclusion of Human Development in Conditional Cash Transfer Programmes in Latin America*, BWPI Working Paper Series 200, Brooks World Poverty Institute, University of Manchester, Manchester.

Bean, C. (1994) 'European Unemployment: A Survey', *Journal of Economic Literature*, vol. 32, pp. 573–619.

Betcherman, G. and Islam, R. (2001) *East Asian Labour Markets and the Economic Crisis: Impacts, Responses and Lessons*, World Bank and International Labour Office, Washington, D.C. and Geneva.

Damerau, T.M. (2011) *Social Protection: A Necessary Condition for Economic Growth? A Guidance for Governance Decisions under Theoretical Uncertainty*, Maastricht Graduate School of Governance, Maastricht University.

Dercon, S. (ed.) (2005) *Insurance against Poverty*, Oxford University Press, Oxford.

Dercon, S. (2011) *Social Protection, Efficiency and Growth*, CSAE Working Paper WPS/2011, 17, Centre for Studies on African Economies, Oxford University, Oxford.

Devereux, S. and Solomon, C. (2006) *Employment Creation Programmes: The International Experience*, Issues in Employment and Poverty: Discussion Paper 24, ILO, Geneva.

Fiszbein, A. and Shady, N. (2009) *Conditional Cash Transfers: Reducing Present and Future Poverty*, World Bank, Washington, D.C.

Forteza, A. and Rama, M. (2002) *Labor Market 'Rigidity' and the Success of Economic Reforms across More than One Hundred Countries*, available at: http://www.lacea.org/meeting2000/AlvaroForteza.pdf.

Ghose, A. (2011) *Addressing the Employment Challenge: India's MGNREGA*, Employment Sector Working Paper No. 105, International Labour Organization, Geneva.

GOI (Government of India) (2006) *Towards Faster and More Inclusive Growth: An Approach to the 11th Five-Year Plan*, Planning Commission, Government of India, New Delhi.

GOI (Government of India) (2012) *MGNREGA Sameeksha: An Anthology of Research Studies on the Mahatma Gandhi National Rural Employment Guarantee Act, 2005, 2006–12*, Ministry of Rural Development, Government of India and Orient Blackswan, New Delhi.

Handa, S. and Davis, B. (2006) 'The Experience of Conditional Cash Transfers in Latin America and the Caribbian', *Development Policy Review*, vol. 24, no. 5, pp. 513–536.

IEG (Independent Evaluation Group) (2011) *Social Safety Nets: An Evaluation of World Bank Support, 2000–2010*, IEG, World Bank, Washington, D.C.

ILO (International Labour Organization) (2000) *World Labour Report 2000*, Geneva.

ILO (International Labour Organization) (2004) *Economic Security for a Better World*, Geneva.

ILO (International Labour Organization) (2006) *Key Indicators of Labour Market (KILM) 4th edition*, Geneva.

ILO (International Labour Organization) (2008) *Can Low Income Countries Afford Basic Social Security?* Social Security Policy Briefings Paper 3, Social Security Department, Geneva.

ILO (International Labour Organization) (2009) *The Financial and Economic Crisis: A Decent Work Response*, International Institute for Labour Studies, Geneva.

ILO (International Labour Organization) (2010) *World Social Security Report 2010/11: Providing Coverage in Times of Crisis and Beyond*, Geneva.

ILO (International Labour Organization) (2012) *Global Wage Report 2012–2013*, Geneva.

ILO (International Labour Organization) (2014) *World of Work Report 2014: Developing with Jobs*, Geneva.

ILO (International Labour Organization) and WHO (World Health Organization) (2009) *Manual and Strategic Framework for Joint UN Country Operations*, Geneva.

IMF (International Monetary Fund) (2007) *World Economic Outlook April 2007*, Washington, D.C.

Islam, I. (2002) *Poverty, Employment and Wages: An Indonesian Perspective*, paper presented at the ILO-JMHLW-Government of Indonesia seminar on 'Strengthening Employment and Labour Market Policies for Poverty Alleviation and Economic Recovery in East and Southeast Asia', Jakarta, 29 April–1 May 2002.

Islam, R. (2003) *Labour Market Policies, Economic Growth and Poverty Reduction: Lessons and Non-lessons from the Comparative Experience of East, South-East and South Asia*, Issues in Employment and Poverty Discussion Paper 8, ILO, Geneva.

Islam, R. (2006) 'The Nexus of Economic Growth, Employment and Poverty Reduction: An Empirical Analysis', in Islam, R. (ed.) *Fighting Poverty: The Development-Employment Link*, Lynn Rienner, Boulder and London, pp. 31–61.

Islam, R. (2009) 'Has Development and Employment through Labour-Intensive Industrialization Become History?' in Basu, K. and Kanbur, R. (eds) *Arguments for a Better World: Essays in Honour of Amartya Sen, Volume 2: Society, Institutions and Development*, Oxford University Press, Oxford, pp. 387–410.

Islam, R. (2013) 'Economic Growth, Employment and Poverty: Evidence and Lessons', in *Yojana, Special Issue on Growth, Employment and Poverty*, October 2013. (Development monthly published by the Ministry of Information, Government of India.)

Islam, R. and Majeres, J. (2001) *Employment-Intensive Growth for Poverty Reduction: What can Labour Based Technology in Infrastructure Contribute?* Paper presented at the International Conference on Employment Creation in Development, University of Witwatersrand, Johannesburg, 2–5 April 2001.

Islam, R., Mujeri, M.K. and Ali, Z. (2011) *Fiscal and Political Space for Crisis Response with a Focus on Employment and Labour Market: A Study of Bangladesh*, ILO Employment Sector Working Paper No. 92, ILO, Geneva.

Jaydev, A. (2007) 'Capital Account Openness and the Labour Share of Income', *Cambridge Journal of Economics*, vol. 31, pp. 423–443.

Khan, A.R. (2007) *Asian Experience on Growth, Employment and Poverty: An Overview with Special reference to the Findings of Some Recent Case Studies*, ILO and UNDP, Geneva and Colombo.

Lee, E. (1998) *The Asian Financial Crisis: The Challenge for Social Policy*, ILO, Geneva.

Moss, T. (2011) *Oil to Cash: Fighting the Resource Curse through Cash Transfers*, Center for Global Development (CGD) Working Paper No. 237, Center for Global Development, Washington, D.C.

Nickel, S. (1997) 'Unemployment and Labour Market Rigidities: Europe versus North America', *Journal of Economic Perspectives*, vol. 11, no. 3, pp. 55–74.

OECD (Organization for Economic Cooperation and Development) (2006) *OECD*

Employment Outlook 2006, available at: www.oecd.org/employment/emp/oecdemploy-mentoutlook2006.htm (accessed 27 October 2014).

Rawlings, L.B. (2004) *A New Approach to Social Assistance: Latin America's Experi-ence with Conditional Cash Transfer Programs*, Social Protection Discussion Paper Series No. 0416, World Bank, Washington, D.C.

Reinhart, C.M. and Rogoff, K. (2009) *This Time is Different: Eight Centuries of Finan-cial Folly*, Princeton University Press, Princeton and Oxford.

Saith, A. (2006) 'Social Protection, Decent Work and Development Discourse', in Ghai, D. (ed.) *Decent Work: Objectives and Strategies*, International Institute for Labour Studies, ILO, Geneva, pp. 127–173.

Schweighofer, J. (2013) 'The US or the European Way of Life?' *Social Europe Journal*, available at: www.social-europe.eu/2013/06/the-us-or-the-european-way-of-life (accessed 20 June 2013).

Wurzel, E. (2006) *Labour Market Reform in Germany: How to Improve Effectiveness*, OECD Economics Department Working Papers No. 512, Paris, September.

10   Conclusions and a way forward

Introduction

This book has evolved against a global context in which the challenge of creating enough jobs and good quality jobs is receiving a great deal of attention among development practitioners and policy makers. The global recession of 2008–09 and the financial crisis that preceded it clearly played a role in galvanizing the attention of the international community on the need for more and better jobs.

This is certainly a welcome development and a refreshing departure from the past. During the 1950s and 1960s, the emphasis on state-led planning and import substituting industrialization placed considerable emphasis on growth, with the optimism that jobs will follow. The 1970s were preoccupied with the notion of basic needs and redistribution with growth, but employment creation as a route to meeting basic needs and sharing the benefits of growth was not at the core of policy debates. The 1980s and 1990s were the era of structural adjustment and the focus shifted to rectifying macroeconomic imbalances in developing countries struggling to cope with debt crises and rampant inflation.

When the Millennium Development Goals (MDGs) were launched in 2000, there was a renewed commitment to poverty reduction. Yet, it was only in 2008 that the need to make significant progress towards full and productive employment for all became a formally recognized target under the goal of reducing extreme poverty. While it remains to be seen what the new development goals will look like as part of the post-2015 agenda, it is unlikely that the theme of jobs will suffer from benign neglect as it did in the past.

Recognizing that the goal of job creation is a central global challenge is not the same as having a common understanding of what that entails in terms of both a conceptual framework and appropriate policy actions. Hence, this treatise argued the case for a shared understanding of key issues and concepts as well as an objective reading of the evidence on the theme of employment and inclusive growth.

What have we learnt? What needs to be done and how do we move forward? Rather than replicating the conclusions that have been reached at the end of each chapter, it would be useful to re-enact a series of refutable propositions that might be regarded as part of conventional wisdom and spell out where common areas of agreement ought to exist. Such common agreement can spawn a shared vision of how to respond to the challenge of attaining inclusive growth in developing countries through the route of employment growth.

One should hasten to add that the propositions that are discussed here should not be associated with any specific individual or institution. The purpose is to highlight proclamations that might lead to misguided actions. With this caveat in mind, the critical reader is asked to ponder over the following propositions. The authors will seek to provide an answer that captures the substance and spirit of the diverse issues that have been discussed at some length in this volume.

1   Growth is good for the poor and good for jobs.
2   Inclusive growth is a redundant concept, given that growth is good for the poor and good for jobs.
3   Macroeconomic stability is fundamental to growth and employment creation.
4   The biggest impediment to structural transformation in developing countries is premature de-industrialization.
5   A rights-based approach to employment raises unrealizable expectations among job seekers.
6   Human capital is at the centre of growth and development, and the major focus should be on primary education.
7   Young men and women find it difficult to get good jobs because they lack the requisite skills.
8   Labour market regulations are the primary constraints on employment creation.
9   Developing countries should be wary of a comprehensive social protection system as it might distort incentives, affect long-term growth and put a burden on public finances.

Growth is good for the poor and good for jobs

It would be foolish to deny the importance of growth for developing countries. Of course, economic growth is not the only end of development, but, as someone once said, the end of growth is the end of development. Yet, one should guard against growth fetishism. This means making the usual distinction between necessary and sufficient condition. Growth is necessary for poverty to decline and for jobs to be created, but it is not sufficient. Both global evidence and country-specific experience suggest that various patterns in the growth–poverty–employment nexus are possible. The rate of poverty reduction can match the rate of growth, but it can also lie above or below it. In more technical terms, the growth elasticity of poverty reduction can take multiple values: well above 1, equal to 1 and below unity. Indeed, it is, in principle, possible for per capita GDP growth rate for a given period to be low, say 0.2 per cent, but poverty to decline by, say, 2 per cent over the same period. In that case, the growth elasticity of poverty will be conspicuously high.[1] In practice, it is most unlikely to happen. Prolonged periods of low growth and stagnation will inevitably cast its baleful influence on the poor. In that fundamental sense, growth is good for the poor.

Similar arguments can be invoked to reflect on the growth–employment nexus. The rate of employment growth can match the rate of economic growth, but it can also lie above or below it. In more technical terms, the employment elasticity of growth can take multiple values: well above 1, equal to 1 and below unity, but there is an important difference in interpretation vis-à-vis the growth elasticity of poverty. When employment growth exceeds the rate of economic growth, it embodies the uncomfortable implication that labour productivity is declining. Thus, there could be a trade-off: economic growth creates more jobs, but not necessarily more productive jobs. Fortunately, country experiences suggest that this trade-off is neither unavoidable nor inevitable. Avoiding the trade-off means caring about the quality of employment. Succumbing to the mind-set that any job is better than no job will merely reinforce the employment–productivity trade-off.

An important message of this book is that policy makers ought to watch out for the phenomenon of 'jobless growth', an undesirable state of affairs in which the rate of per capita growth is satisfactory, but jobs barely grow. This is not uncommon and requires requisite policy actions. In sum, growth is good for employment in the fundamental sense that prolonged periods of low growth and stagnation is unlikely to produce widespread job opportunities. Yet, one cannot rely on growth alone to deliver more and productive employment. Hence, pro-growth policies – such as more investment – are necessary but not sufficient. They need to be accompanied by complementary interventions ranging across macroeconomic, sectoral and labour market policies.

Inclusive growth is a redundant concept, given that growth is good for the poor and good for jobs

The term inclusive growth is widely used, but rarely defined. Indeed, this book drew attention to the fact that international organizations that are closely associated with global and regional development are struggling to come up with an agreed definition of inclusive growth. This does not mean that the concept is redundant. The previous discussion has established that a focus on growth alone is not sufficient to ensure that the benefits of economic growth are widely shared. This is where it becomes important to make the distinction between growth and inclusive growth.

This volume offered a stylized characterization of inclusive growth in which employment is an integral part of the concept. Thus, any notion of inclusive growth should embody the following essential elements:

- Rapid, stable and sustainable per capita GDP growth;
- Sustained decline in income poverty;
- Sustained improvement in human development indicators, such as health, nutrition and education;

- Growth of productive employment that matches or exceeds labour force growth;
- Reduction in inequality;
- Social protection for all.

The critical reader might note that there is no explicit reference to gender, young men and women and environmental concerns. The issue of the particular experiences of young people is indeed taken up in this book but is not highlighted in the definition of inclusive growth that has guided the various chapters. The rationale is that the definition adopted here emphasizes its universalistic attributes and thus applies with equal force to adults and young people, men and women. At the same time, the emphasis on sustainable growth means that environmental concerns are implicit in the definition of inclusive growth. It is not possible for growth to be sustainable if it entails the depletion and destruction of scarce environmental resources.

Macroeconomic stability is fundamental to growth and employment creation

A key message of this book is that one should eschew a fundamentalist notion of the role that macroeconomic stability plays in supporting growth and employment. Once again, making the customary distinction between necessary and sufficient condition is helpful. Macroeconomic stability is a necessary condition for growth and employment, but it is not sufficient. Hyperinflation and out-of-control budget deficits can lead to growth collapses. Restoring macroeconomic stability by itself will avert a crisis, but it is unlikely to kick-start self-sustaining growth and structural change that lies at the core of job creation. Extreme macroeconomic instability is a relatively rare occurrence and its baleful influence can be readily demonstrated. It is more difficult to argue that a country experiencing a 5 per cent inflation rate is somehow likely to experience growth and labour market outcomes that are rather better than a country enduring a long run inflation rate of, say, 7 per cent. Indeed, it has turned out to be surprisingly difficult to assemble hard evidence in favour of the view that macroeconomic stability is fundamental to growth and jobs.

This does not mean that the conventional emphasis on macroeconomic instability is misplaced. Governments in developing countries should act as guardians of stability, but they should also act as agents of development. This means protecting citizens from the vagaries of economic volatility, engaging in a sustainable resource mobilization strategy to finance core development needs, promoting a competitive and inclusive financial system, ensuring that exchange rates do not become badly misaligned and engaging in prudent management of the capital account. This is by no means a radical agenda but an incremental adjustment to the conventional macroeconomic policy framework that can reap substantial growth and employment dividends.

The biggest impediment to structural transformation in developing countries is premature de-industrialization

This treatise highlighted the debate on the pros and cons of structural transformation as it has evolved in developing countries. The essence of this debate can be captured in the notion of 'premature de-industrialization'. This thesis, the book noted, has two dimensions: (a) a descriptive statement on the changing relationship between employment shares of manufacturing and per capita income; (b) a normative statement that developing economies in many parts of the world have experienced growth-reducing structural change. The implication of (b) is that labour and resources move into low productivity non-manufacturing activities from low productivity agriculture. In the language of decomposition of aggregate productivity, one can say that, for any given level of changes in within-sector productivity, changes in between-sector productivity are negative which acts as a drag on growth and employment. More importantly, this deleterious outcome can be attributed to the fact that developing countries have de-industrialized at a rate that is faster than the historical norm. Hence, the manufacturing sector is unable to absorb the growing labour force in developing countries entailing a concomitant expansion of low productivity activities in the non-manufacturing sector.

This volume assessed the relevant evidence on premature de-industrialization and concluded that while (a) as stated above was largely valid, the veracity of (b) was less clear. It built on this argument to suggest that one should not adopt the view that manufacturing-led industrialization is the only route to economic prosperity. Certainly, this route led to unprecedented prosperity in the post-industrial societies in the Western world as well as to a distinctive group of East Asian economies in the 1960s and 1970s. On the other hand, one cannot ignore the structural reality that, in large parts of the developing world of today, non-manufacturing activities are the primary sources of livelihood and will remain so in the long term. Furthermore, in low and lower middle income economies the agricultural sector will continue to be a major source of livelihood for decades. At the same time, the non-renewable natural resources sector plays a crucial role in many low income countries, especially in Sub-Saharan Africa. These structural realities need to be addressed in a way that goes beyond the pessimism of premature de-industrialization.

A rights-based approach to employment raises unrealizable expectations among job seekers

Is the right to work equivalent to a human right? Who in this case is the 'right holder' and who is the 'duty bearer'? In a developing country market economy where approximately 90 per cent of the jobs are created by the private sector, can the government really enforce the right to work for all? In that case, it might be legitimately argued that a rights-based approach to employment can unleash unrealizable aspirations among 'right holders' or job seekers. This will affect the credibility of governments as they struggle to respond to unrealistic expectations. What, then, is the way forward?

This treatise made a distinction between the government as a direct provider of jobs and the government as an enabler of policies that support productive employment creation. Certainly, the public sector is a significant employer; it can also be an employer of last resort through public employment programmes, but these should be seen only as some elements of an overall strategy for promoting jobs. Such an overall strategy provides the basis for a government to build a rights-based approach to work through ratification of international covenants and national legislation.

This book suggested how one can use ILO conventions and instruments, most notably C.122, to operationalize the notion of the right to work. Such conventions and instruments apply to two situations. One is in countries that have ratified the Conventions: they are required to bring their legal and administrative frameworks in line with the requirements of the Conventions. Even in those situations, the system is not entirely legalistic; much is done through the ILO's system of consultation, monitoring and reporting. The second situation obtains in countries that have not ratified the relevant Convention(s). They also are brought within the purview of ILO's monitoring mechanism. Hence, if this system is applied in spirit, all countries would be obliged not only to declare employment for all as a goal but also to adopt appropriate measures to move towards that goal. Governments might be seen as the primary 'duty bearer', but others in the society including employers and workers have a collective responsibility to support policies and programmes that facilitate job creation.

It is also important to make a distinction between right *to* work and rights *at* work. There is considerable consensus on the latter, with the vast majority of ILO member states having ratified the eight fundamental conventions pertaining to freedom of association, forced labour, discrimination and child labour.[2] Hence, a rights-based approach to employment, entailing both right to work and rights at work is not as impractical as it seems.

Human capital is at the centre of growth and development and the major focus should be on primary education

This volume recognizes that shortage of human capital may emerge as a major constraint on the growth of economies in developing countries. While noting that education and skills training plays a pivotal role in reducing poverty and inequality and in improving the employability of potential job-seekers, this book pointed out that a particular issue has not yet received detailed analysis in development literature, namely, how the pattern of demand for education and skills changes with the level of economic development. For example, a country with a good base of elementary education may be able to achieve economic growth up to a certain level and yet face constraints arising from the shortage of skilled workers at a higher level of development. If that is the case, countries would need to keep upgrading the level of their human capital as they achieve higher levels of economic development.

In highlighting the importance of changing skill requirements as economic growth takes place, this volume drew attention to the need for demand-side analysis of the human capital requirements of a country. In policy terms, what this implies is the need to avoid a 'supply side bias'. Simply increasing the pool of workers through the education and training system in an undifferentiated way is unlikely to respond to the changing requirements of the labour market. The net outcome is likely to be unemployed and underemployed educated workers representing a waste of human resources. Hence, human capital can play its due role in the development process provided a framework is in place that entails an appropriate utilization of the skills and talents embodied in the work-force and tailors policy interventions to anticipated changes in patterns of labour demand. This is easier said than done and remains a major challenge for policy makers in developing countries.

Young men and women find it difficult to get good jobs because they lack the requisite skills

The current concerns about the global employment challenge are also driven by concerns about lack of suitable employment opportunities for young people. While youth unemployment was much higher than adult unemployment even during normal times, young people were hit by the global recession of 2008–09. And many faced the danger of a 'scarring effect' with long-term negative impact on their careers and earnings.

An analysis of the causes of youth unemployment in both developed and developing countries indicates that a variety of factors operating from both the demand and supply side are in force. Poor macroeconomic conditions reduce the demand for labour in general and the demand for the labour services provided by young people in particular. They are the first to be fired when bad times hit firms and businesses. At the same time, it takes time for young people to make the transition from the world of learning to the world of work. Many successfully make this transition, but many do not as they are hampered by lack of appropriate skills and competencies. The school-to-work transition is also contingent on the business cycle. A booming economy means an easier passage to jobs, for any given set of skills; slow growth and recessions make that passage more difficult.

Despite the reasonable view that poor youth employment outcomes are the product of demand and supply side factors that work in tandem, strategies and policies adopted at the national level are often found to be biased towards supply side interventions. When governments find it difficult to cope with fluctuations in aggregate demand either because they are committed to an economic austerity programme (as in the European Union today) or because such fluctuations stem from external sources, there is a tendency to look for an expedient explanation. This is conveniently provided by the notion that young people lack the requisite skills to meet the imperatives of a changing labour market. This usually paves the way for calls to revamp the education and training system, special initiatives such as youth entrepreneurship training, apprenticeship schemes and other activation measures to keep young people focused on the need to nurture marketeable skills. They are certainly laudable interventions and governments can readily demonstrate that they are making an effort to look after the needs of young people. But these initiatives are a partial solution to the problem of mass youth unemployment that often emerges in the wake of a major global recession. A strategy of inclusive growth demands that governments across the world recognize that poor youth employment outcomes are best handled by policy interventions that operate on both the demand and supply side of the economy.

Labour market regulations are the primary constraints on employment creation

Labour market market regulations are enacted to protect the rights of workers (such as the right to collective bargaining) and to empower them to cope with economic insecurity. Critics allege that, however well meaning, specific labour regulations – such as high minimum wages and employment protection legislation – depress the demand for labour. The price, it is claimed, is borne by workers, especially low skilled and young workers, who are then 'priced out' of the labour market. Such workers often have to endure long spells of unemployment or move into the 'informal economy' and join an interminable queue to obtain formal sector jobs that are in scarce supply. Thus, attenuating or removing onerous labour market regulations reduces the incidence of informality, empowers young and marginalized workers to gain a foothold in the formal labour market and contributes to the goal of inclusive development.

This volume argued that an objective reading of the evidence does not enable one to make the claim that labour regulations represent the primary constraint on employment creation. Indeed, the evidence suggest that, across all regions of the world, firms identify multiple constraints on business operations, labour market regulations being one of them, but by no means the most important one. The quality of governance, access to finance, use of a reliable transport network and reliable supply of electricity are usually more important constraints from a business perspective than labour regulations. Hence, if labour regulations are either substantially attenuated or removed, one cannot expect a major expansion of the private sector unless other remaining and more significant constraints are also tackled.

In light of the prevailing evidence, influential international organizations, such as the World Bank, have offered a nuanced view: too much flexibility is bad for employment as is too little flexibility. Within these limits, there is a 'plateau' in which labour market regulations are essentially benign with respect to their impact on employment while engendering redistributive benefits.[3] On the other hand, the G20 appears to advocate an agenda of structural reforms in which labour market flexibility re-emerges as a key policy initiative. Hence, the issue of labour market flexibility remains as contentious as ever. Arriving at a consensus on this issue is crucial for progress to be made on the agenda of employment and inclusive growth.

Developing countries should be wary of a comprehensive social protection system as it is likely to distort incentives, affect long-term growth and put a strain on public finances

This volume pointed out that when the MDGs were unveiled in 2000, they did not make a distinction between those who are in chronic poverty and those who are at risk of poverty, or in a state of vulnerability. Someone might not be poor today, but become poor tomorrow, at least for a transitory period, as a result of idiosyncratic or system-wide shocks. The incidence of vulnerability is higher than the incidence of chronic poverty. Hence, the state – both in developed and developing countries – has an obligation to empower households, families and individuals to cope with economic insecurity. These considerations led to the adoption by the UN system of a 2009 resolution that all member states should strive to provide a 'social protection floor' (SPF) for its citizens. As the book noted, one interpretation of the SPF is that developing countries should strive to provide (1) access to basic/essential healthcare benefits, (2) income security for children at least at the poverty level through various family/child benefits, (3) targeted income support to the poor and the unemployed in the active age group, and (4) income security for the old and the disabled – at least at the poverty level – through pensions for old age, disability and survivors. Whether a social protection floor should rest on means-tested schemes or rely on unconditional benefits is left to the discretion of the state.

Despite the 2009 resolution, there is a tendency among some agencies and analysts to focus on the notion of a 'social safety net' which is essentially means-tested income transfers directed only towards the poor and usually to be activated during periods of crises. The components pertaining to child benefits and unconditional transfers targeted towards the old and disabled are usually absent in discussions of social safety nets. This narrow conceptualization is justified on the ground that it is attuned to the budgetary realities of developing countries and minimizes any negative impact on incentives to work. Furthermore, one could argue that, by devoting more resources to large-scale income transfers (as would be the case under an SPF), developing country governments might find that they are less able to devote adequate resources to investment, thus damaging long-run growth prospects.

This volume took the view that the evidence does not support such concerns. Income transfers under a social protection floor are best seen as investment in human development rather than as unproductive current expenditure. Hence, they are compatible with a growth promoting strategy. The negative impact on incentives to work is not significant, while, on average, social protection floors can be financed on a sustainable basis. In any case, developing countries have demonstrated that they are capable of institutional innovations in the field of social protection as the popularity of conditional cash transfers and the relative success of employment guarantee schemes testify. The aim is to translate the principle of social protection within the particular environment of developing countries rather than seeking to replicate a Western-style social welfare state.

Notes

1 World Bank (n/d) *Growth Elasticity of Poverty*, available at: http://web.worldbank.org/WBSITE/EXTERNAL/TOPICS/EXTPOVERTY/EXTPGI/0,,contentMDK:21932026~menuPK:5461555~pagePK:210058~piPK:210062~theSitePK:342771,00.html (accessed 1 August, 2014).
2 See Chapter 5.
3 See Chapter 8.

Index

Page numbers in *italics* denote tables, those in **bold** denote figures.

For Product Safety Concerns and Information please contact our EU
representative GPSR@taylorandfrancis.com
Taylor & Francis Verlag GmbH, Kaufingerstraße 24, 80331 München, Germany